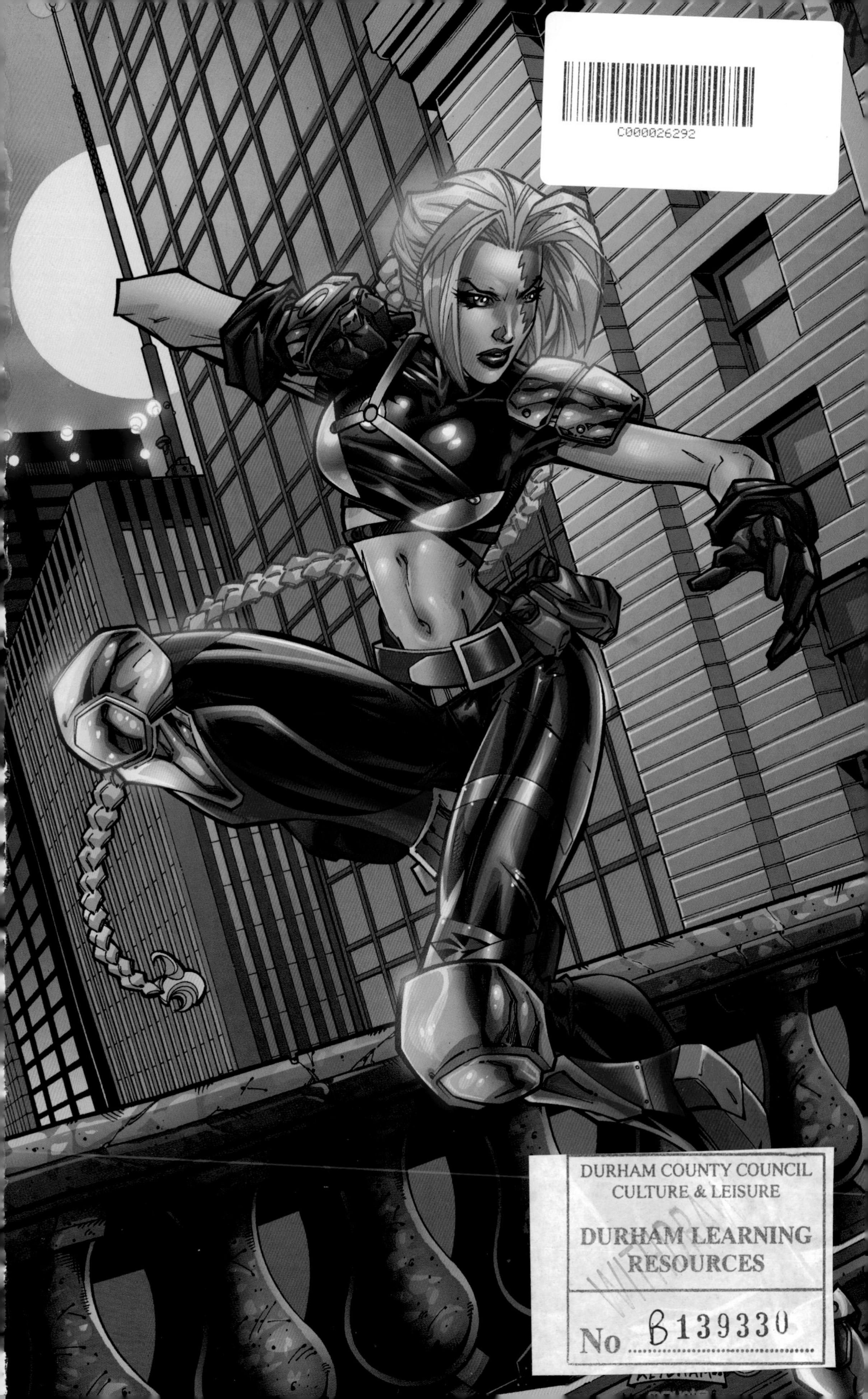

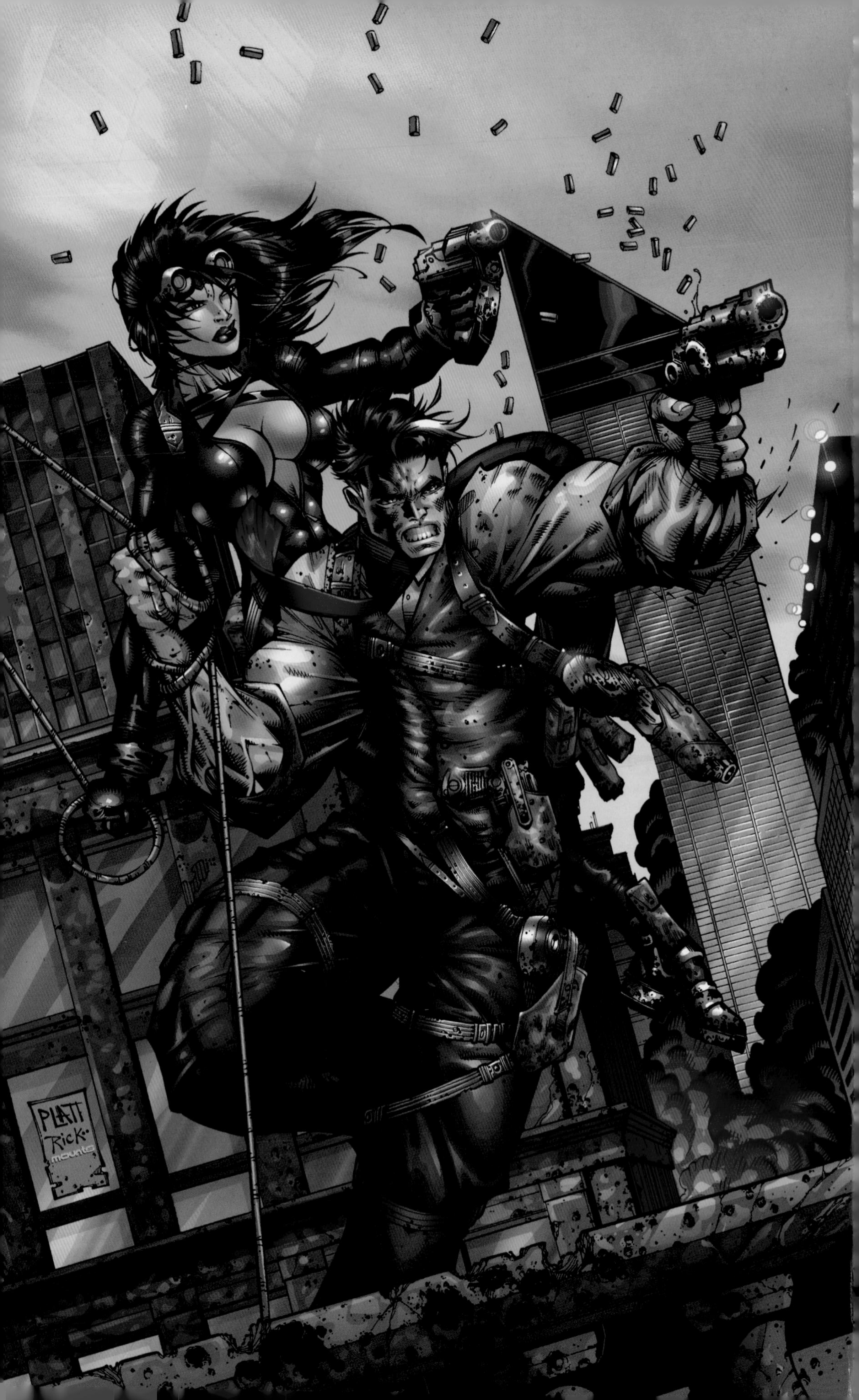
PLATT
Rick
mounts

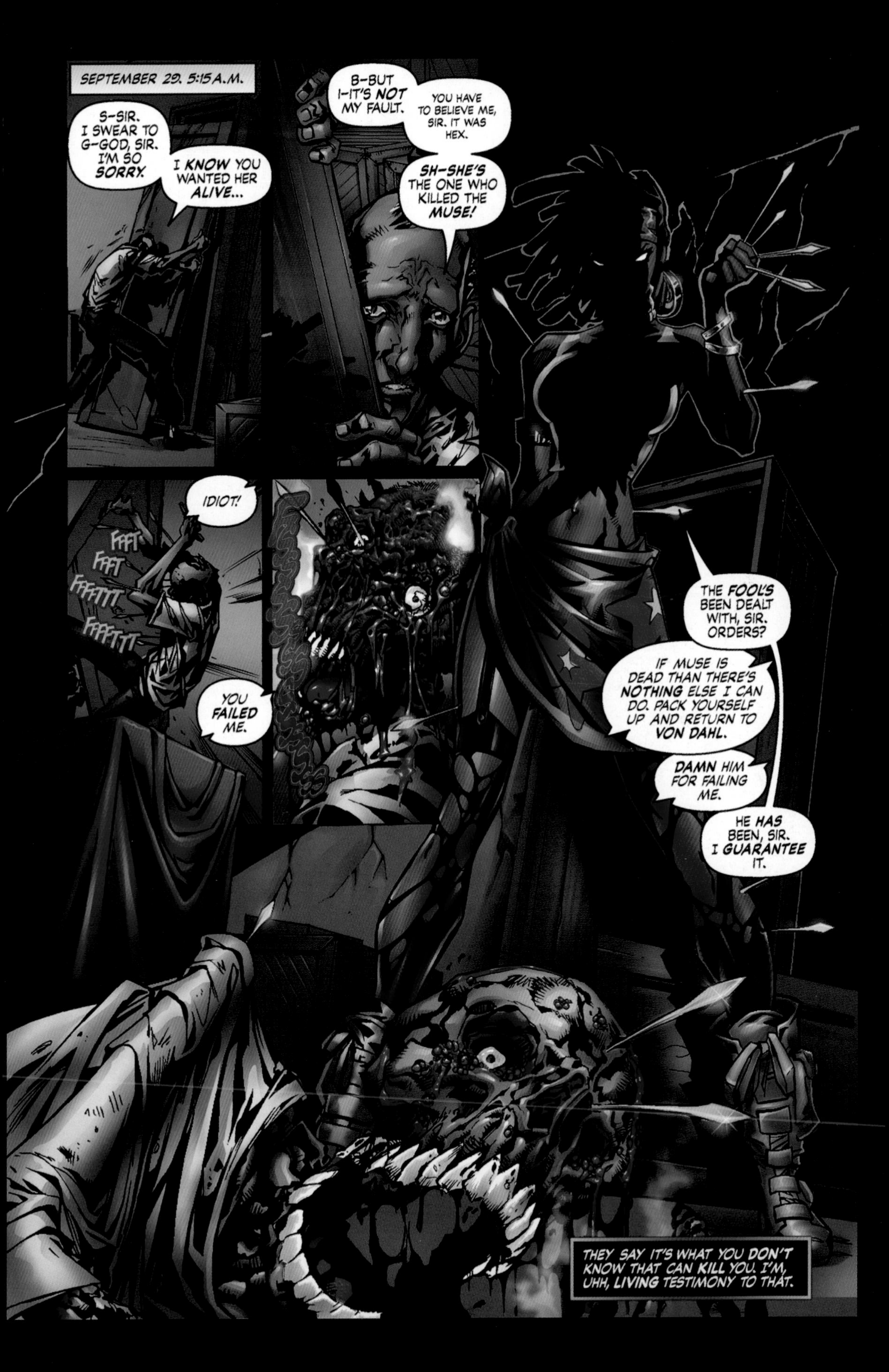
SEPTEMBER 29. 5:15 A.M.
S-SIR. I SWEAR TO G-GOD, SIR. I'M SO SORRY.
I KNOW YOU WANTED HER ALIVE...
B-BUT I-IT'S NOT MY FAULT.
YOU HAVE TO BELIEVE ME, SIR. IT WAS HEX.
SH-SHE'S THE ONE WHO KILLED THE MUSE!
IDIOT!
FFFT
FFFT
FFFFTTT
FFFFTTT
YOU FAILED ME.
THE FOOL'S BEEN DEALT WITH, SIR. ORDERS?
IF MUSE IS DEAD THAN THERE'S NOTHING ELSE I CAN DO. PACK YOURSELF UP AND RETURN TO VON DAHL.
DAMN HIM FOR FAILING ME.
HE HAS BEEN, SIR. I GUARANTEE IT.
THEY SAY IT'S WHAT YOU DON'T KNOW THAT CAN KILL YOU. I'M, UHH, LIVING TESTIMONY TO THAT.

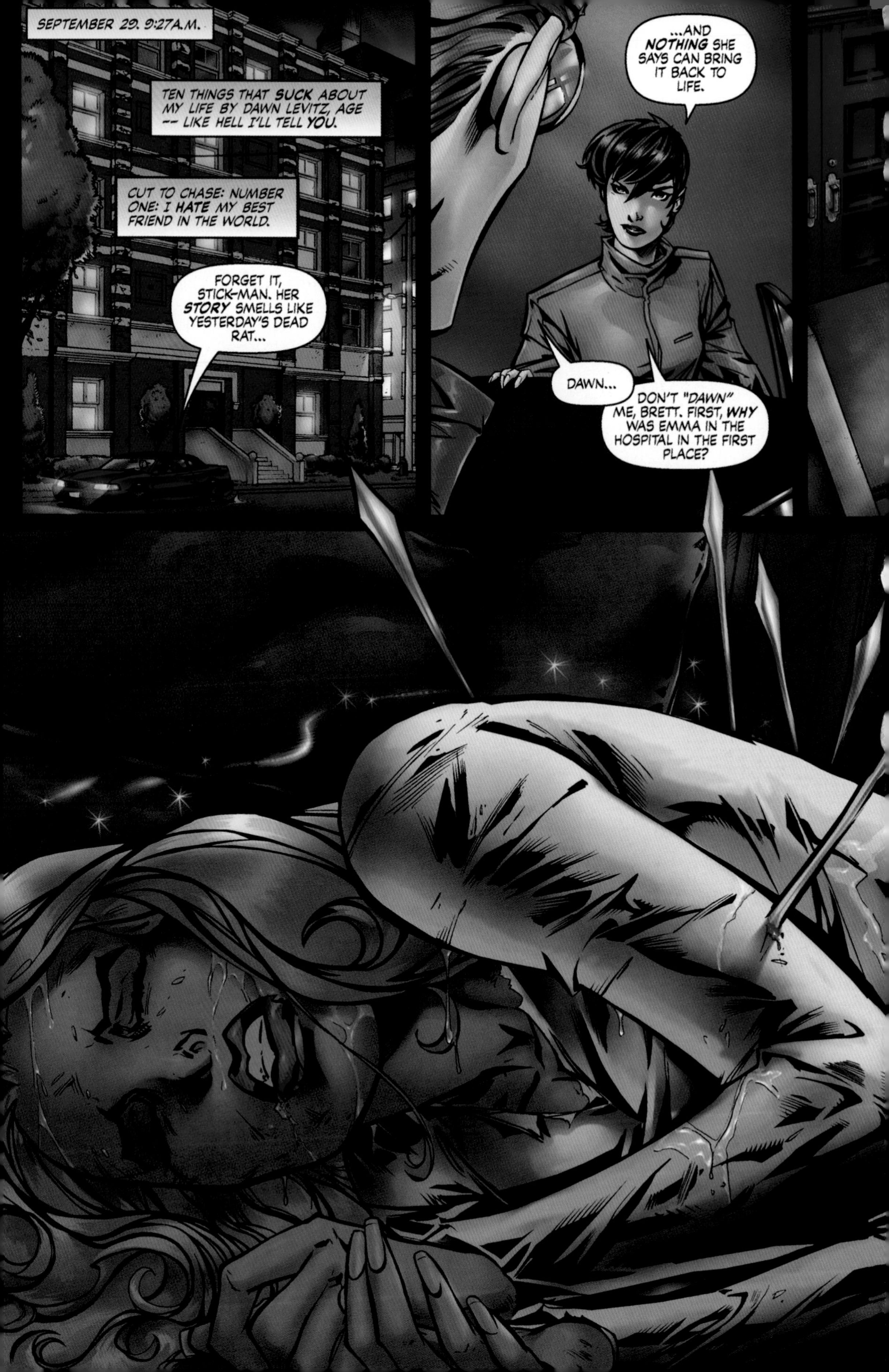
SEPTEMBER 29. 9:27A.M.
TEN THINGS THAT SUCK ABOUT MY LIFE BY DAWN LEVITZ, AGE -- LIKE HELL I'LL TELL YOU.
CUT TO CHASE: NUMBER ONE: I HATE MY BEST FRIEND IN THE WORLD.
FORGET IT, STICK-MAN. HER STORY SMELLS LIKE YESTERDAY'S DEAD RAT...
...AND NOTHING SHE SAYS CAN BRING IT BACK TO LIFE.
DAWN...
DON'T "DAWN" ME, BRETT. FIRST, WHY WAS EMMA IN THE HOSPITAL IN THE FIRST PLACE?

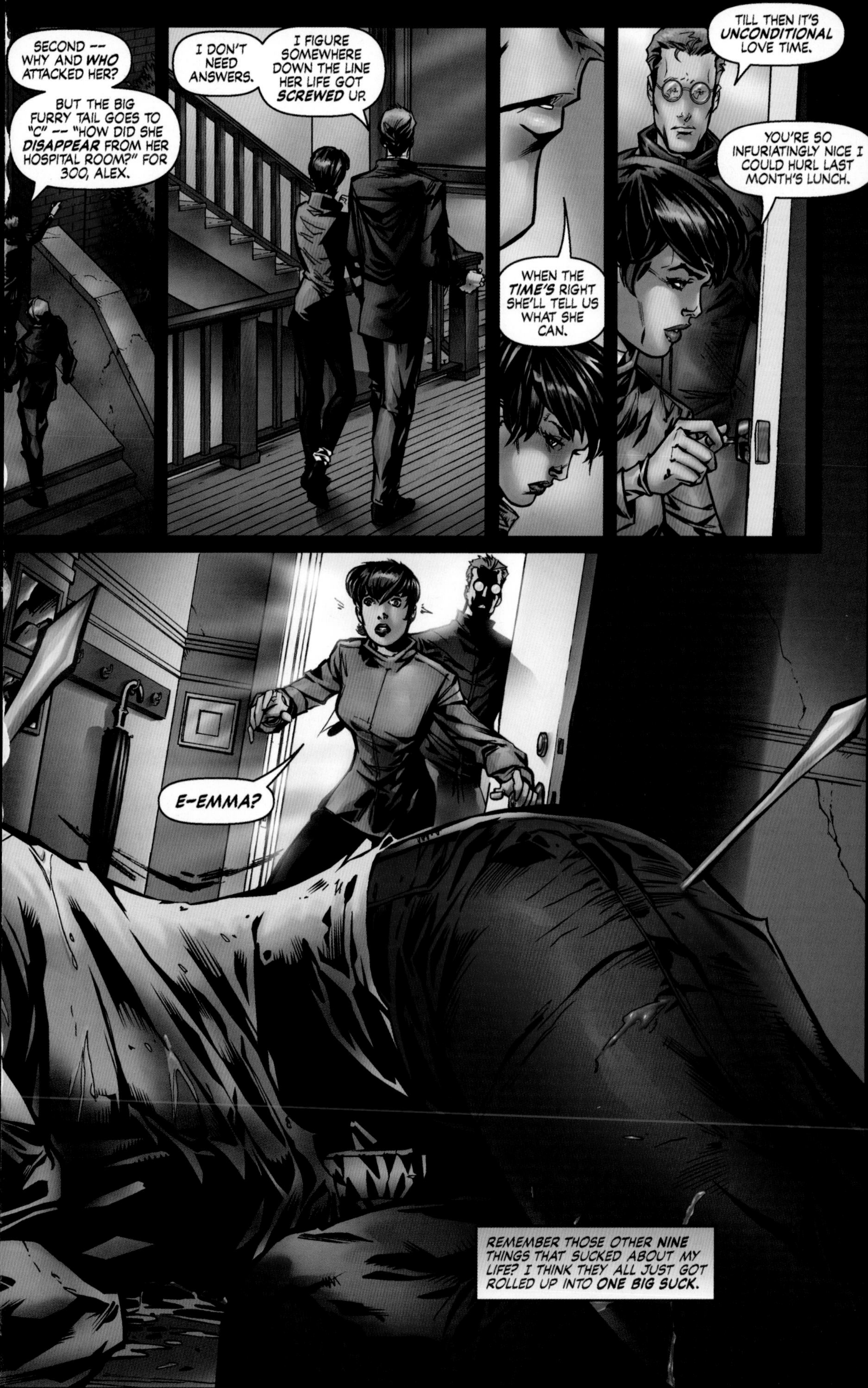
SECOND -- WHY AND WHO ATTACKED HER?
BUT THE BIG FURRY TAIL GOES TO "C" -- "HOW DID SHE DISAPPEAR FROM HER HOSPITAL ROOM?" FOR 300, ALEX.
I DON'T NEED ANSWERS.
I FIGURE SOMEWHERE DOWN THE LINE HER LIFE GOT SCREWED UP.
WHEN THE TIME'S RIGHT SHE'LL TELL US WHAT SHE CAN.
TILL THEN IT'S UNCONDITIONAL LOVE TIME.
YOU'RE SO INFURIATINGLY NICE I COULD HURL LAST MONTH'S LUNCH.
E-EMMA?
REMEMBER THOSE OTHER NINE THINGS THAT SUCKED ABOUT MY LIFE? I THINK THEY ALL JUST GOT ROLLED UP INTO ONE BIG SUCK.

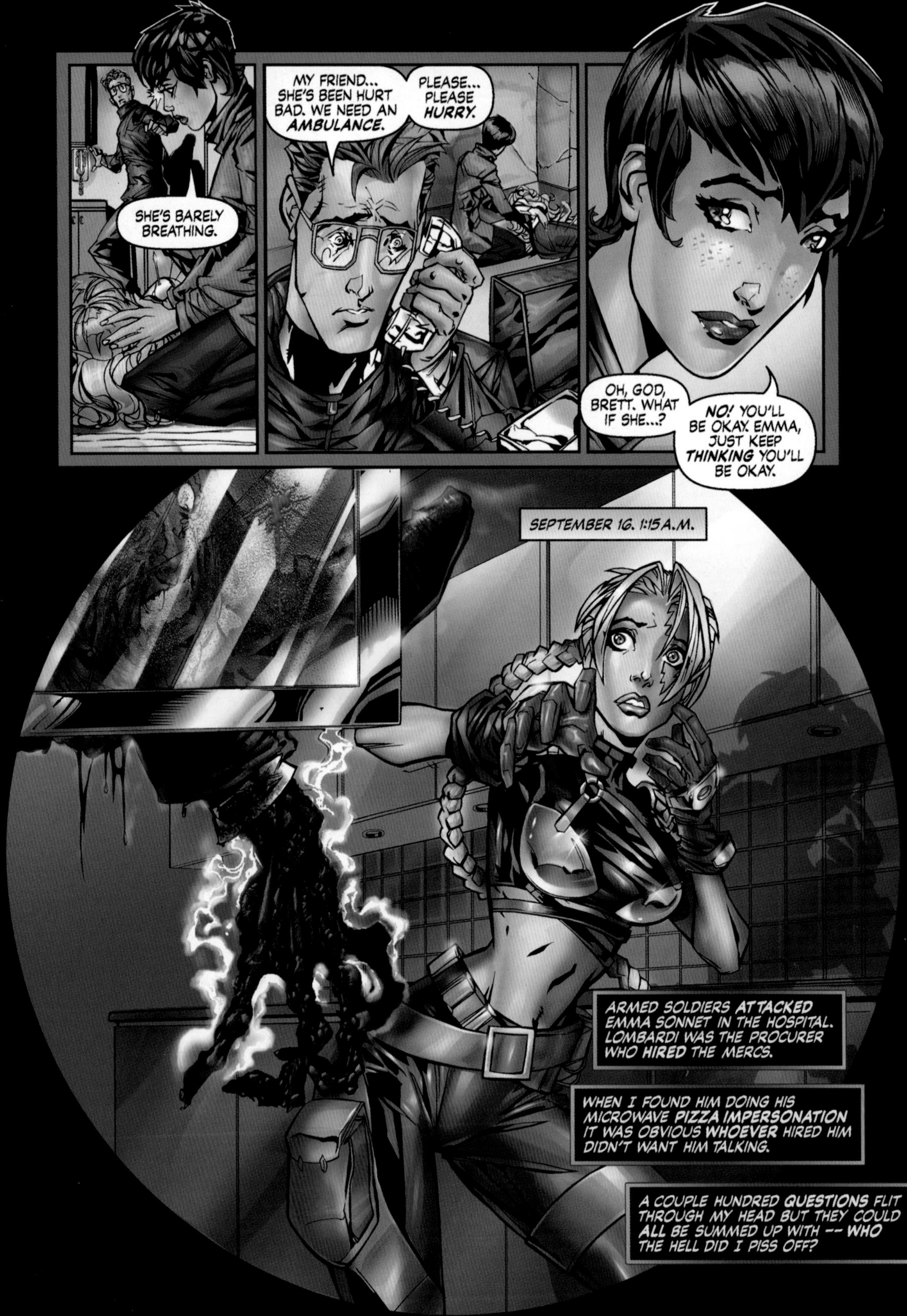
SHE'S BARELY BREATHING.
MY FRIEND... SHE'S BEEN HURT BAD. WE NEED AN AMBULANCE.
PLEASE... PLEASE HURRY.
OH, GOD, BRETT. WHAT IF SHE...?
NO! YOU'LL BE OKAY. EMMA, JUST KEEP THINKING YOU'LL BE OKAY.
SEPTEMBER 16. 1:15 A.M.
ARMED SOLDIERS ATTACKED EMMA SONNET IN THE HOSPITAL. LOMBARDI WAS THE PROCURER WHO HIRED THE MERCS.
WHEN I FOUND HIM DOING HIS MICROWAVE PIZZA IMPERSONATION IT WAS OBVIOUS WHOEVER HIRED HIM DIDN'T WANT HIM TALKING.
A COUPLE HUNDRED QUESTIONS FLIT THROUGH MY HEAD BUT THEY COULD ALL BE SUMMED UP WITH -- WHO THE HELL DID I PISS OFF?

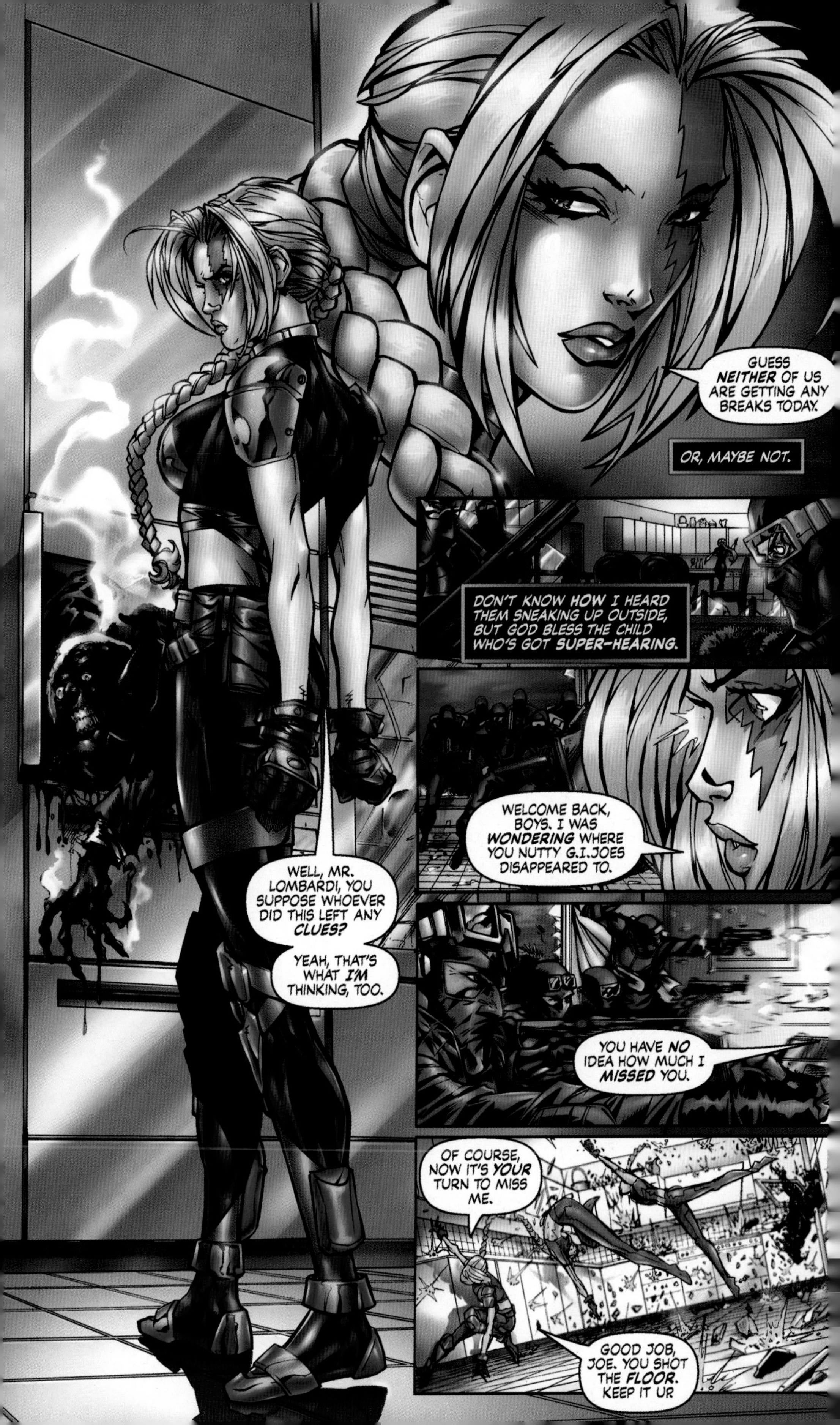
GUESS NEITHER OF US ARE GETTING ANY BREAKS TODAY.
WELL, MR. LOMBARDI, YOU SUPPOSE WHOEVER DID THIS LEFT ANY CLUES?
YEAH, THAT'S WHAT I'M THINKING, TOO.
OR, MAYBE NOT.
DON'T KNOW HOW I HEARD THEM SNEAKING UP OUTSIDE, BUT GOD BLESS THE CHILD WHO'S GOT SUPER-HEARING.
WELCOME BACK, BOYS. I WAS WONDERING WHERE YOU NUTTY G.I.JOES DISAPPEARED TO.
YOU HAVE NO IDEA HOW MUCH I MISSED YOU.
OF COURSE, NOW IT'S YOUR TURN TO MISS ME.
GOOD JOB, JOE. YOU SHOT THE FLOOR. KEEP IT UP.

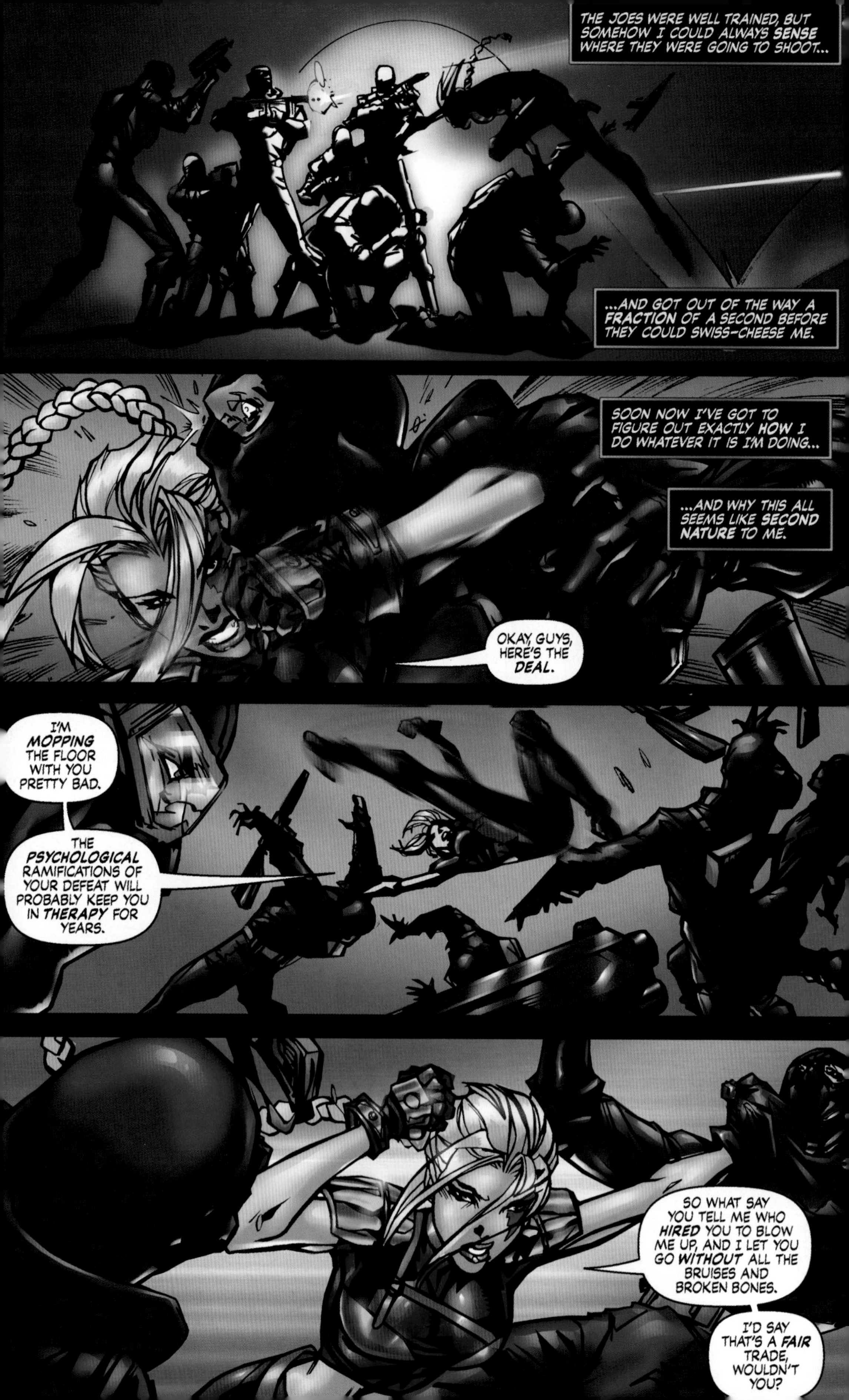
THE JOES WERE WELL TRAINED, BUT SOMEHOW I COULD ALWAYS SENSE WHERE THEY WERE GOING TO SHOOT...
...AND GOT OUT OF THE WAY A FRACTION OF A SECOND BEFORE THEY COULD SWISS-CHEESE ME.
SOON NOW I'VE GOT TO FIGURE OUT EXACTLY HOW I DO WHATEVER IT IS I'M DOING...
...AND WHY THIS ALL SEEMS LIKE SECOND NATURE TO ME.
OKAY, GUYS, HERE'S THE DEAL.
I'M MOPPING THE FLOOR WITH YOU PRETTY BAD.
THE PSYCHOLOGICAL RAMIFICATIONS OF YOUR DEFEAT WILL PROBABLY KEEP YOU IN THERAPY FOR YEARS.
SO WHAT SAY YOU TELL ME WHO HIRED YOU TO BLOW ME UP, AND I LET YOU GO WITHOUT ALL THE BRUISES AND BROKEN BONES.
I'D SAY THAT'S A FAIR TRADE, WOULDN'T YOU?

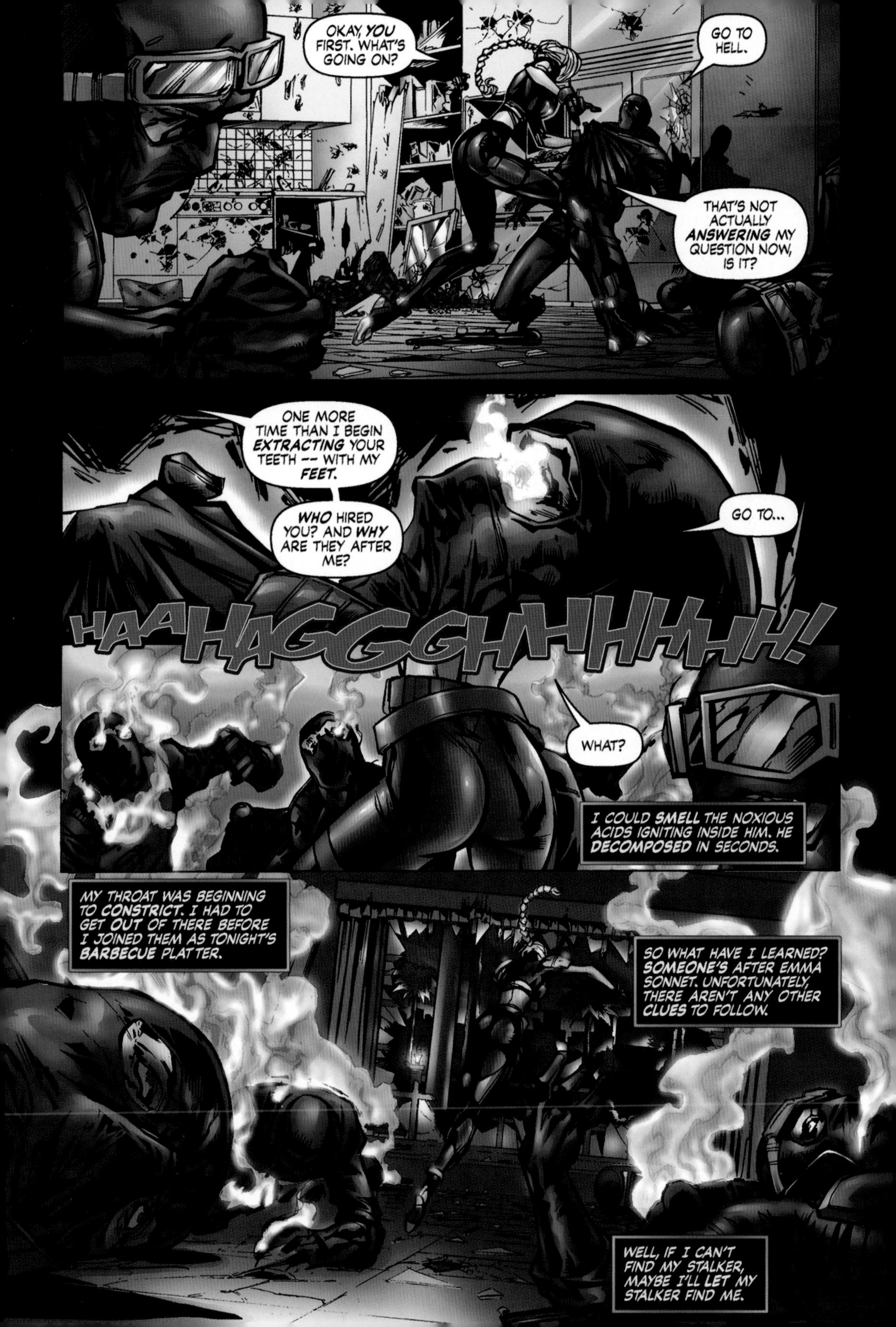

OKAY, YOU FIRST. WHAT'S GOING ON?
GO TO HELL.
THAT'S NOT ACTUALLY ANSWERING MY QUESTION NOW, IS IT?
ONE MORE TIME THAN I BEGIN EXTRACTING YOUR TEETH -- WITH MY FEET.
WHO HIRED YOU? AND WHY ARE THEY AFTER ME?
GO TO...
HAAHAGGGHHHHHHH!
WHAT?
I COULD SMELL THE NOXIOUS ACIDS IGNITING INSIDE HIM. HE DECOMPOSED IN SECONDS.
MY THROAT WAS BEGINNING TO CONSTRICT. I HAD TO GET OUT OF THERE BEFORE I JOINED THEM AS TONIGHT'S BARBECUE PLATTER.
SO WHAT HAVE I LEARNED? SOMEONE'S AFTER EMMA SONNET. UNFORTUNATELY, THERE AREN'T ANY OTHER CLUES TO FOLLOW.
WELL, IF I CAN'T FIND MY STALKER, MAYBE I'LL LET MY STALKER FIND ME.

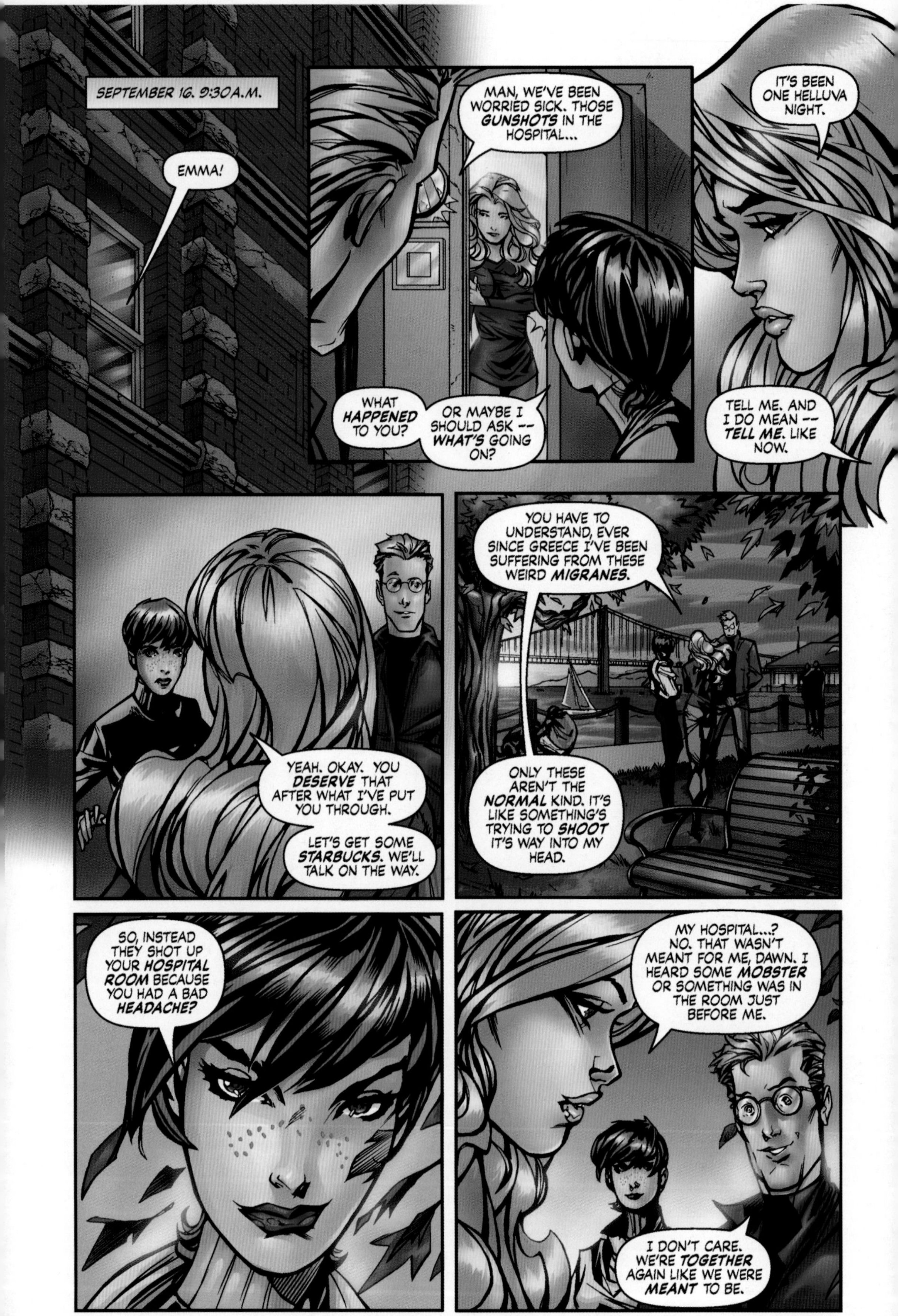
SEPTEMBER 16. 9:30A.M.
EMMA!
MAN, WE'VE BEEN WORRIED SICK. THOSE GUNSHOTS IN THE HOSPITAL...
WHAT HAPPENED TO YOU?
OR MAYBE I SHOULD ASK -- WHAT'S GOING ON?
IT'S BEEN ONE HELLUVA NIGHT.
TELL ME. AND I DO MEAN -- TELL ME. LIKE NOW.
YEAH. OKAY. YOU DESERVE THAT AFTER WHAT I'VE PUT YOU THROUGH.
LET'S GET SOME STARBUCKS. WE'LL TALK ON THE WAY.
YOU HAVE TO UNDERSTAND, EVER SINCE GREECE I'VE BEEN SUFFERING FROM THESE WEIRD MIGRANES.
ONLY THESE AREN'T THE NORMAL KIND. IT'S LIKE SOMETHING'S TRYING TO SHOOT IT'S WAY INTO MY HEAD.
SO, INSTEAD THEY SHOT UP YOUR HOSPITAL ROOM BECAUSE YOU HAD A BAD HEADACHE?
MY HOSPITAL...? NO. THAT WASN'T MEANT FOR ME, DAWN. I HEARD SOME MOBSTER OR SOMETHING WAS IN THE ROOM JUST BEFORE ME.
I DON'T CARE. WE'RE TOGETHER AGAIN LIKE WE WERE MEANT TO BE.

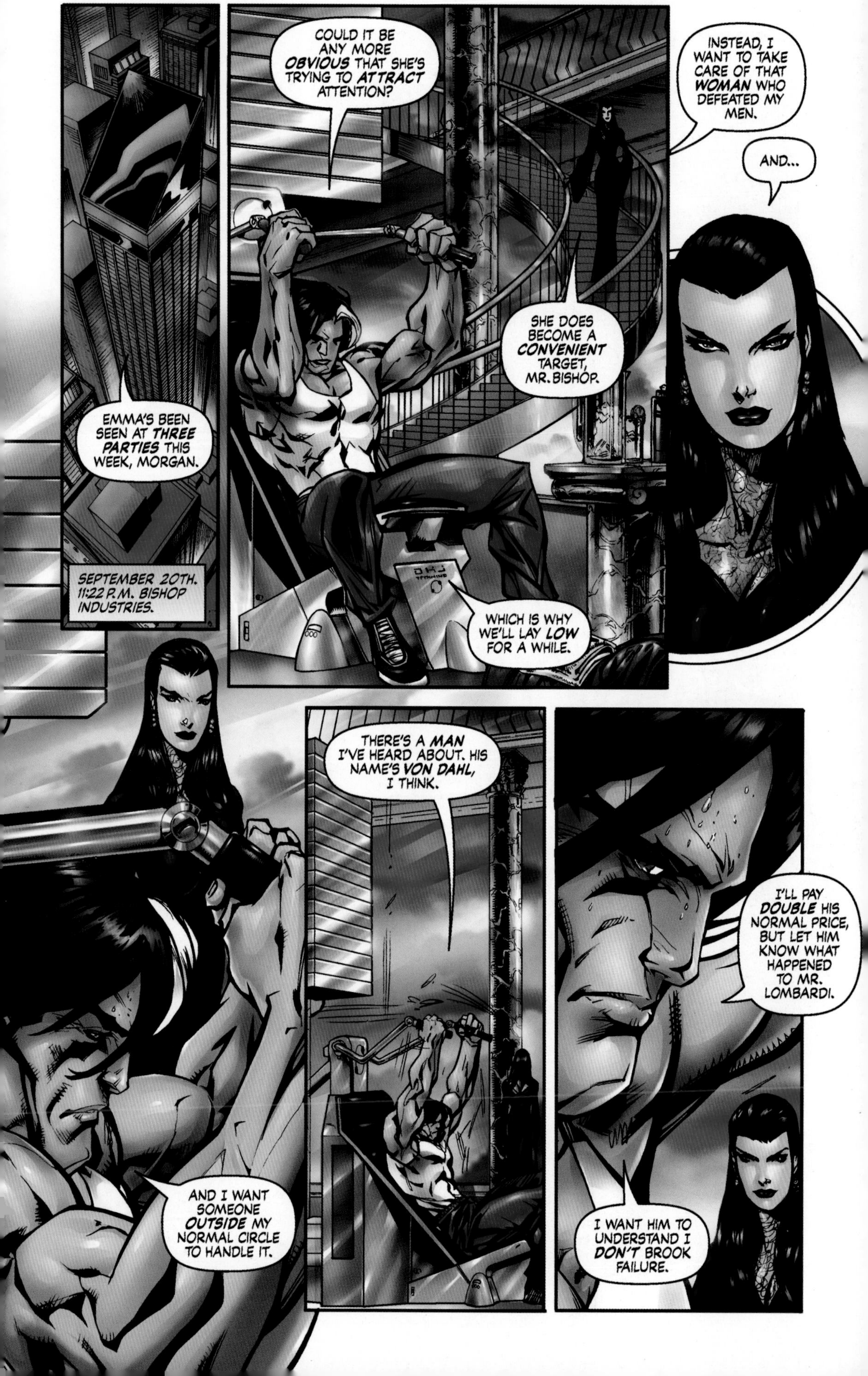
SEPTEMBER 20TH. 11:22 P.M. BISHOP INDUSTRIES.
EMMA'S BEEN SEEN AT THREE PARTIES THIS WEEK, MORGAN.
COULD IT BE ANY MORE OBVIOUS THAT SHE'S TRYING TO ATTRACT ATTENTION?
SHE DOES BECOME A CONVENIENT TARGET, MR. BISHOP.
WHICH IS WHY WE'LL LAY LOW FOR A WHILE.
INSTEAD, I WANT TO TAKE CARE OF THAT WOMAN WHO DEFEATED MY MEN.
AND...
AND I WANT SOMEONE OUTSIDE MY NORMAL CIRCLE TO HANDLE IT.
THERE'S A MAN I'VE HEARD ABOUT. HIS NAME'S VON DAHL, I THINK.
I'LL PAY DOUBLE HIS NORMAL PRICE, BUT LET HIM KNOW WHAT HAPPENED TO MR. LOMBARDI.
I WANT HIM TO UNDERSTAND I DON'T BROOK FAILURE.

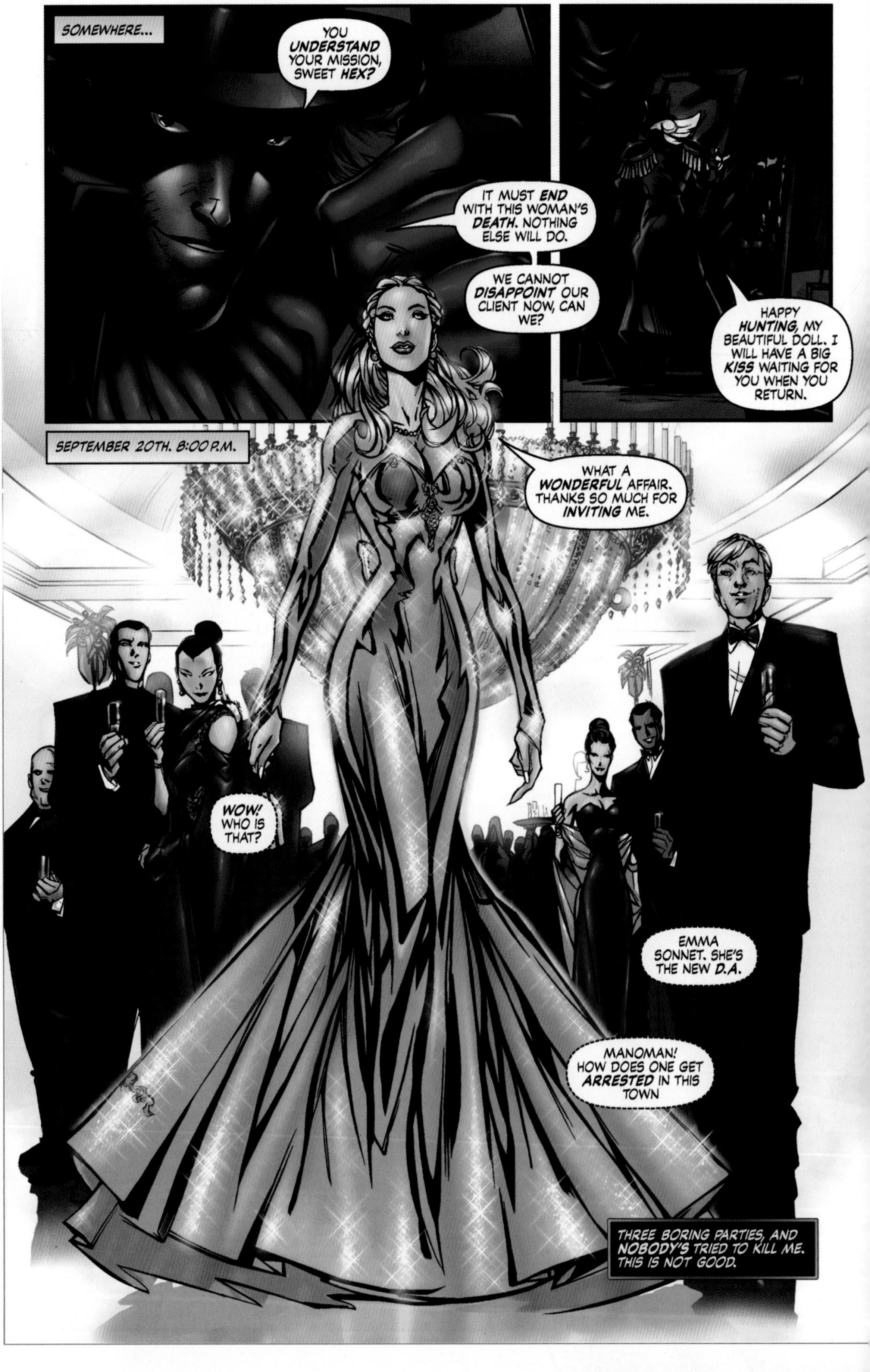
SOMEWHERE...
YOU UNDERSTAND YOUR MISSION, SWEET HEX?
IT MUST END WITH THIS WOMAN'S DEATH. NOTHING ELSE WILL DO.
WE CANNOT DISAPPOINT OUR CLIENT NOW, CAN WE?
HAPPY HUNTING, MY BEAUTIFUL DOLL. I WILL HAVE A BIG KISS WAITING FOR YOU WHEN YOU RETURN.
SEPTEMBER 20TH. 8:00 P.M.
WHAT A WONDERFUL AFFAIR. THANKS SO MUCH FOR INVITING ME.
WOW! WHO IS THAT?
EMMA SONNET. SHE'S THE NEW D.A.
MANOMAN! HOW DOES ONE GET ARRESTED IN THIS TOWN
THREE BORING PARTIES, AND NOBODY'S TRIED TO KILL ME. THIS IS NOT GOOD.

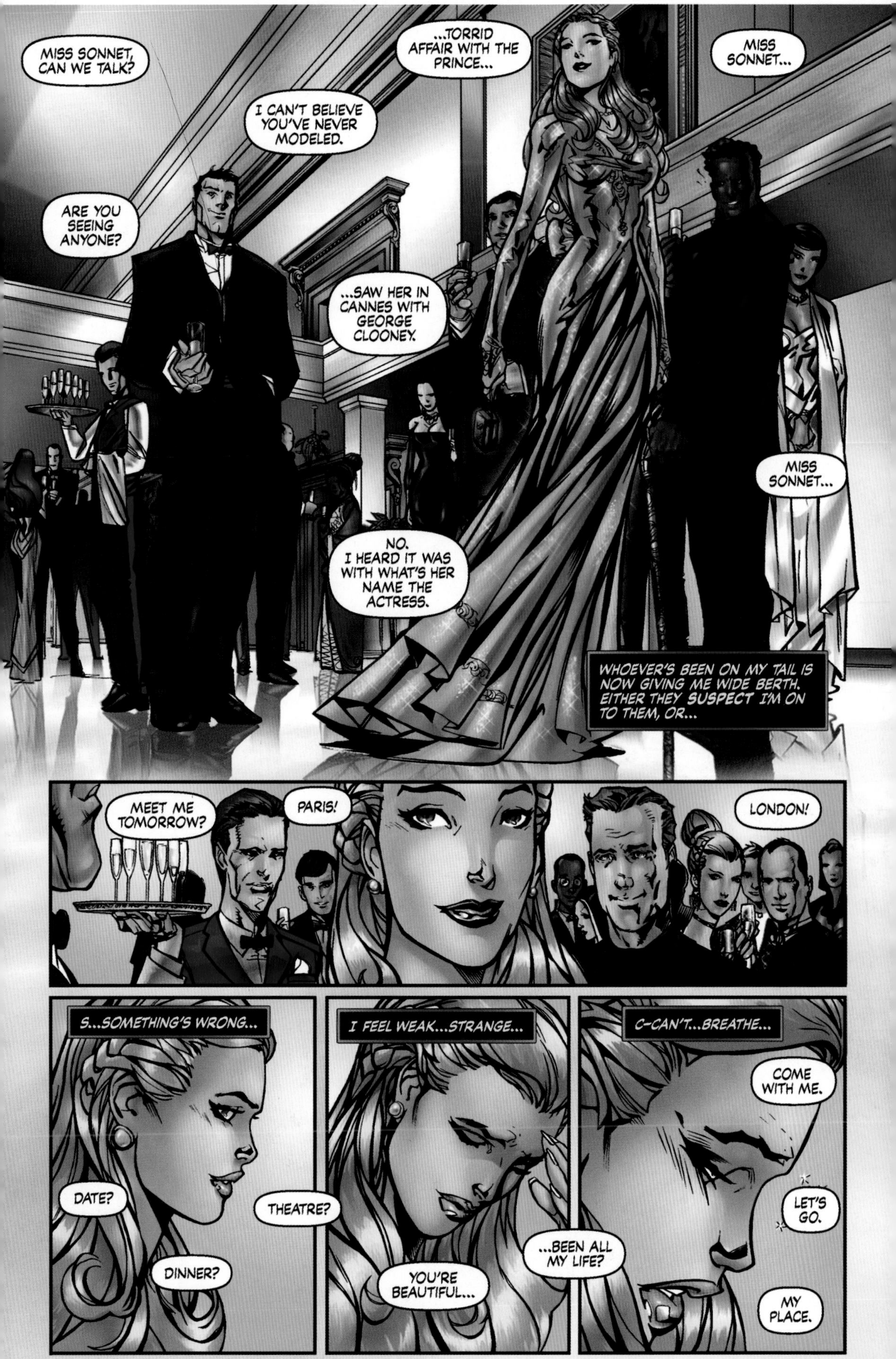
MISS SONNET, CAN WE TALK?
I CAN'T BELIEVE YOU'VE NEVER MODELED.
...TORRID AFFAIR WITH THE PRINCE...
MISS SONNET...
ARE YOU SEEING ANYONE?
...SAW HER IN CANNES WITH GEORGE CLOONEY.
MISS SONNET...
NO. I HEARD IT WAS WITH WHAT'S HER NAME THE ACTRESS.
WHOEVER'S BEEN ON MY TAIL IS NOW GIVING ME WIDE BERTH. EITHER THEY SUSPECT I'M ON TO THEM, OR...
MEET ME TOMORROW?
PARIS!
LONDON!
S...SOMETHING'S WRONG...
DATE?
DINNER?
THEATRE?
I FEEL WEAK...STRANGE...
YOU'RE BEAUTIFUL...
...BEEN ALL MY LIFE?
C-CAN'T...BREATHE...
COME WITH ME.
LET'S GO.
MY PLACE.

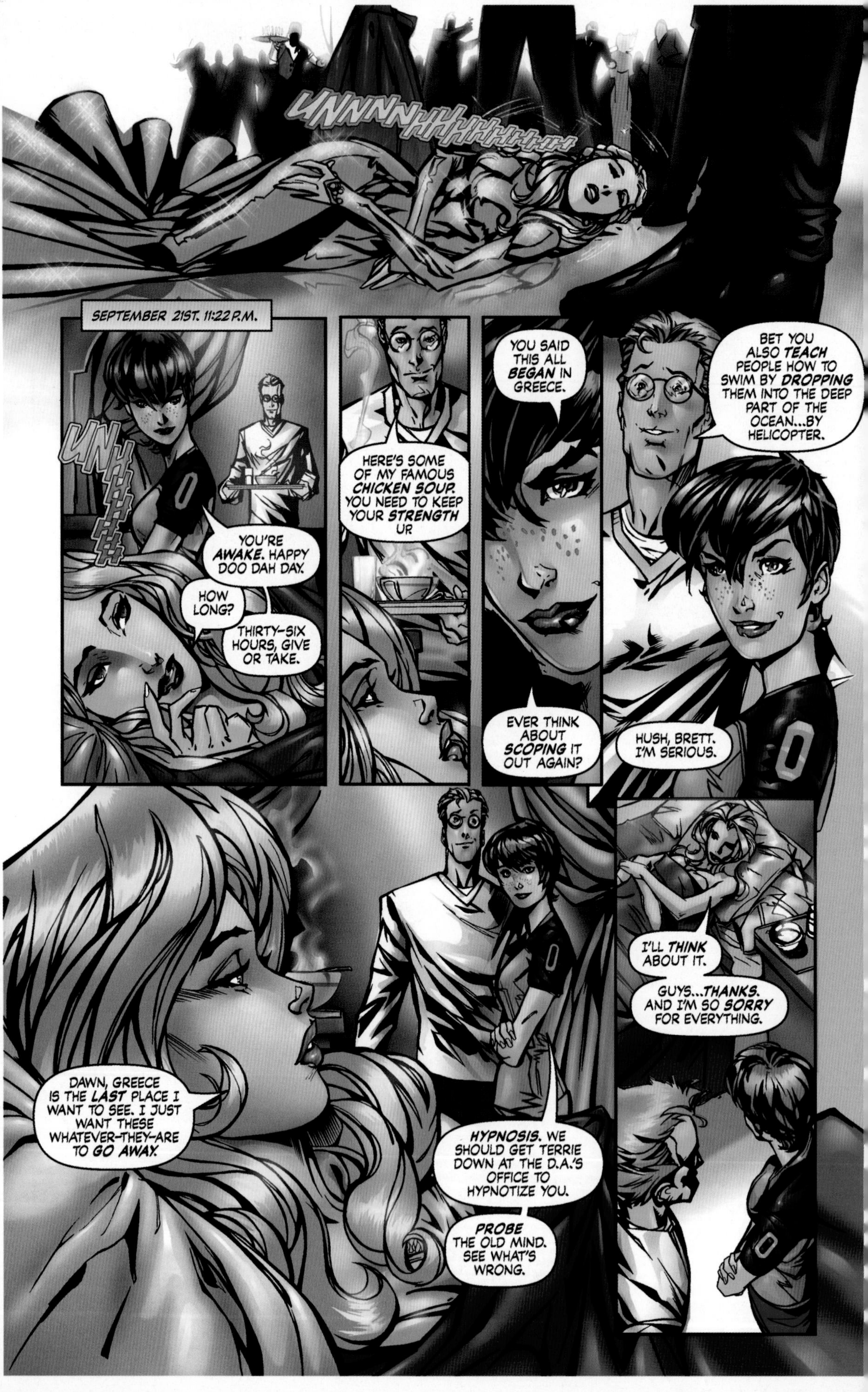
UNNNNHHHHHHHHHHH
SEPTEMBER 21ST. 11:22 P.M.
UNHHHHHH
YOU'RE AWAKE. HAPPY DOO DAH DAY.
HOW LONG?
THIRTY-SIX HOURS, GIVE OR TAKE.
HERE'S SOME OF MY FAMOUS CHICKEN SOUP. YOU NEED TO KEEP YOUR STRENGTH UP.
YOU SAID THIS ALL BEGAN IN GREECE.
EVER THINK ABOUT SCOPING IT OUT AGAIN?
BET YOU ALSO TEACH PEOPLE HOW TO SWIM BY DROPPING THEM INTO THE DEEP PART OF THE OCEAN...BY HELICOPTER.
HUSH, BRETT. I'M SERIOUS.
DAWN, GREECE IS THE LAST PLACE I WANT TO SEE. I JUST WANT THESE WHATEVER-THEY-ARE TO GO AWAY.
HYPNOSIS. WE SHOULD GET TERRIE DOWN AT THE D.A.'S OFFICE TO HYPNOTIZE YOU.
PROBE THE OLD MIND. SEE WHAT'S WRONG.
I'LL THINK ABOUT IT.
GUYS...THANKS. AND I'M SO SORRY FOR EVERYTHING.

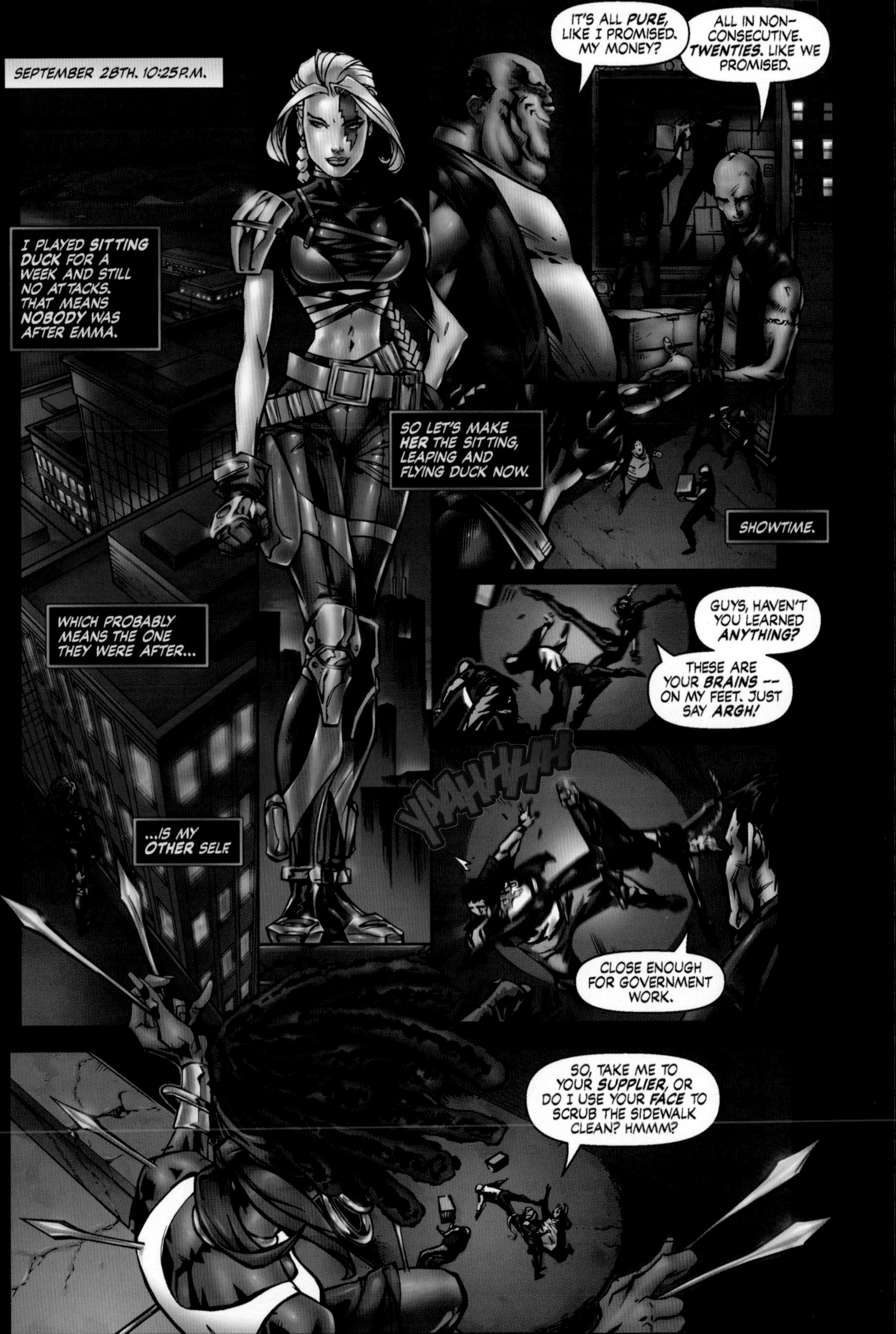

SEPTEMBER 28TH. 10:25P.M.
I PLAYED SITTING DUCK FOR A WEEK AND STILL NO ATTACKS. THAT MEANS NOBODY WAS AFTER EMMA.
WHICH PROBABLY MEANS THE ONE THEY WERE AFTER...
...IS MY OTHER SELF.
IT'S ALL PURE, LIKE I PROMISED. MY MONEY?
ALL IN NON-CONSECUTIVE. TWENTIES. LIKE WE PROMISED.
SO LET'S MAKE HER THE SITTING, LEAPING AND FLYING DUCK NOW.
SHOWTIME.
GUYS, HAVEN'T YOU LEARNED ANYTHING?
THESE ARE YOUR BRAINS -- ON MY FEET. JUST SAY ARGH!
YAAHHHHH
CLOSE ENOUGH FOR GOVERNMENT WORK.
SO, TAKE ME TO YOUR SUPPLIER, OR DO I USE YOUR FACE TO SCRUB THE SIDEWALK CLEAN? HMMM?

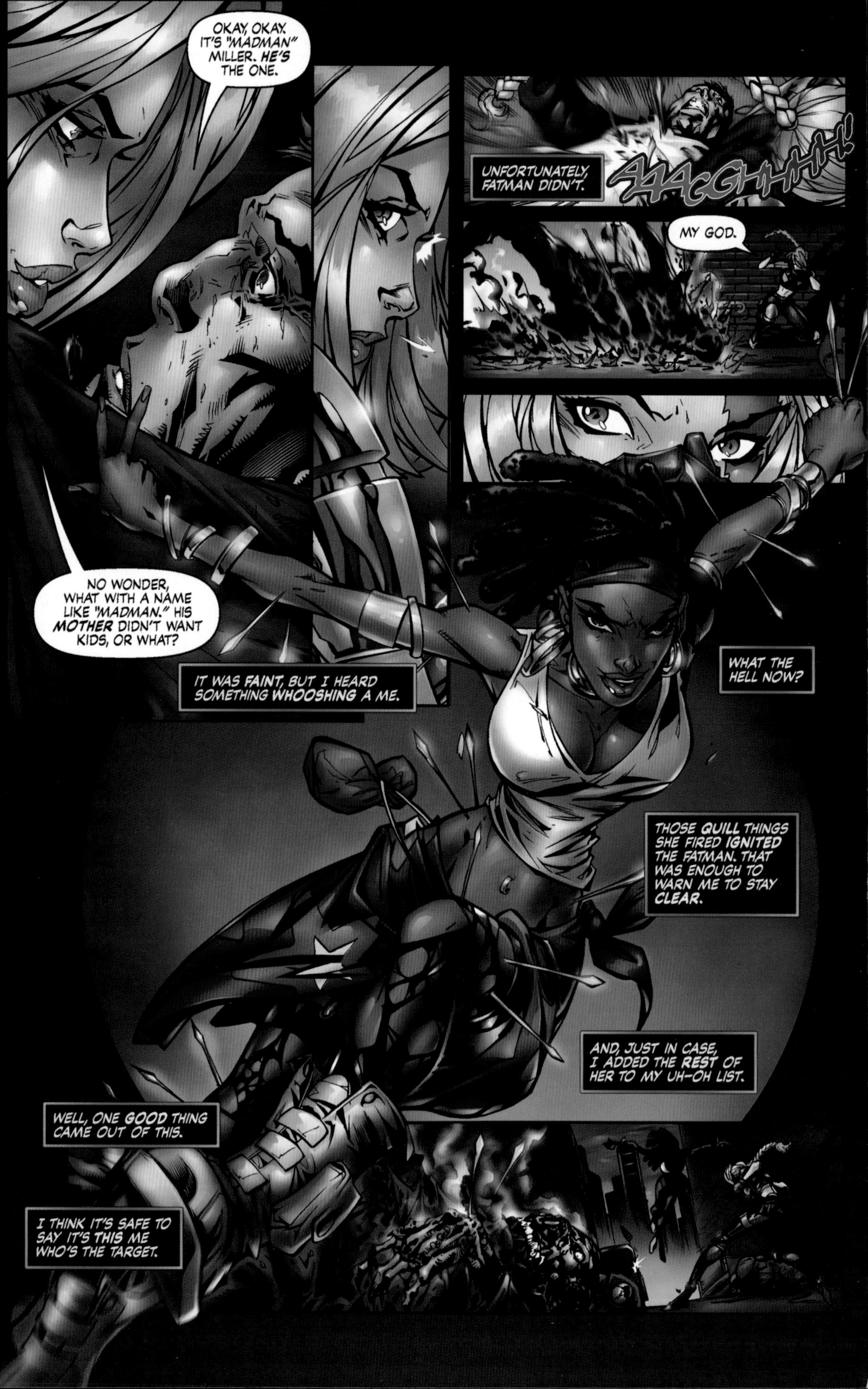

OKAY, OKAY. IT'S "MADMAN" MILLER. HE'S THE ONE.
UNFORTUNATELY, FATMAN DIDN'T.
AAAGGHHHH!
MY GOD.
NO WONDER, WHAT WITH A NAME LIKE "MADMAN." HIS MOTHER DIDN'T WANT KIDS, OR WHAT?
IT WAS FAINT, BUT I HEARD SOMETHING WHOOSHING A ME.
WHAT THE HELL NOW?
THOSE QUILL THINGS SHE FIRED IGNITED THE FATMAN. THAT WAS ENOUGH TO WARN ME TO STAY CLEAR.
AND, JUST IN CASE, I ADDED THE REST OF HER TO MY UH-OH LIST.
WELL, ONE GOOD THING CAME OUT OF THIS.
I THINK IT'S SAFE TO SAY IT'S THIS ME WHO'S THE TARGET.

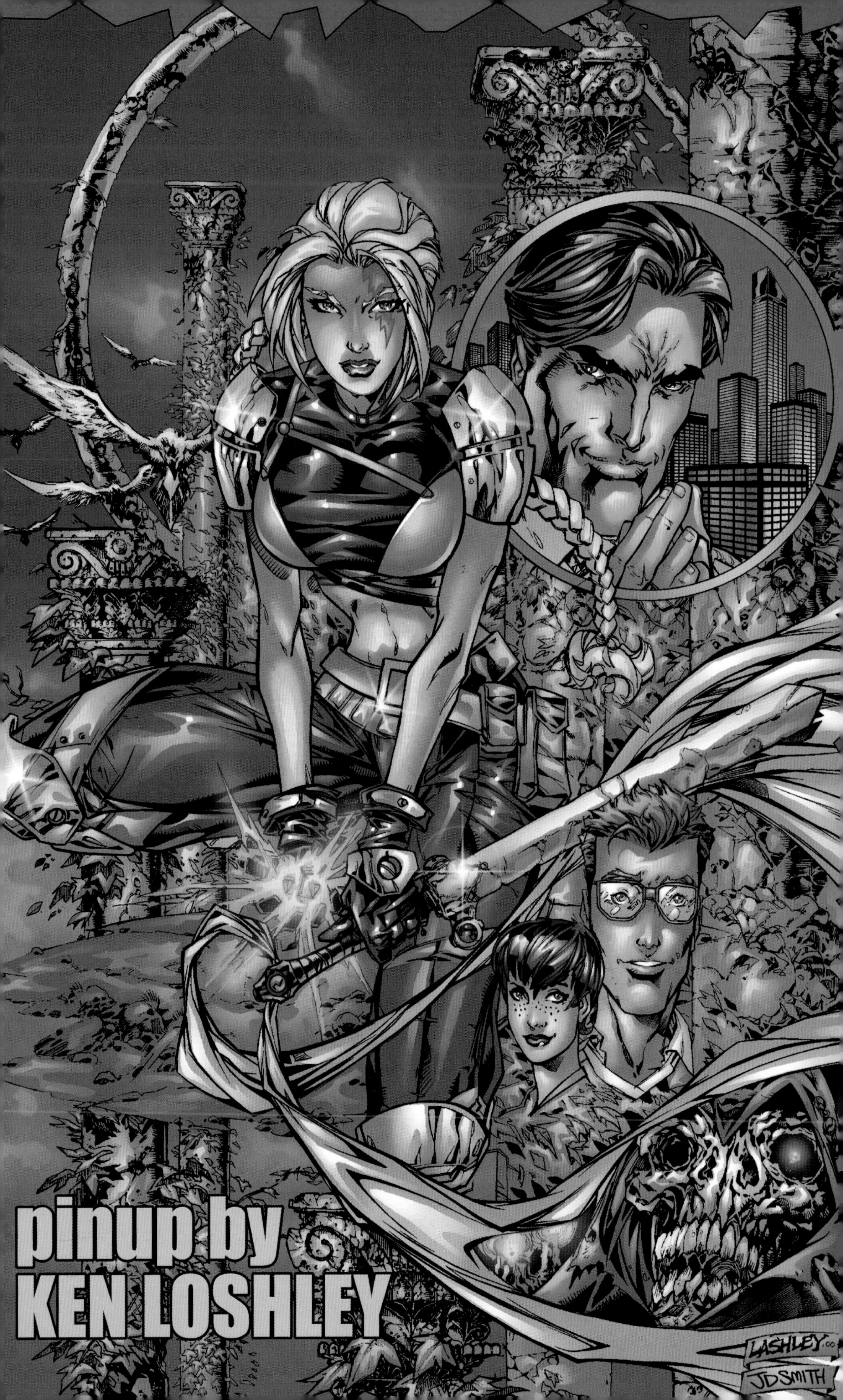
LASHLEY.00
JD SMITH

pinup by
KEN LOSHLEY

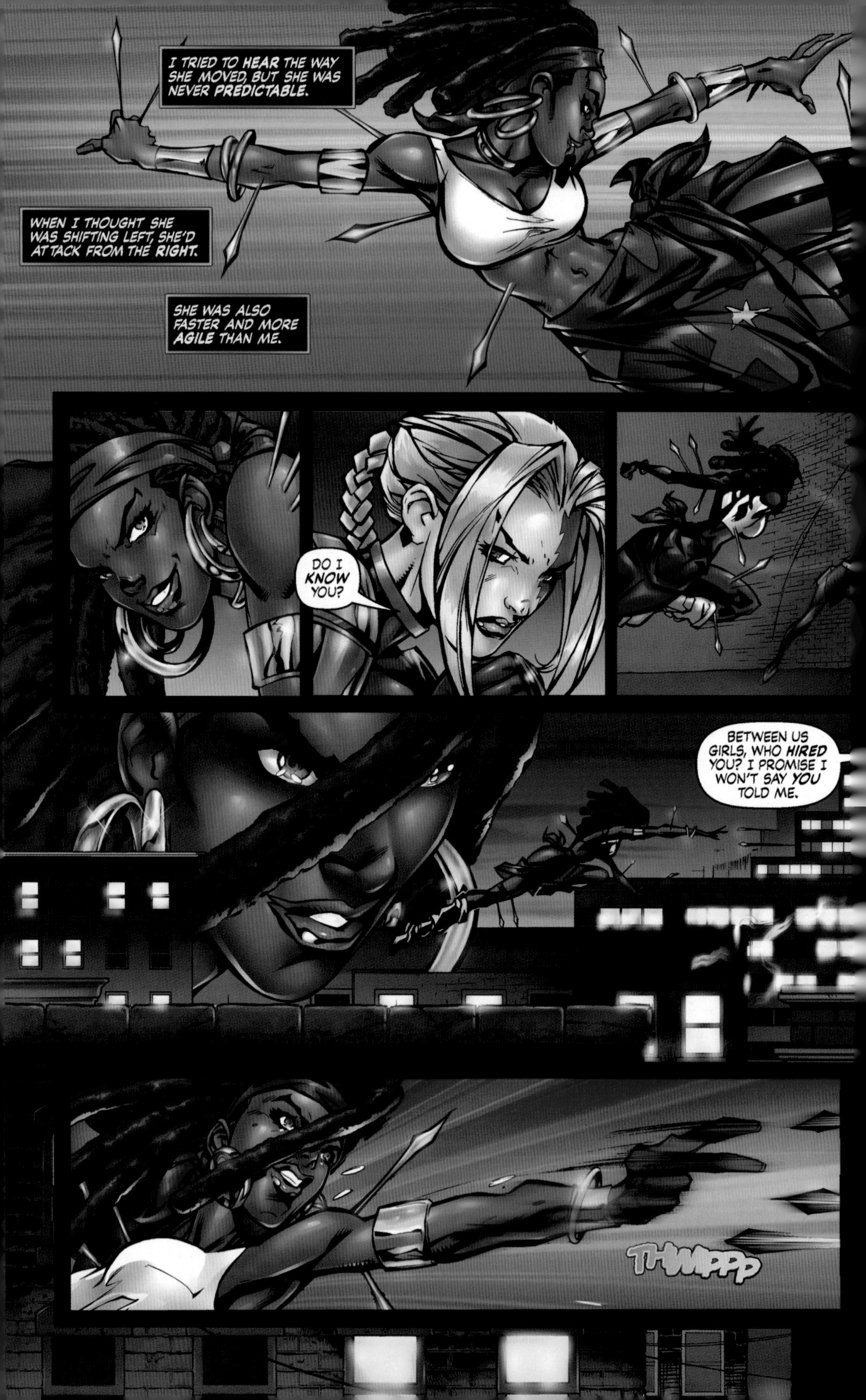
I TRIED TO HEAR THE WAY SHE MOVED, BUT SHE WAS NEVER PREDICTABLE.
WHEN I THOUGHT SHE WAS SHIFTING LEFT, SHE'D ATTACK FROM THE RIGHT.
SHE WAS ALSO FASTER AND MORE AGILE THAN ME.
DO I KNOW YOU?
BETWEEN US GIRLS, WHO HIRED YOU? I PROMISE I WON'T SAY YOU TOLD ME.
THWIPPP

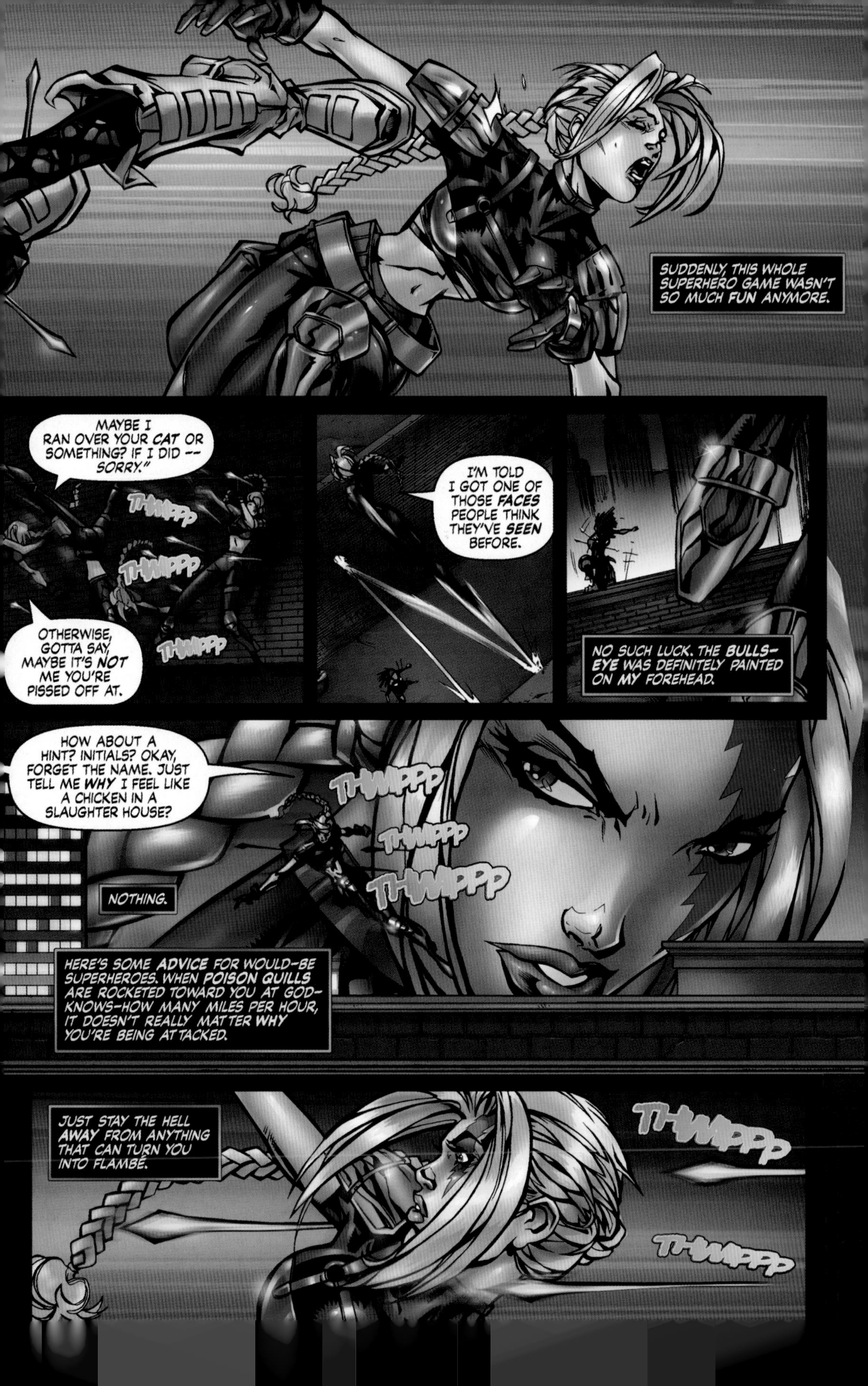
SUDDENLY, THIS WHOLE SUPERHERO GAME WASN'T SO MUCH FUN ANYMORE.
MAYBE I RAN OVER YOUR CAT OR SOMETHING? IF I DID -- SORRY."
THWIPPP
THWIPPP
THWIPPP
OTHERWISE, GOTTA SAY, MAYBE IT'S NOT ME YOU'RE PISSED OFF AT.
I'M TOLD I GOT ONE OF THOSE FACES PEOPLE THINK THEY'VE SEEN BEFORE.
NO SUCH LUCK. THE BULLS-EYE WAS DEFINITELY PAINTED ON MY FOREHEAD.
HOW ABOUT A HINT? INITIALS? OKAY, FORGET THE NAME. JUST TELL ME WHY I FEEL LIKE A CHICKEN IN A SLAUGHTER HOUSE?
THWIPPP
THWIPPP
THWIPPP
NOTHING.
HERE'S SOME ADVICE FOR WOULD-BE SUPERHEROES. WHEN POISON QUILLS ARE ROCKETED TOWARD YOU AT GOD-KNOWS-HOW MANY MILES PER HOUR, IT DOESN'T REALLY MATTER WHY YOU'RE BEING ATTACKED.
JUST STAY THE HELL AWAY FROM ANYTHING THAT CAN TURN YOU INTO FLAMBÉ.
THWIPPP
THWIPPP

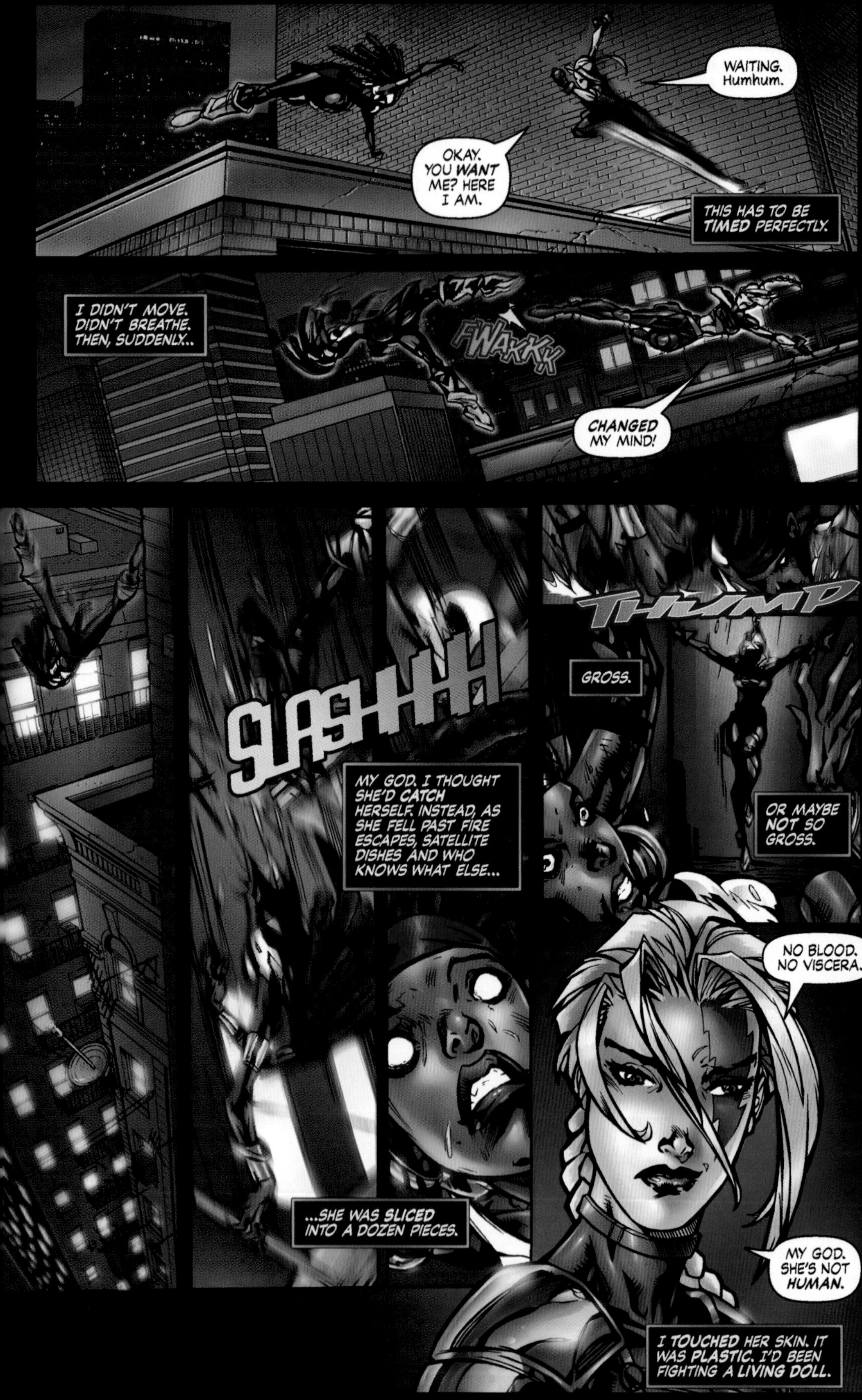

WAITING. Humhum.
OKAY. YOU WANT ME? HERE I AM.
THIS HAS TO BE TIMED PERFECTLY.
I DIDN'T MOVE. DIDN'T BREATHE. THEN, SUDDENLY..
FWAKKK
CHANGED MY MIND!
SLASHHHH
MY GOD. I THOUGHT SHE'D CATCH HERSELF. INSTEAD, AS SHE FELL PAST FIRE ESCAPES, SATELLITE DISHES AND WHO KNOWS WHAT ELSE...
...SHE WAS SLICED INTO A DOZEN PIECES.
THUMP
GROSS.
OR MAYBE NOT SO GROSS.
NO BLOOD. NO VISCERA.
MY GOD. SHE'S NOT HUMAN.
I TOUCHED HER SKIN. IT WAS PLASTIC. I'D BEEN FIGHTING A LIVING DOLL.

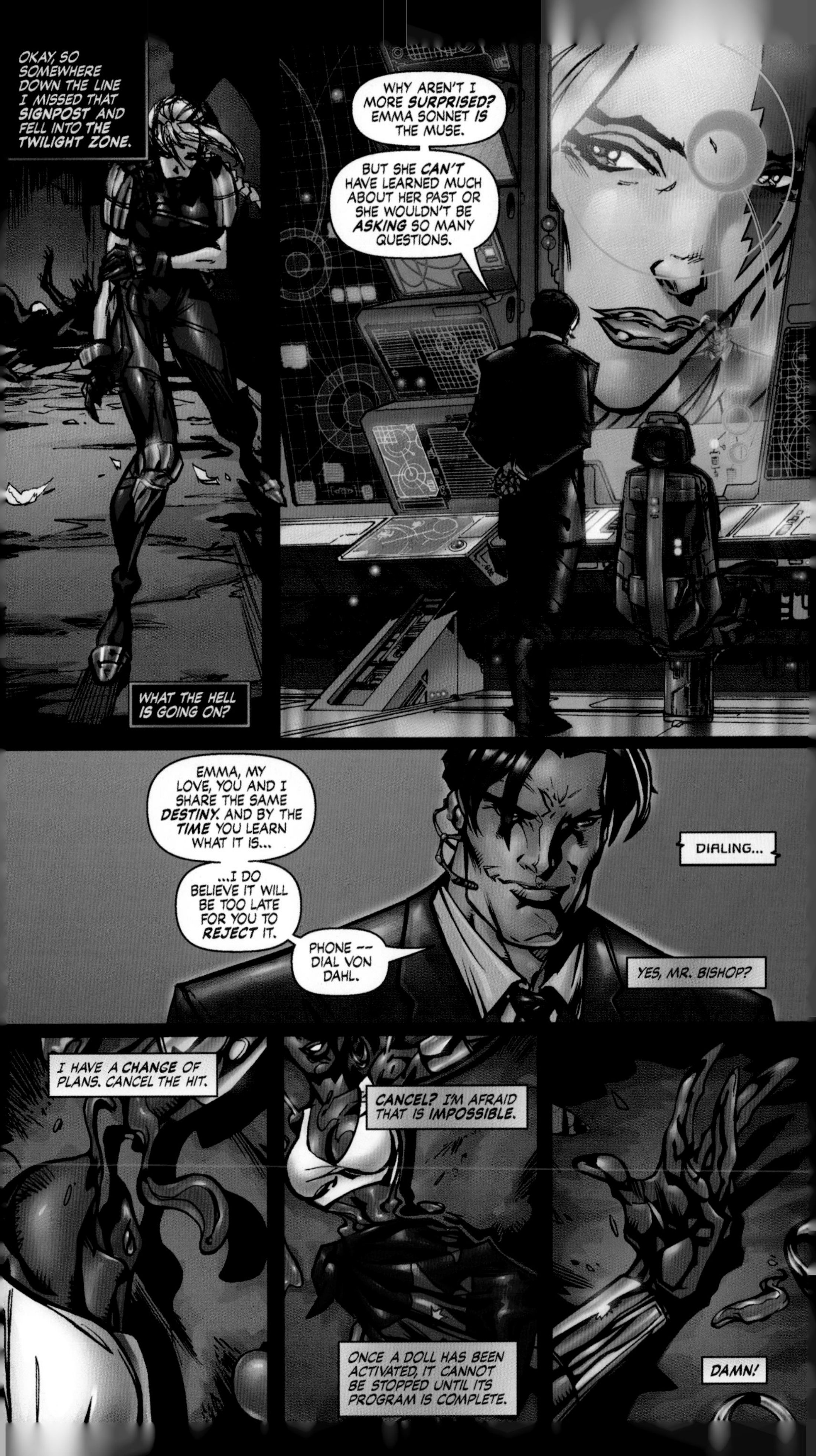
OKAY, SO SOMEWHERE DOWN THE LINE I MISSED THAT SIGNPOST AND FELL INTO THE TWILIGHT ZONE.
WHAT THE HELL IS GOING ON?
WHY AREN'T I MORE SURPRISED? EMMA SONNET IS THE MUSE.
BUT SHE CAN'T HAVE LEARNED MUCH ABOUT HER PAST OR SHE WOULDN'T BE ASKING SO MANY QUESTIONS.
EMMA, MY LOVE, YOU AND I SHARE THE SAME DESTINY. AND BY THE TIME YOU LEARN WHAT IT IS...
...I DO BELIEVE IT WILL BE TOO LATE FOR YOU TO REJECT IT.
PHONE -- DIAL VON DAHL.
DIALING...
YES, MR. BISHOP?
I HAVE A CHANGE OF PLANS. CANCEL THE HIT.
CANCEL? I'M AFRAID THAT IS IMPOSSIBLE.
ONCE A DOLL HAS BEEN ACTIVATED, IT CANNOT BE STOPPED UNTIL ITS PROGRAM IS COMPLETE.
DAMN!

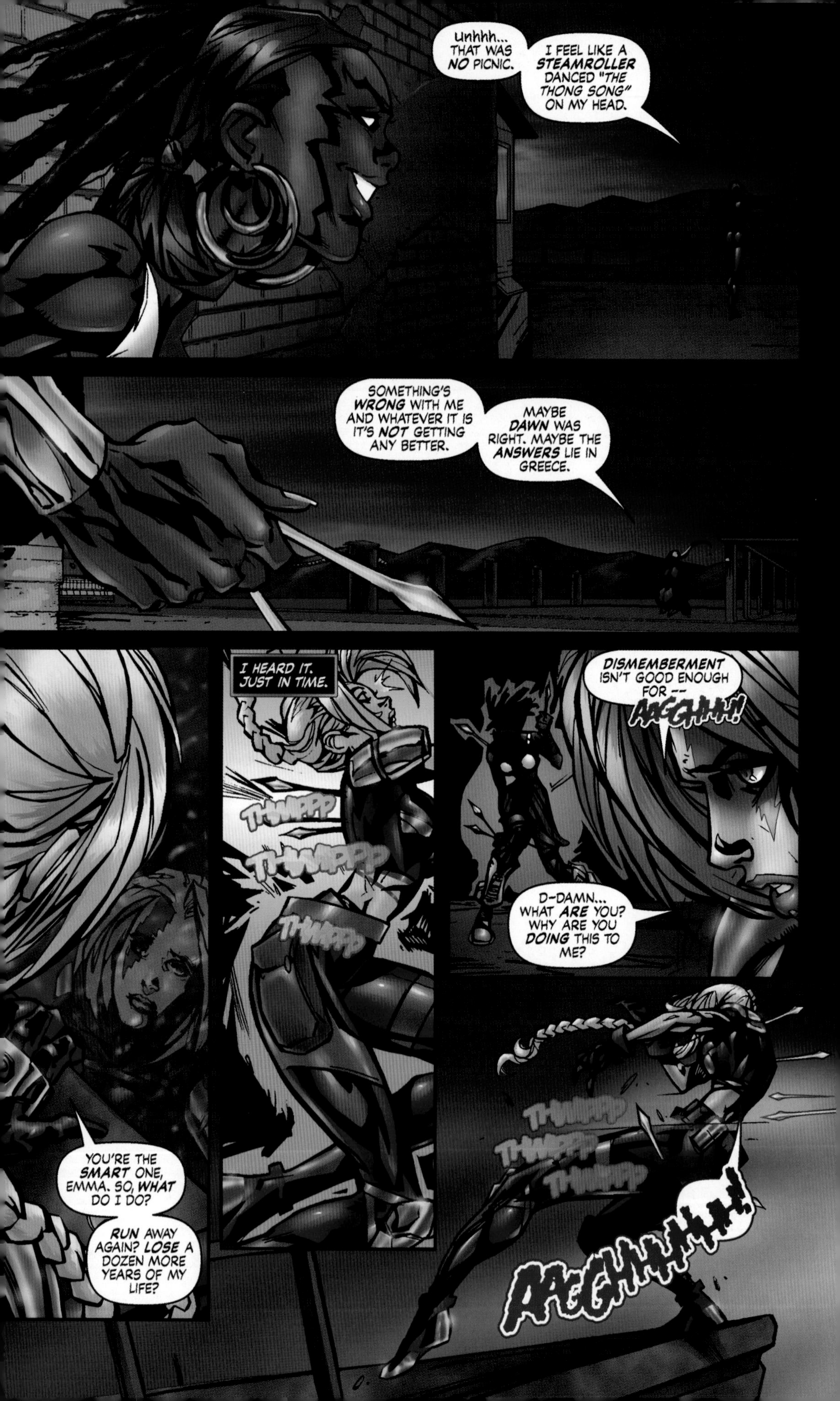

unhhh... THAT WAS NO PICNIC.
I FEEL LIKE A STEAMROLLER DANCED "THE THONG SONG" ON MY HEAD.
SOMETHING'S WRONG WITH ME AND WHATEVER IT IS IT'S NOT GETTING ANY BETTER.
MAYBE DAWN WAS RIGHT. MAYBE THE ANSWERS LIE IN GREECE.
YOU'RE THE SMART ONE, EMMA. SO, WHAT DO I DO?
RUN AWAY AGAIN? LOSE A DOZEN MORE YEARS OF MY LIFE?
I HEARD IT. JUST IN TIME.
THWIPPP
THWIPPP
THWIPPP
DISMEMBERMENT ISN'T GOOD ENOUGH FOR --
AAGHHH!
D-DAMN... WHAT ARE YOU? WHY ARE YOU DOING THIS TO ME?
THWIPPP
THWIPPP
THWIPPP
AAGHHHH!

LET GO!

I DON'T KNOW WHY I HADN'T BURNED UP YET, BUT I COULD FEEL HER *POISONS* FLOWING THROUGH MY VEINS, MAKING THEIR WAY TO MY *HEART.*

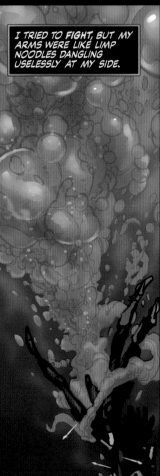

I TRIED TO *FIGHT,* BUT MY ARMS WERE LIKE LIMP NOODLES DANGLING USELESSLY AT MY SIDE.

I HAD NO STRENGTH. I HAD NO BREATH LEFT.

AND EXCEPT FOR THAT GRINNING *GHOUL* FACE LAUGHING AT ME, I HAD *NOTHING* TO HOPE FOR BUT A SLOW, PAINFUL *DEATH.*

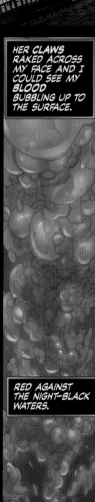

HER *CLAWS* RAKED ACROSS MY FACE AND I COULD SEE MY *BLOOD* BUBBLING UP TO THE SURFACE.

RED AGAINST THE NIGHT-BLACK WATERS.

SO PRETTY.

MY VERY *LAST SIGHT.*

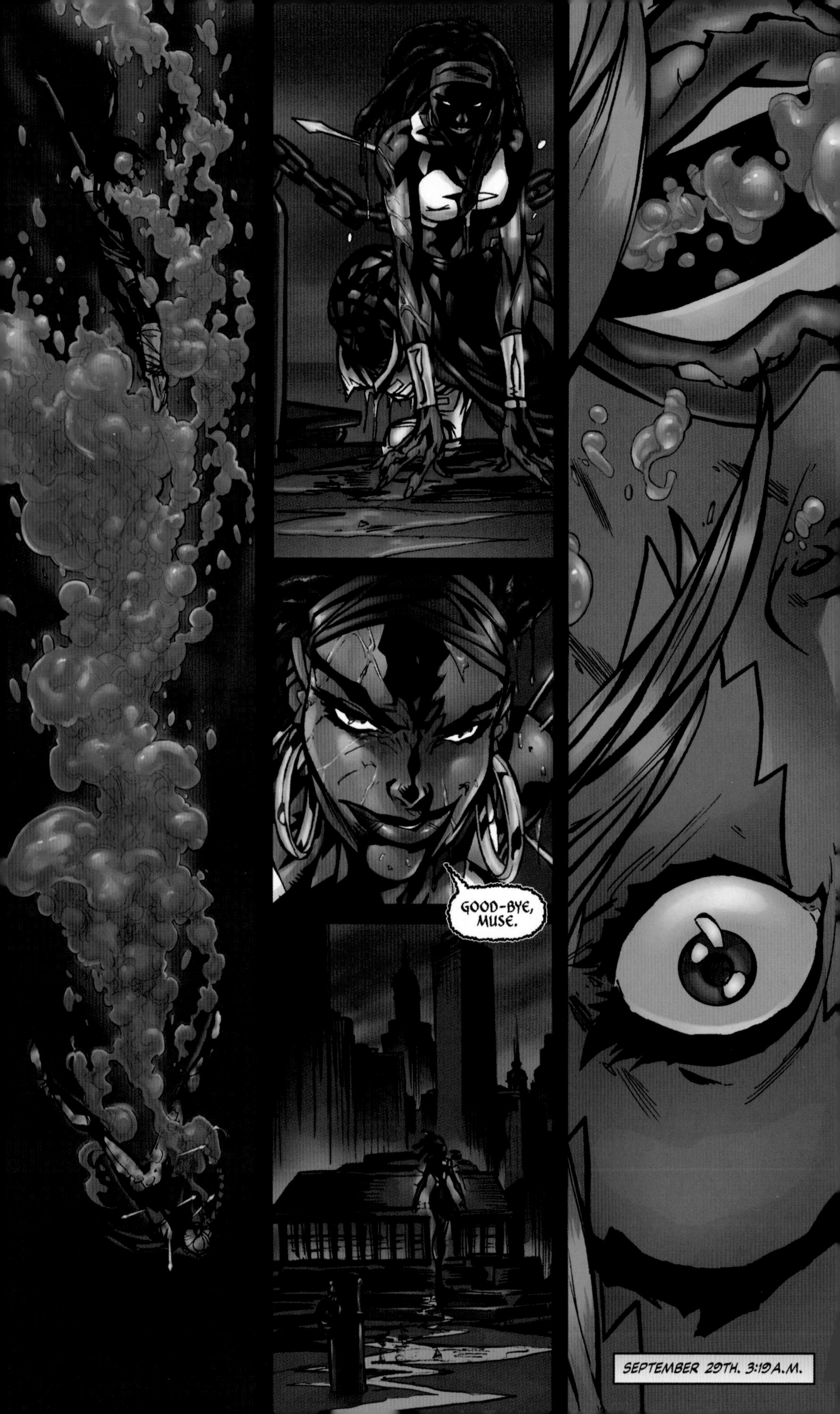
GOOD-BYE, MUSE.
SEPTEMBER 29TH. 3:19A.M.

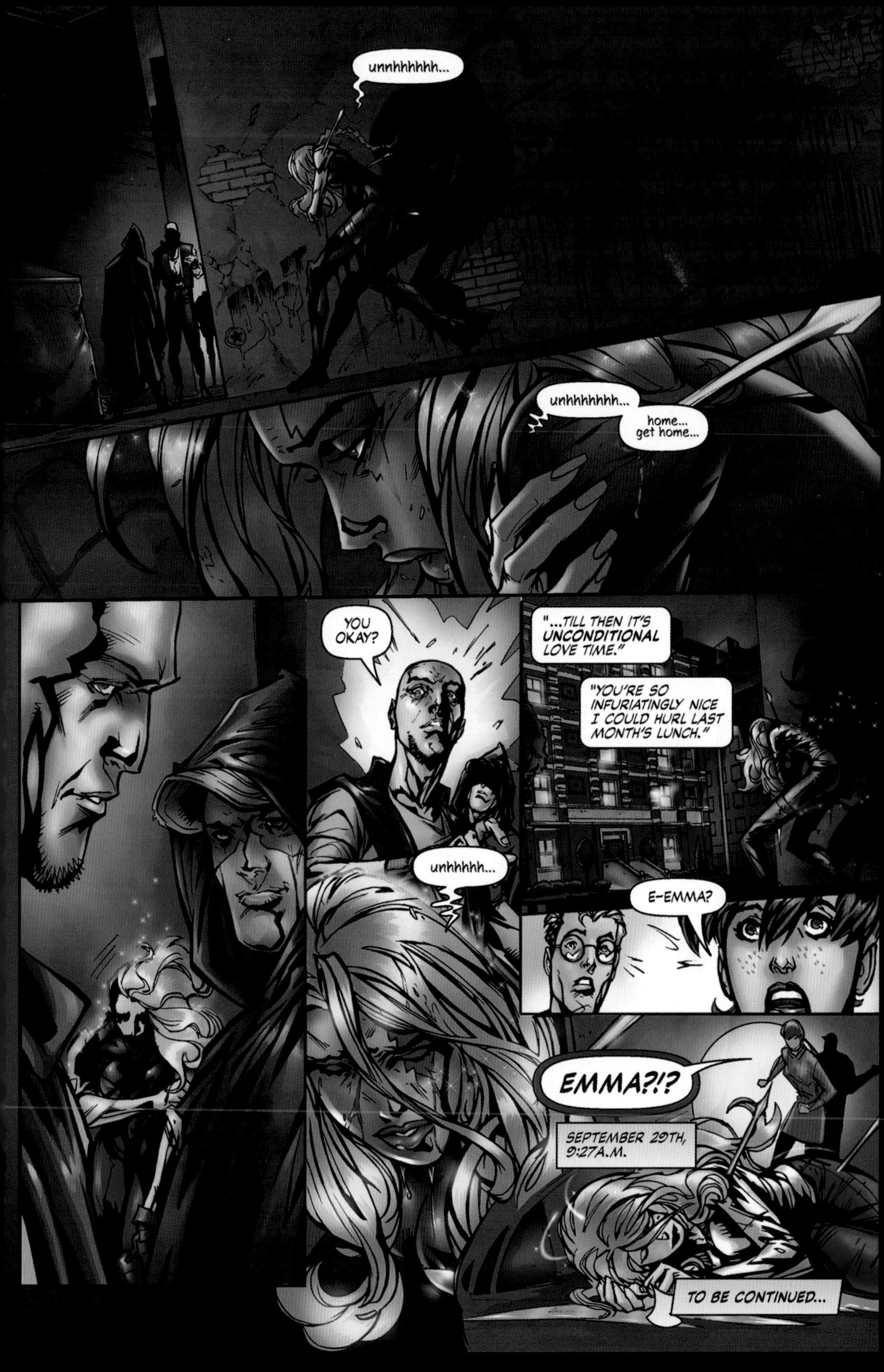
unnhhhhhh...
unnhhhhhh...
home... get home...
YOU OKAY?
unhhhhh...
"...TILL THEN IT'S UNCONDITIONAL LOVE TIME."
"YOU'RE SO INFURIATINGLY NICE I COULD HURL LAST MONTH'S LUNCH."
E-EMMA?
EMMA?!?
SEPTEMBER 29TH, 9:27A.M.
TO BE CONTINUED...

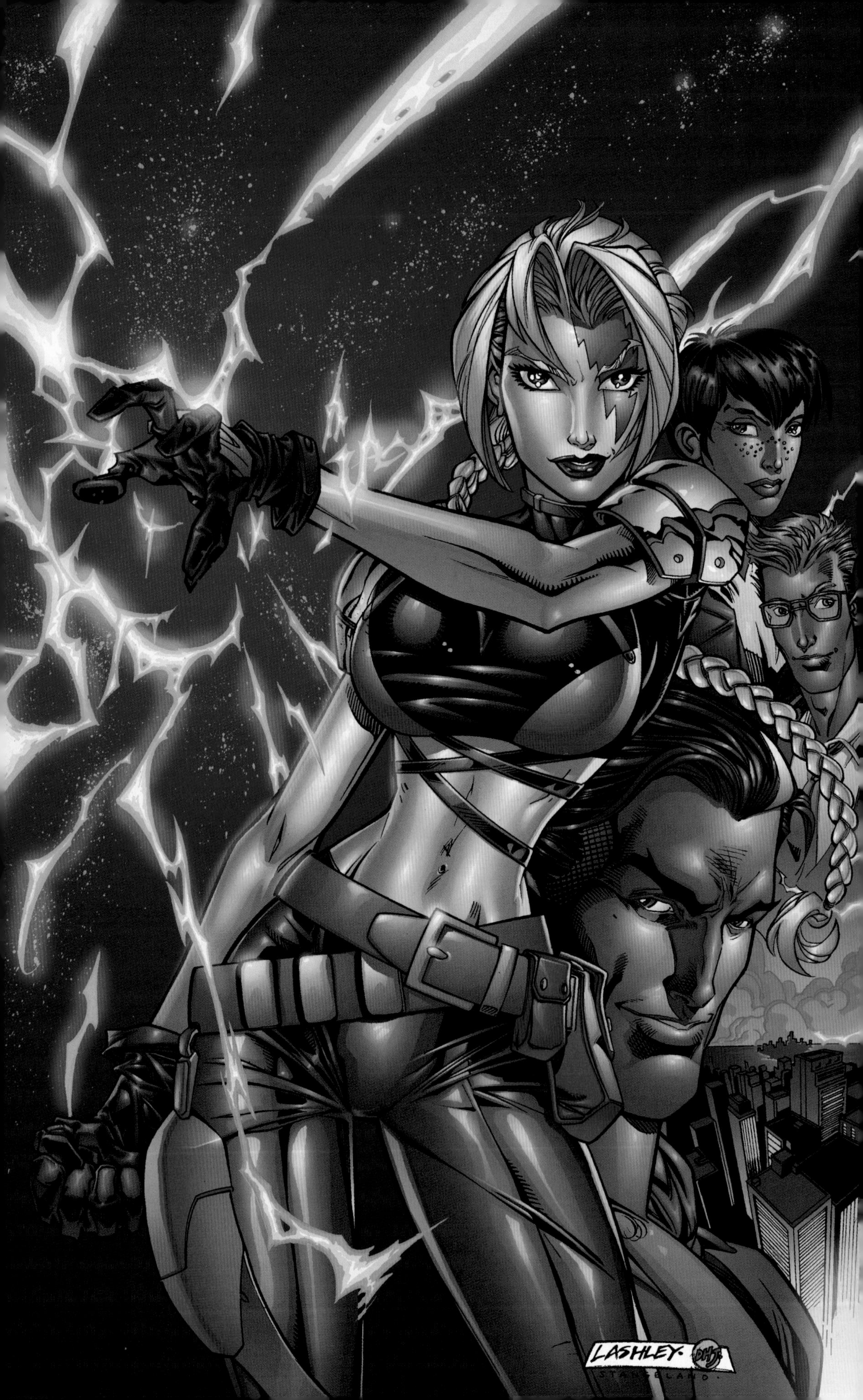
LASHLEY.

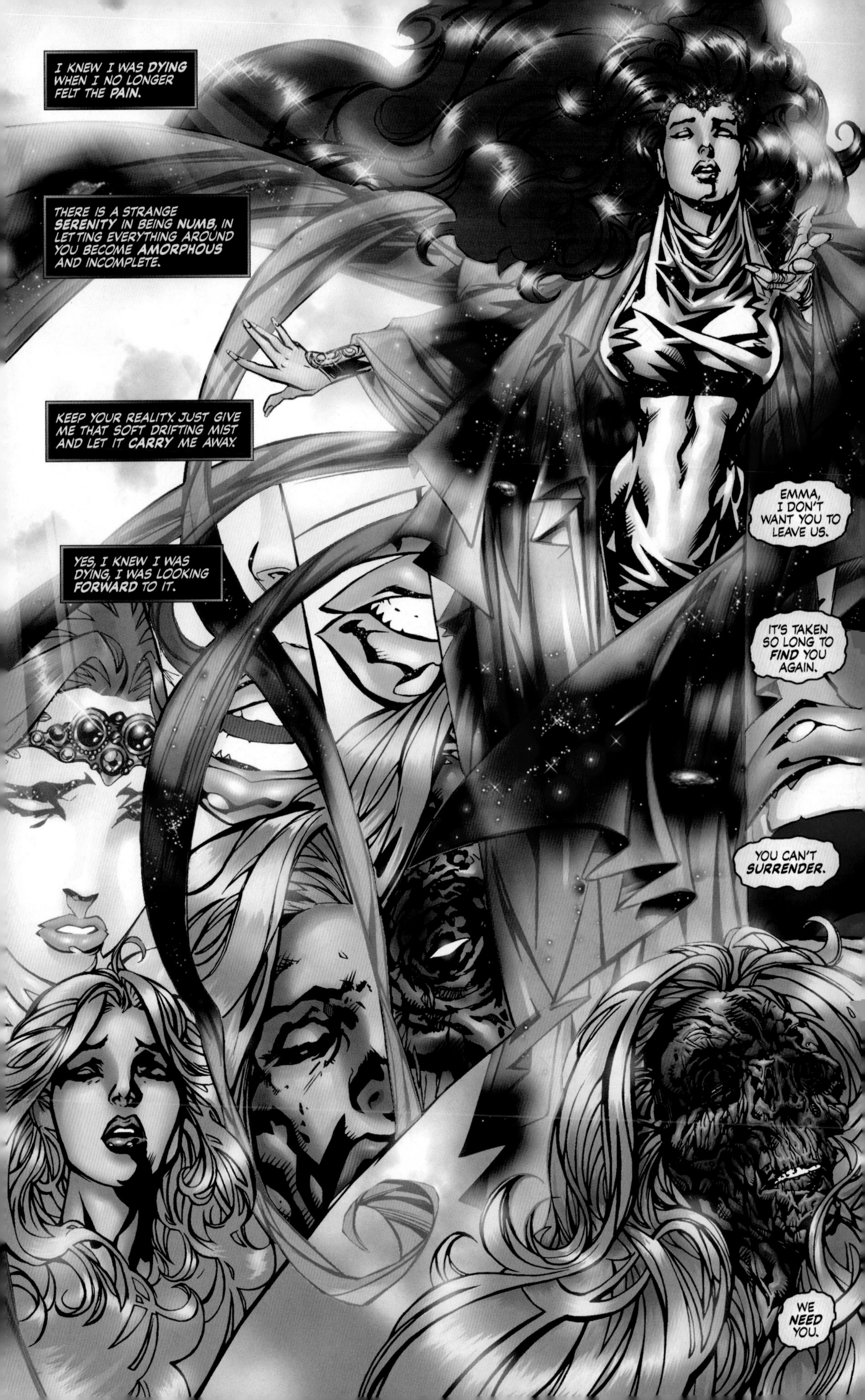
I KNEW I WAS DYING WHEN I NO LONGER FELT THE PAIN.
THERE IS A STRANGE SERENITY IN BEING NUMB, IN LETTING EVERYTHING AROUND YOU BECOME AMORPHOUS AND INCOMPLETE.
KEEP YOUR REALITY. JUST GIVE ME THAT SOFT DRIFTING MIST AND LET IT CARRY ME AWAY.
YES, I KNEW I WAS DYING, I WAS LOOKING FORWARD TO IT.
EMMA, I DON'T WANT YOU TO LEAVE US.
IT'S TAKEN SO LONG TO FIND YOU AGAIN.
YOU CAN'T SURRENDER.
WE NEED YOU.

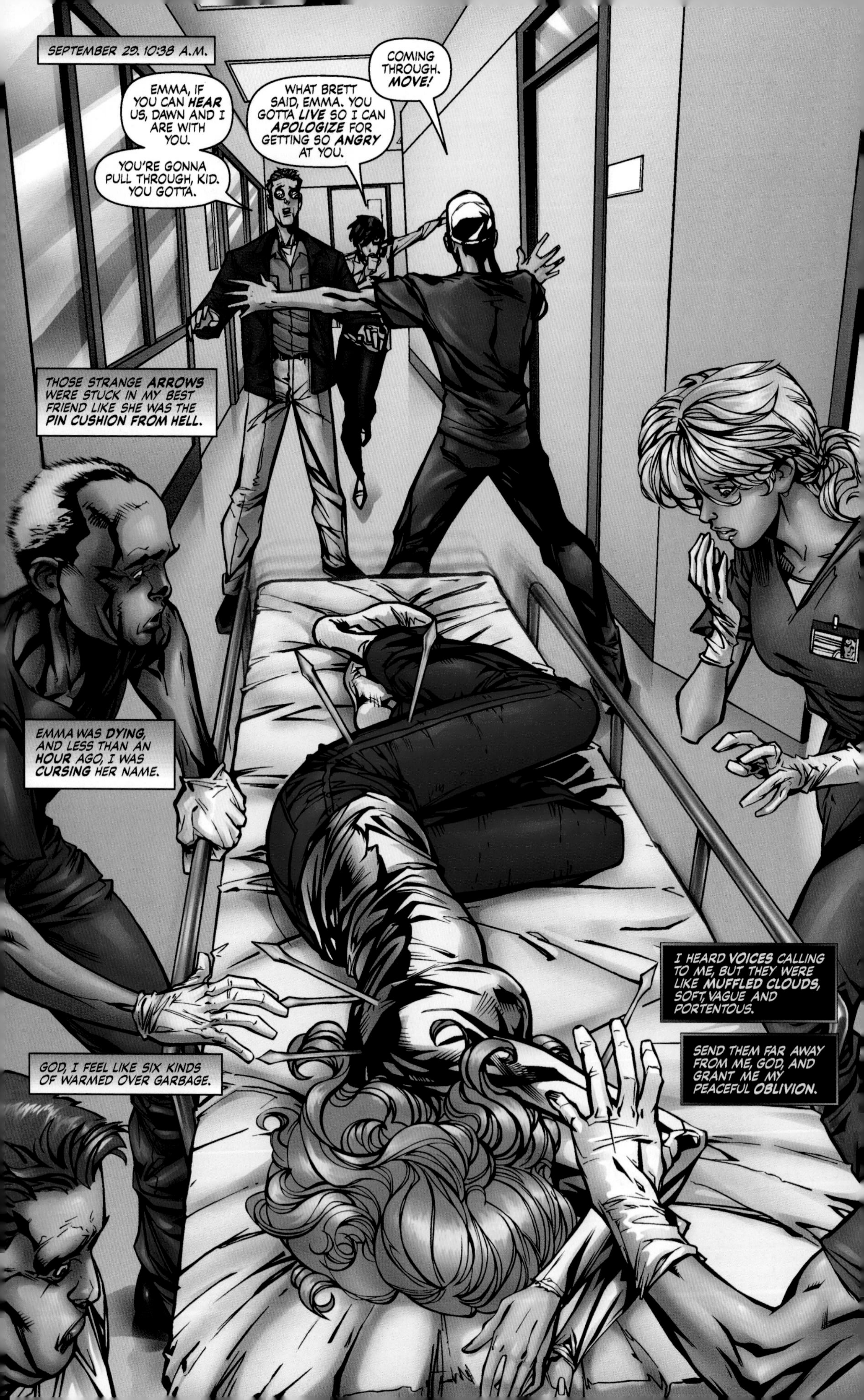
SEPTEMBER 29. 10:38 A.M.
EMMA, IF YOU CAN HEAR US, DAWN AND I ARE WITH YOU.
YOU'RE GONNA PULL THROUGH, KID. YOU GOTTA.
WHAT BRETT SAID, EMMA. YOU GOTTA LIVE SO I CAN APOLOGIZE FOR GETTING SO ANGRY AT YOU.
COMING THROUGH. MOVE!
THOSE STRANGE ARROWS WERE STUCK IN MY BEST FRIEND LIKE SHE WAS THE PIN CUSHION FROM HELL.
EMMA WAS DYING, AND LESS THAN AN HOUR AGO, I WAS CURSING HER NAME.
GOD, I FEEL LIKE SIX KINDS OF WARMED OVER GARBAGE.
I HEARD VOICES CALLING TO ME, BUT THEY WERE LIKE MUFFLED CLOUDS, SOFT, VAGUE AND PORTENTOUS.
SEND THEM FAR AWAY FROM ME, GOD, AND GRANT ME MY PEACEFUL OBLIVION.

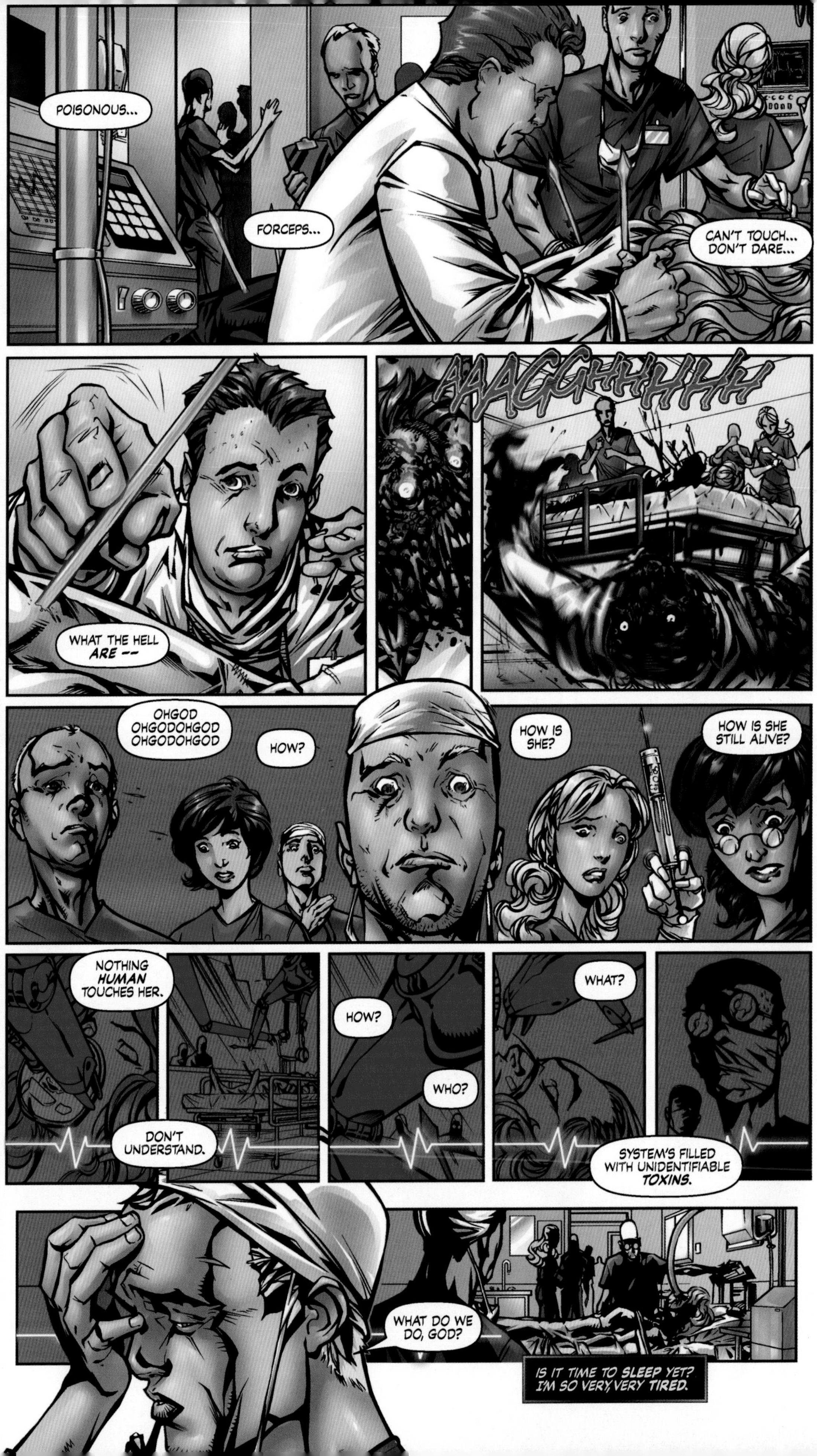
POISONOUS...
FORCEPS...
CAN'T TOUCH... DON'T DARE...
WHAT THE HELL *ARE* --
AAAGGHHHHHH
OHGOD OHGODOHGOD OHGODOHGOD
HOW?
HOW IS SHE?
HOW IS SHE STILL ALIVE?
NOTHING *HUMAN* TOUCHES HER.
DON'T UNDERSTAND.
HOW?
WHO?
WHAT?
SYSTEM'S FILLED WITH UNIDENTIFIABLE *TOXINS.*
WHAT DO WE DO, GOD?
IS IT TIME TO *SLEEP* YET? I'M SO VERY, VERY *TIRED.*

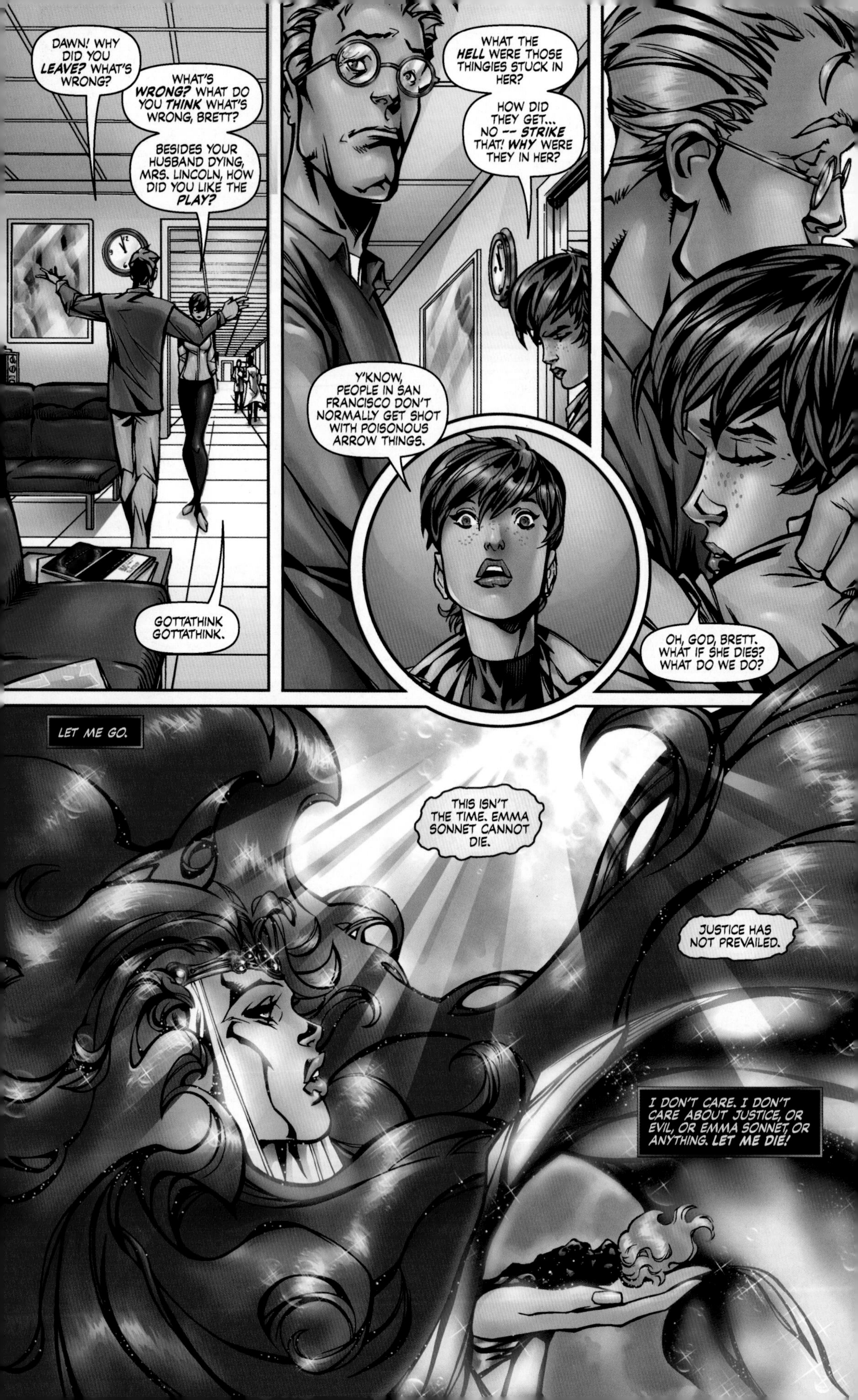
DAWN! WHY DID YOU LEAVE? WHAT'S WRONG?
WHAT'S WRONG? WHAT DO YOU THINK WHAT'S WRONG, BRETT?
BESIDES YOUR HUSBAND DYING, MRS. LINCOLN, HOW DID YOU LIKE THE PLAY?
GOTTATHINK GOTTATHINK.
WHAT THE HELL WERE THOSE THINGIES STUCK IN HER?
HOW DID THEY GET... NO -- STRIKE THAT! WHY WERE THEY IN HER?
Y'KNOW, PEOPLE IN SAN FRANCISCO DON'T NORMALLY GET SHOT WITH POISONOUS ARROW THINGS.
OH, GOD, BRETT. WHAT IF SHE DIES? WHAT DO WE DO?
LET ME GO.
THIS ISN'T THE TIME. EMMA SONNET CANNOT DIE.
JUSTICE HAS NOT PREVAILED.
I DON'T CARE. I DON'T CARE ABOUT JUSTICE, OR EVIL, OR EMMA SONNET, OR ANYTHING. LET ME DIE!

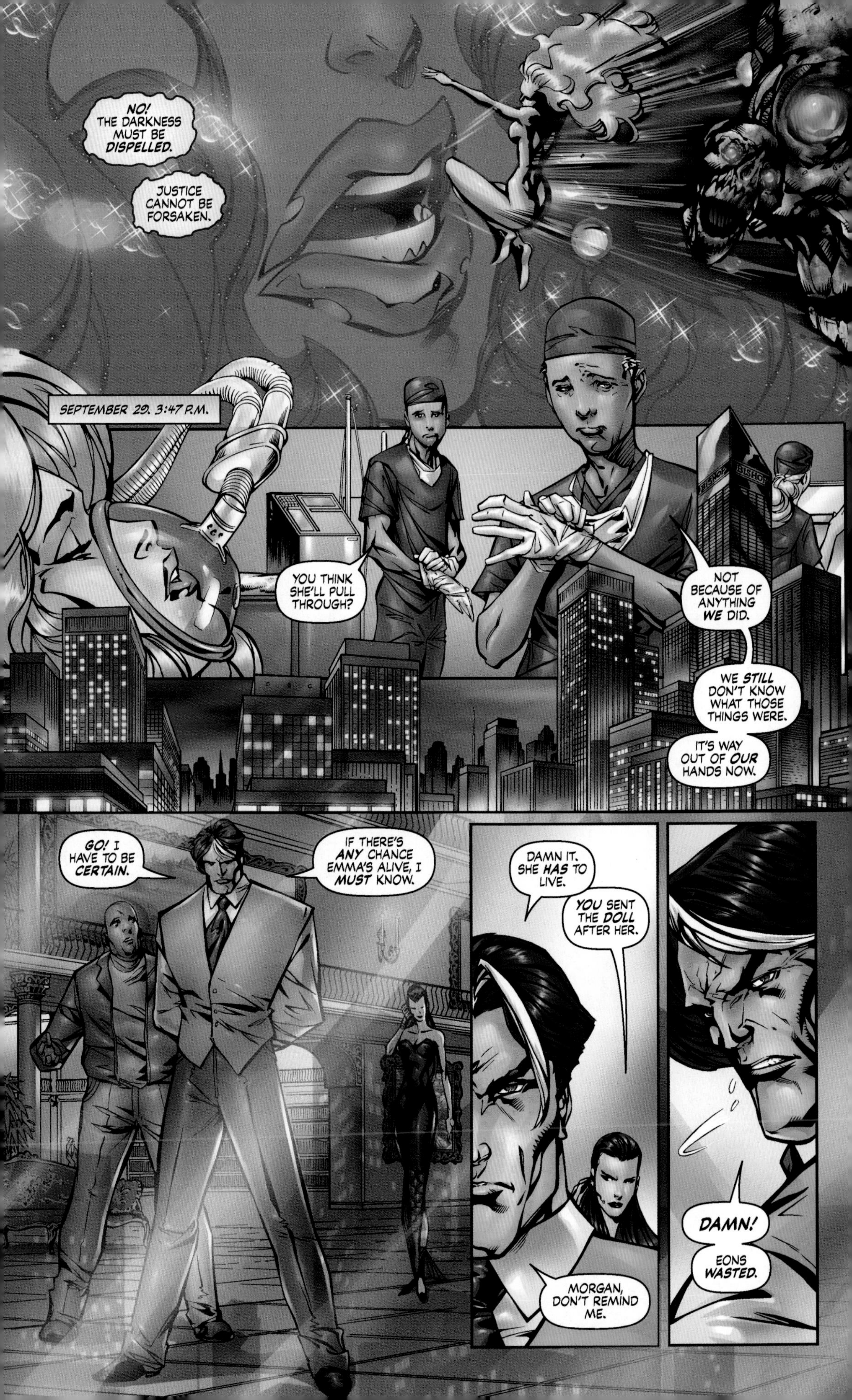
NO! THE DARKNESS MUST BE DISPELLED.
JUSTICE CANNOT BE FORSAKEN.
SEPTEMBER 29. 3:47 P.M.
YOU THINK SHE'LL PULL THROUGH?
NOT BECAUSE OF ANYTHING WE DID.
WE STILL DON'T KNOW WHAT THOSE THINGS WERE.
IT'S WAY OUT OF OUR HANDS NOW.
GO! I HAVE TO BE CERTAIN.
IF THERE'S ANY CHANCE EMMA'S ALIVE, I MUST KNOW.
DAMN IT. SHE HAS TO LIVE.
YOU SENT THE DOLL AFTER HER.
MORGAN, DON'T REMIND ME.
DAMN!
EONS WASTED.

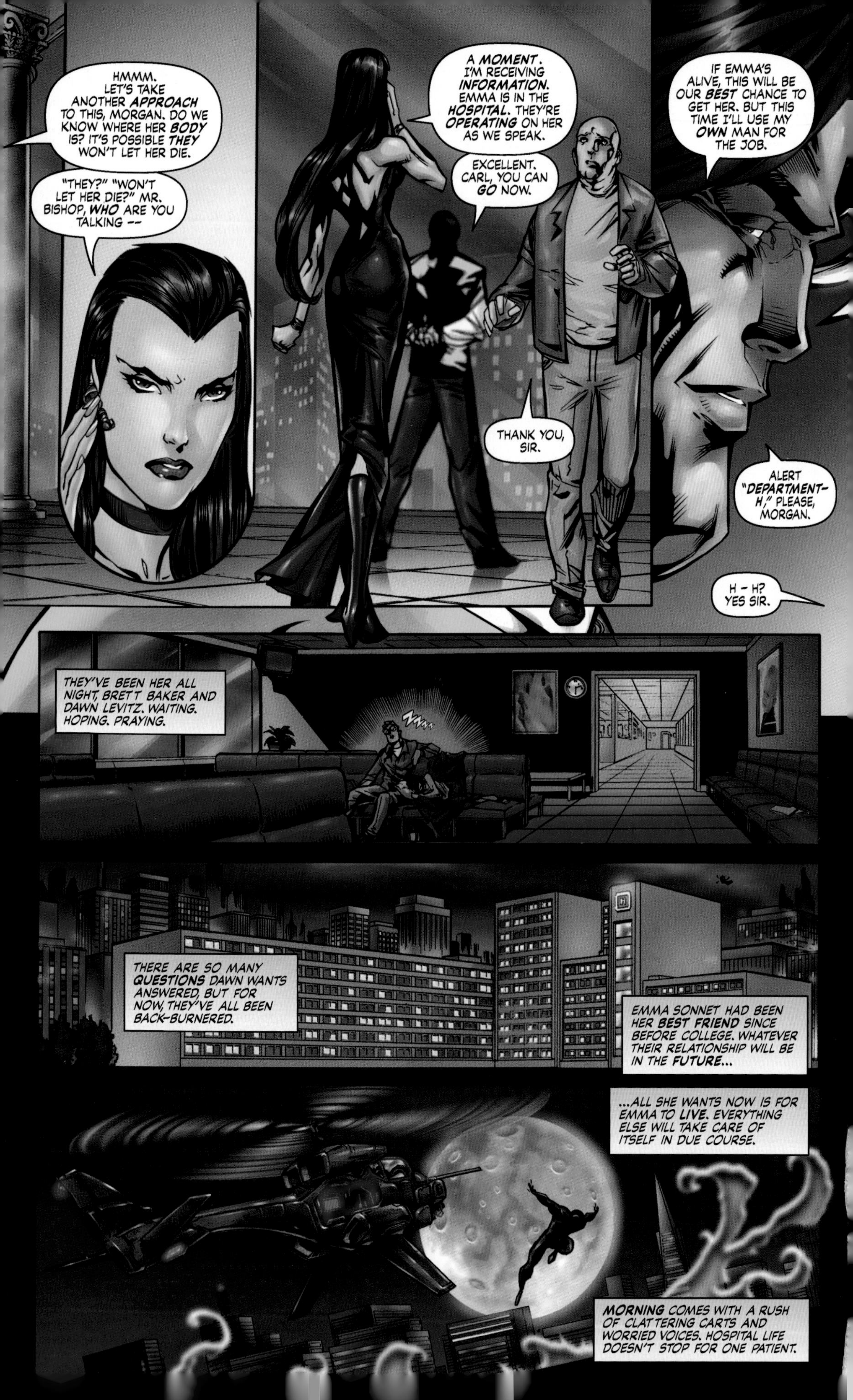
HMMM. LET'S TAKE ANOTHER APPROACH TO THIS, MORGAN. DO WE KNOW WHERE HER BODY IS? IT'S POSSIBLE THEY WON'T LET HER DIE.
"THEY?" "WON'T LET HER DIE?" MR. BISHOP, WHO ARE YOU TALKING --
A MOMENT. I'M RECEIVING INFORMATION. EMMA IS IN THE HOSPITAL. THEY'RE OPERATING ON HER AS WE SPEAK.
EXCELLENT. CARL, YOU CAN GO NOW.
THANK YOU, SIR.
IF EMMA'S ALIVE, THIS WILL BE OUR BEST CHANCE TO GET HER. BUT THIS TIME I'LL USE MY OWN MAN FOR THE JOB.
ALERT "DEPARTMENT-H," PLEASE, MORGAN.
H - H? YES SIR.
THEY'VE BEEN HER ALL NIGHT, BRETT BAKER AND DAWN LEVITZ. WAITING. HOPING. PRAYING.
THERE ARE SO MANY QUESTIONS DAWN WANTS ANSWERED, BUT FOR NOW, THEY'VE ALL BEEN BACK-BURNERED.
EMMA SONNET HAD BEEN HER BEST FRIEND SINCE BEFORE COLLEGE. WHATEVER THEIR RELATIONSHIP WILL BE IN THE FUTURE...
...ALL SHE WANTS NOW IS FOR EMMA TO LIVE. EVERYTHING ELSE WILL TAKE CARE OF ITSELF IN DUE COURSE.
MORNING COMES WITH A RUSH OF CLATTERING CARTS AND WORRIED VOICES. HOSPITAL LIFE DOESN'T STOP FOR ONE PATIENT.

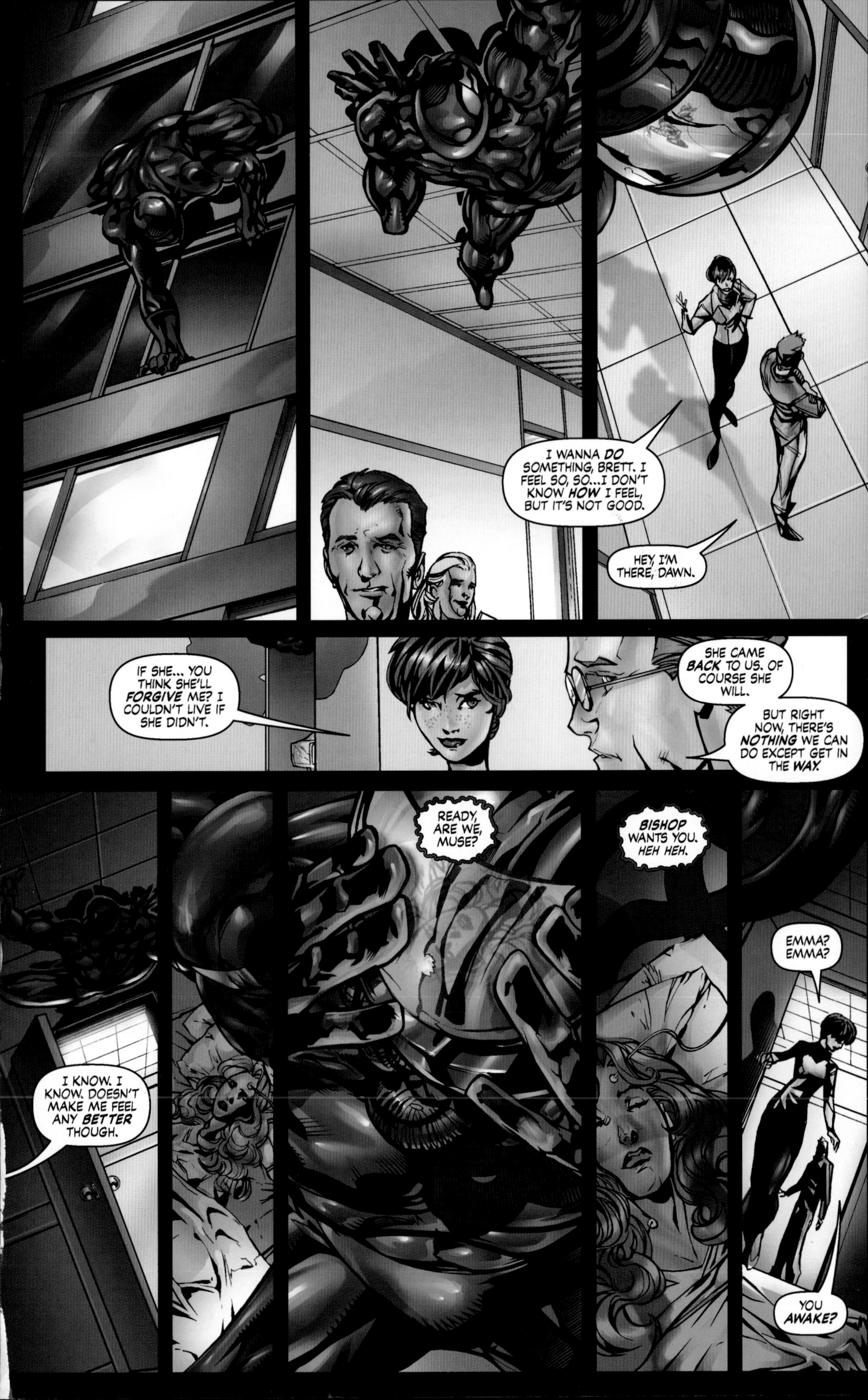
I WANNA *DO* SOMETHING, BRETT. I FEEL SO, SO...I DON'T KNOW *HOW* I FEEL, BUT IT'S NOT GOOD.
HEY, I'M THERE, DAWN.
IF SHE... YOU THINK SHE'LL *FORGIVE* ME? I COULDN'T LIVE IF SHE DIDN'T.
SHE CAME *BACK* TO US. OF COURSE SHE WILL.
BUT RIGHT NOW, THERE'S *NOTHING* WE CAN DO EXCEPT GET IN THE *WAY.*
I KNOW. I KNOW. DOESN'T MAKE ME FEEL ANY *BETTER* THOUGH.
READY, ARE WE, MUSE?
BISHOP WANTS YOU. *HEH HEH.*
EMMA? EMMA?
YOU *AWAKE?*

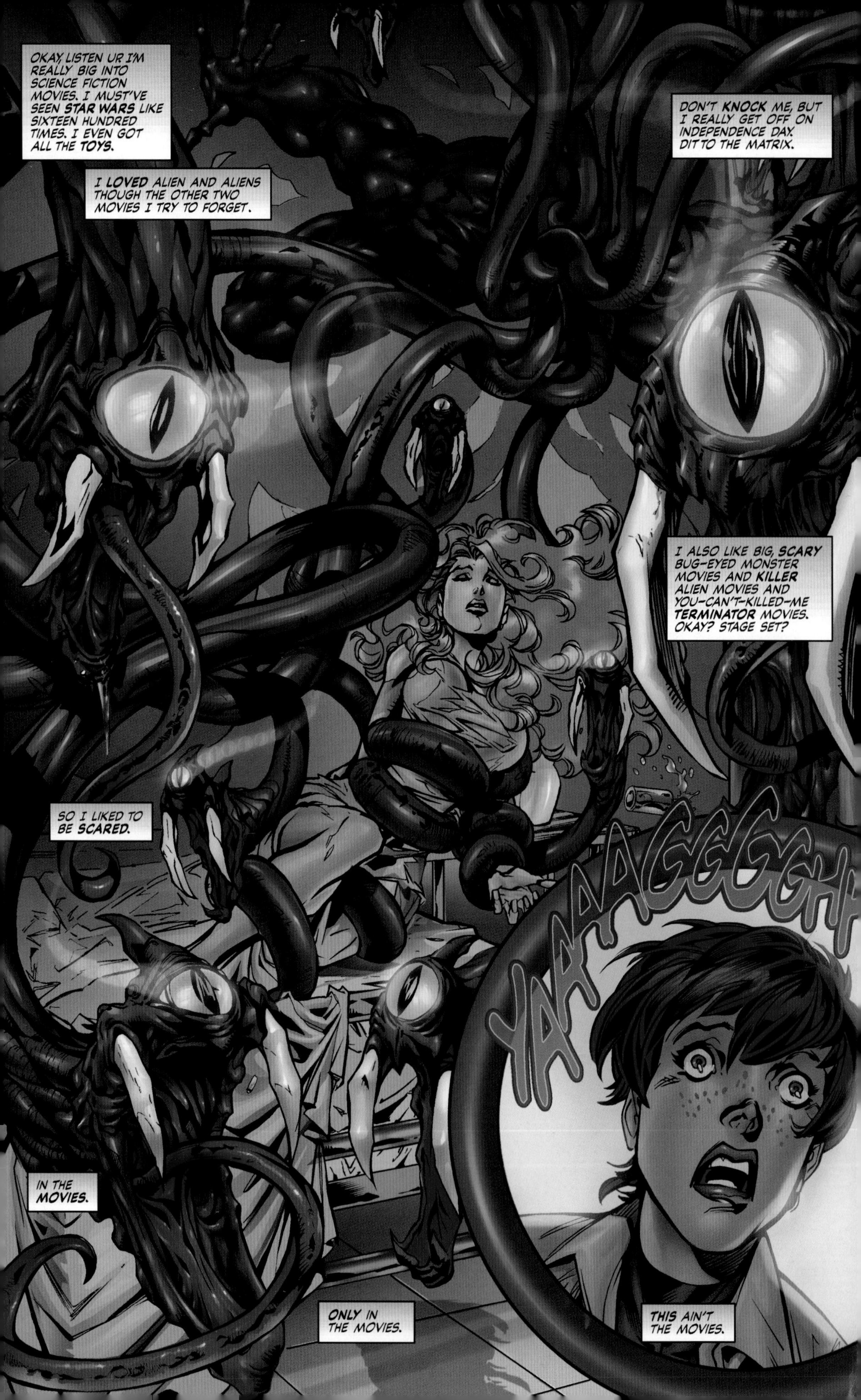
OKAY, LISTEN UP. I'M REALLY BIG INTO SCIENCE FICTION MOVIES. I MUST'VE SEEN STAR WARS LIKE SIXTEEN HUNDRED TIMES. I EVEN GOT ALL THE TOYS.
I LOVED ALIEN AND ALIENS THOUGH THE OTHER TWO MOVIES I TRY TO FORGET.
DON'T KNOCK ME, BUT I REALLY GET OFF ON INDEPENDENCE DAY. DITTO THE MATRIX.
I ALSO LIKE BIG, SCARY BUG-EYED MONSTER MOVIES AND KILLER ALIEN MOVIES AND YOU-CAN'T-KILLED-ME TERMINATOR MOVIES. OKAY? STAGE SET?
SO I LIKED TO BE SCARED.
YAAAAGGGGH
IN THE MOVIES.
ONLY IN THE MOVIES.
THIS AIN'T THE MOVIES.

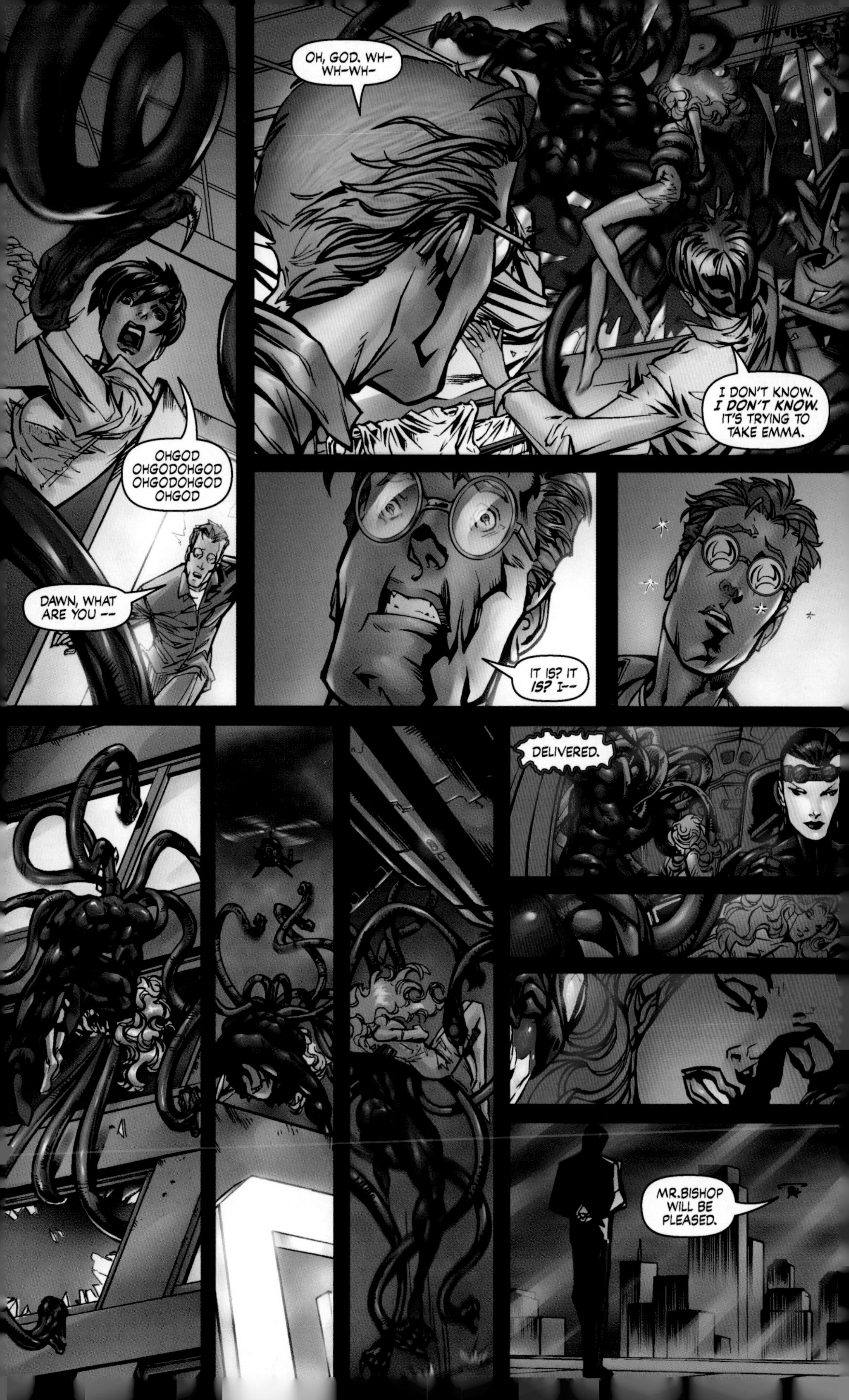
OH, GOD. WH- WH-WH-
I DON'T KNOW. *I DON'T KNOW.* IT'S TRYING TO TAKE EMMA.
OHGOD OHGODOHGOD OHGODOHGOD OHGOD
DAWN, WHAT ARE YOU --
IT IS? IT *IS?* I--
DELIVERED.
MR.BISHOP WILL BE PLEASED.

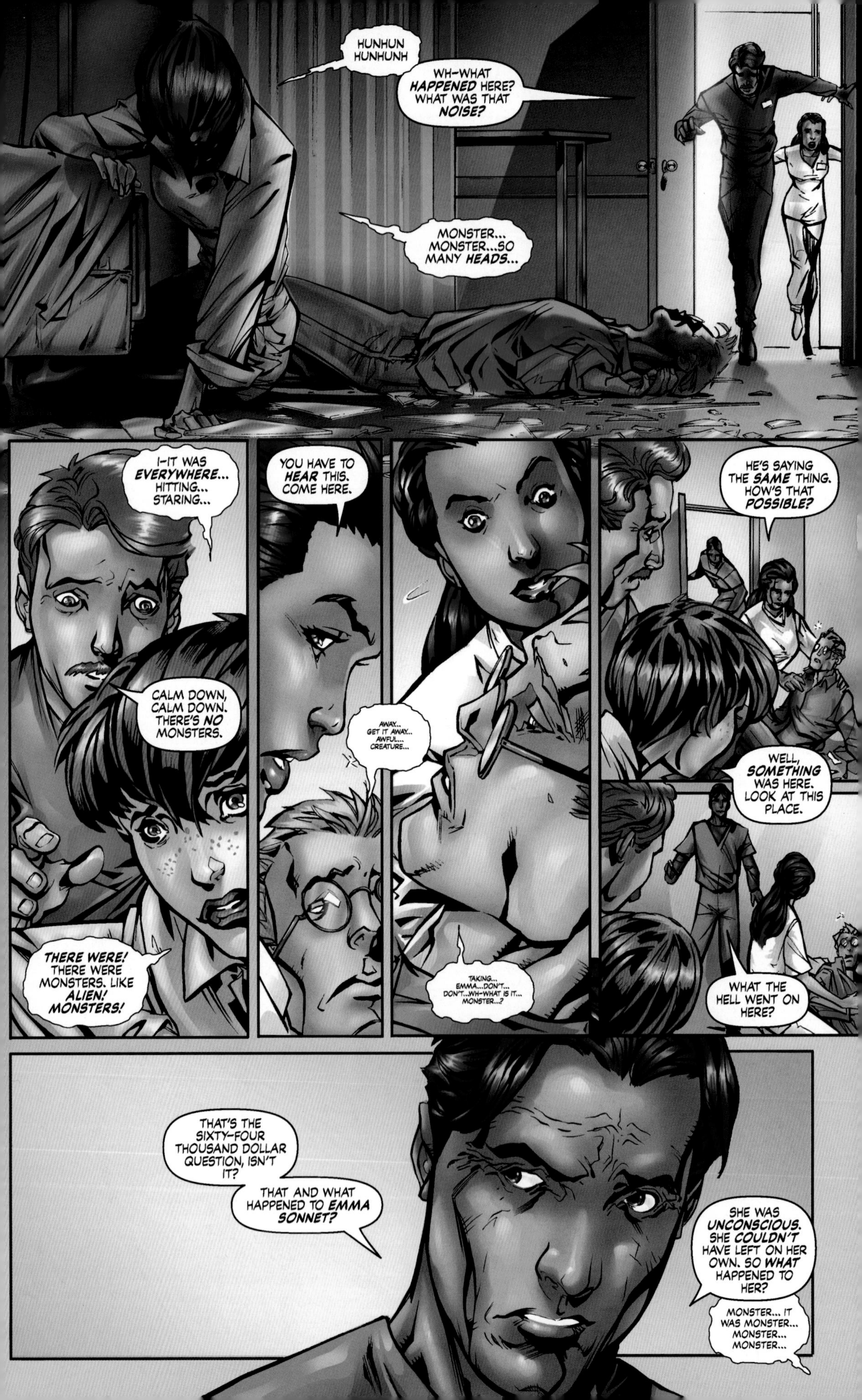
HUNHUN HUNHUNH
WH-WHAT HAPPENED HERE? WHAT WAS THAT NOISE?
MONSTER... MONSTER...SO MANY HEADS...
I-IT WAS EVERYWHERE... HITTING... STARING...
CALM DOWN, CALM DOWN. THERE'S NO MONSTERS.
THERE WERE! THERE WERE MONSTERS. LIKE ALIEN! MONSTERS!
YOU HAVE TO HEAR THIS. COME HERE.
AWAY... GET IT AWAY... AWFUL... CREATURE...
TAKING... EMMA...DON'T... DON'T...WH-WHAT IS IT... MONSTER...?
HE'S SAYING THE SAME THING. HOW'S THAT POSSIBLE?
WELL, SOMETHING WAS HERE. LOOK AT THIS PLACE.
WHAT THE HELL WENT ON HERE?
THAT'S THE SIXTY-FOUR THOUSAND DOLLAR QUESTION, ISN'T IT?
THAT AND WHAT HAPPENED TO EMMA SONNET?
SHE WAS UNCONSCIOUS. SHE COULDN'T HAVE LEFT ON HER OWN. SO WHAT HAPPENED TO HER?
MONSTER... IT WAS MONSTER... MONSTER... MONSTER...

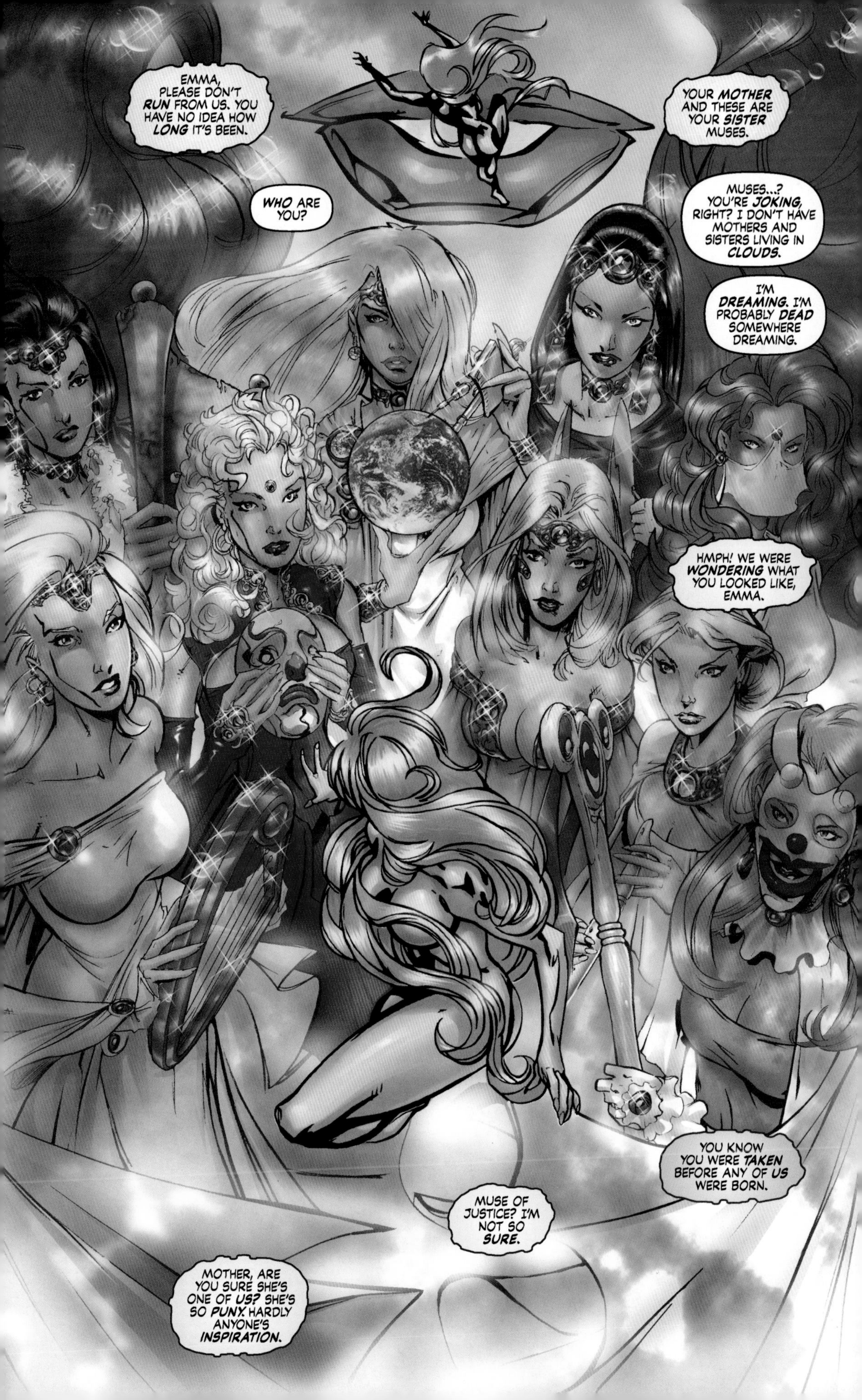
EMMA, PLEASE DON'T RUN FROM US. YOU HAVE NO IDEA HOW LONG IT'S BEEN.
YOUR MOTHER AND THESE ARE YOUR SISTER MUSES.
WHO ARE YOU?
MUSES...? YOU'RE JOKING, RIGHT? I DON'T HAVE MOTHERS AND SISTERS LIVING IN CLOUDS.
I'M DREAMING. I'M PROBABLY DEAD SOMEWHERE DREAMING.
HMPH! WE WERE WONDERING WHAT YOU LOOKED LIKE, EMMA.
YOU KNOW YOU WERE TAKEN BEFORE ANY OF US WERE BORN.
MUSE OF JUSTICE? I'M NOT SO SURE.
MOTHER, ARE YOU SURE SHE'S ONE OF US? SHE'S SO PUNY. HARDLY ANYONE'S INSPIRATION.

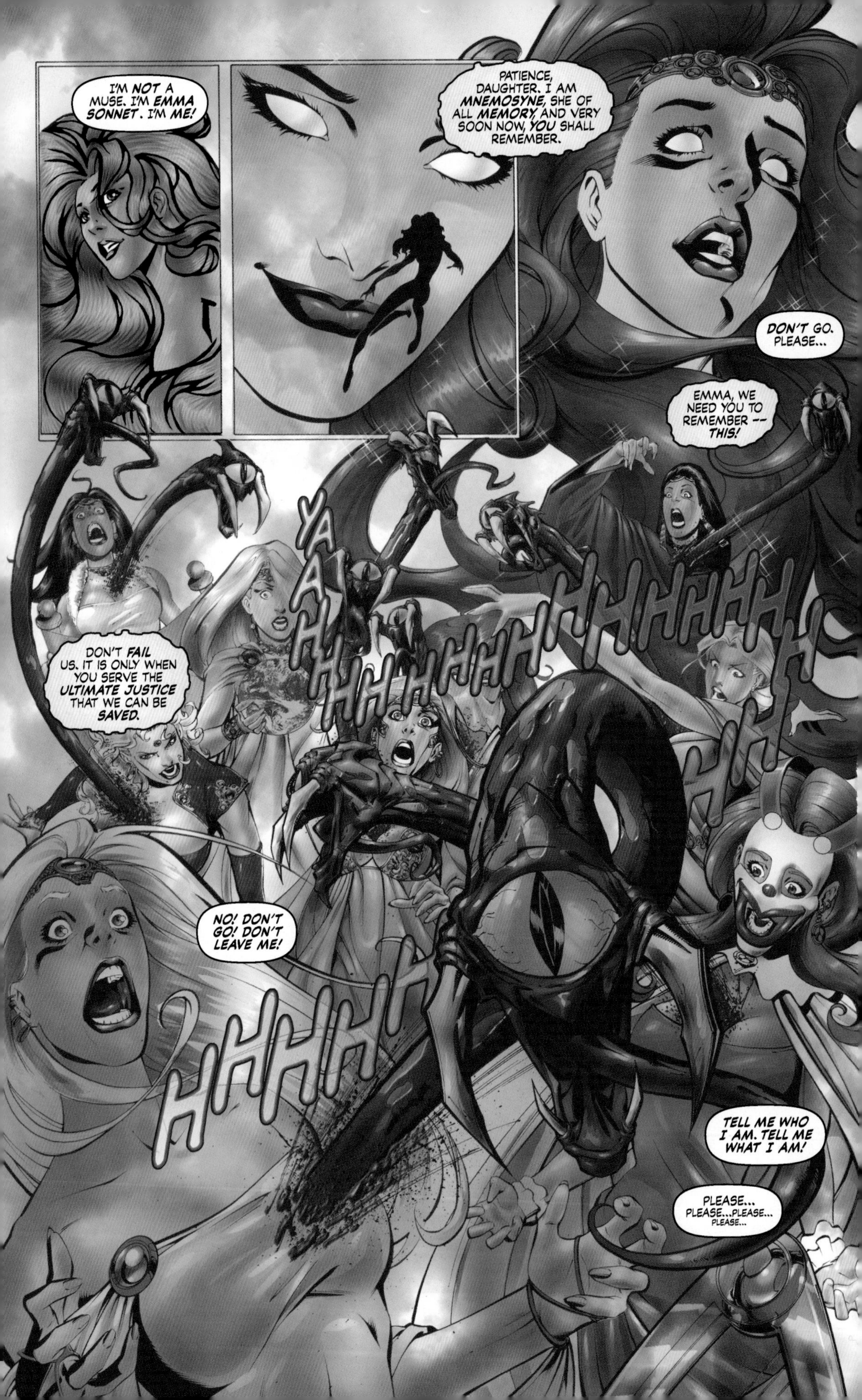
I'M NOT A MUSE. I'M EMMA SONNET. I'M ME!
PATIENCE, DAUGHTER. I AM MNEMOSYNE, SHE OF ALL MEMORY, AND VERY SOON NOW, YOU SHALL REMEMBER.
DON'T GO. PLEASE...
EMMA, WE NEED YOU TO REMEMBER -- THIS!
YAAAHHHHHHHHHHHHHHHHHH
DON'T FAIL US. IT IS ONLY WHEN YOU SERVE THE ULTIMATE JUSTICE THAT WE CAN BE SAVED.
NO! DON'T GO! DON'T LEAVE ME!
HHHHHH
TELL ME WHO I AM. TELL ME WHAT I AM!
PLEASE... PLEASE...PLEASE... PLEASE...

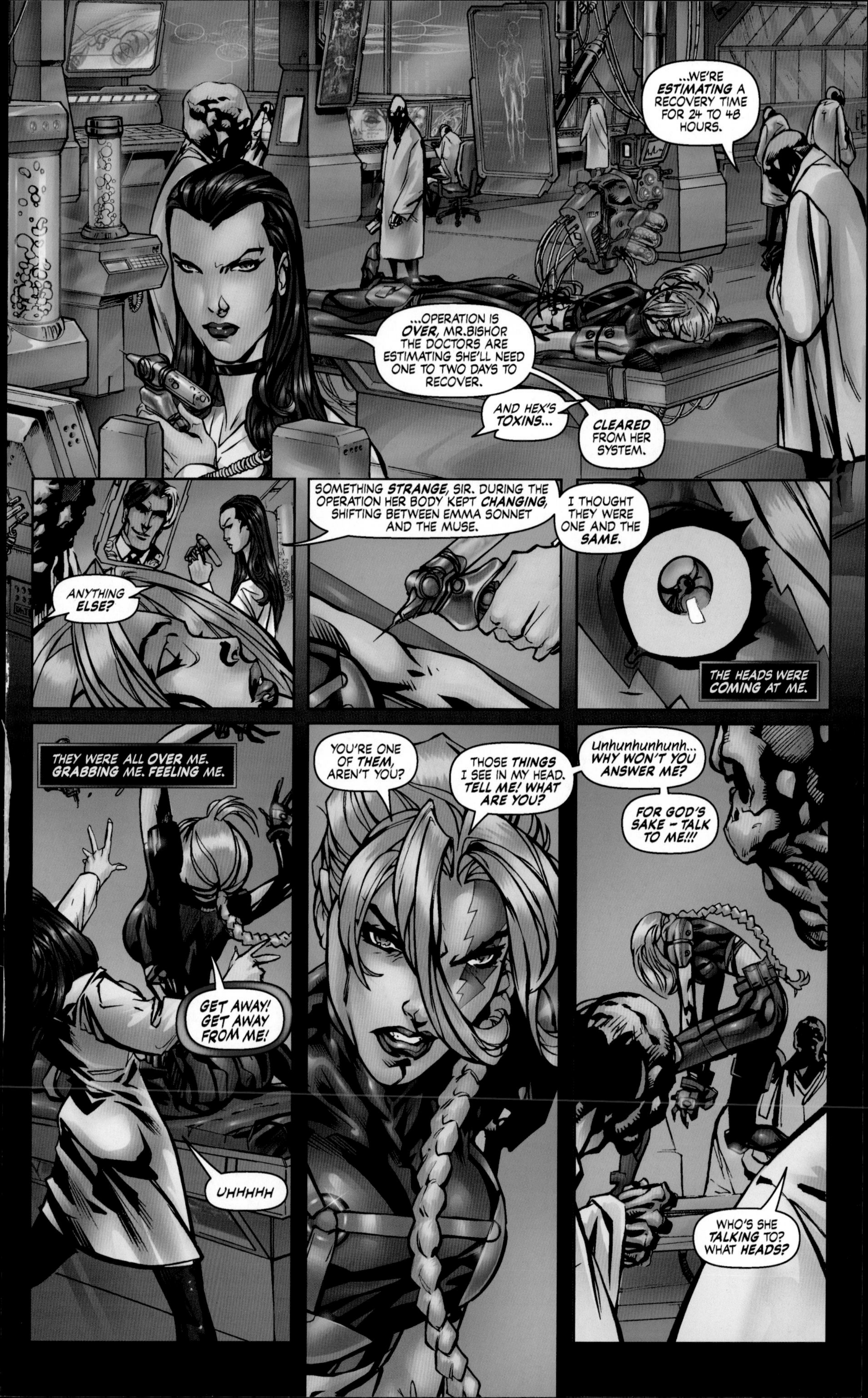
...WE'RE ESTIMATING A RECOVERY TIME FOR 24 TO 48 HOURS.
...OPERATION IS OVER, MR.BISHOP THE DOCTORS ARE ESTIMATING SHE'LL NEED ONE TO TWO DAYS TO RECOVER.
AND HEX'S TOXINS...
CLEARED FROM HER SYSTEM.
ANYTHING ELSE?
SOMETHING STRANGE, SIR. DURING THE OPERATION HER BODY KEPT CHANGING, SHIFTING BETWEEN EMMA SONNET AND THE MUSE.
I THOUGHT THEY WERE ONE AND THE SAME.
THE HEADS WERE COMING AT ME.
THEY WERE ALL OVER ME. GRABBING ME. FEELING ME.
GET AWAY! GET AWAY FROM ME!
UHHHHH
YOU'RE ONE OF THEM, AREN'T YOU?
THOSE THINGS I SEE IN MY HEAD. TELL ME! WHAT ARE YOU?
Unhunhunhunh... WHY WON'T YOU ANSWER ME?
FOR GOD'S SAKE - TALK TO ME!!!
WHO'S SHE TALKING TO? WHAT HEADS?

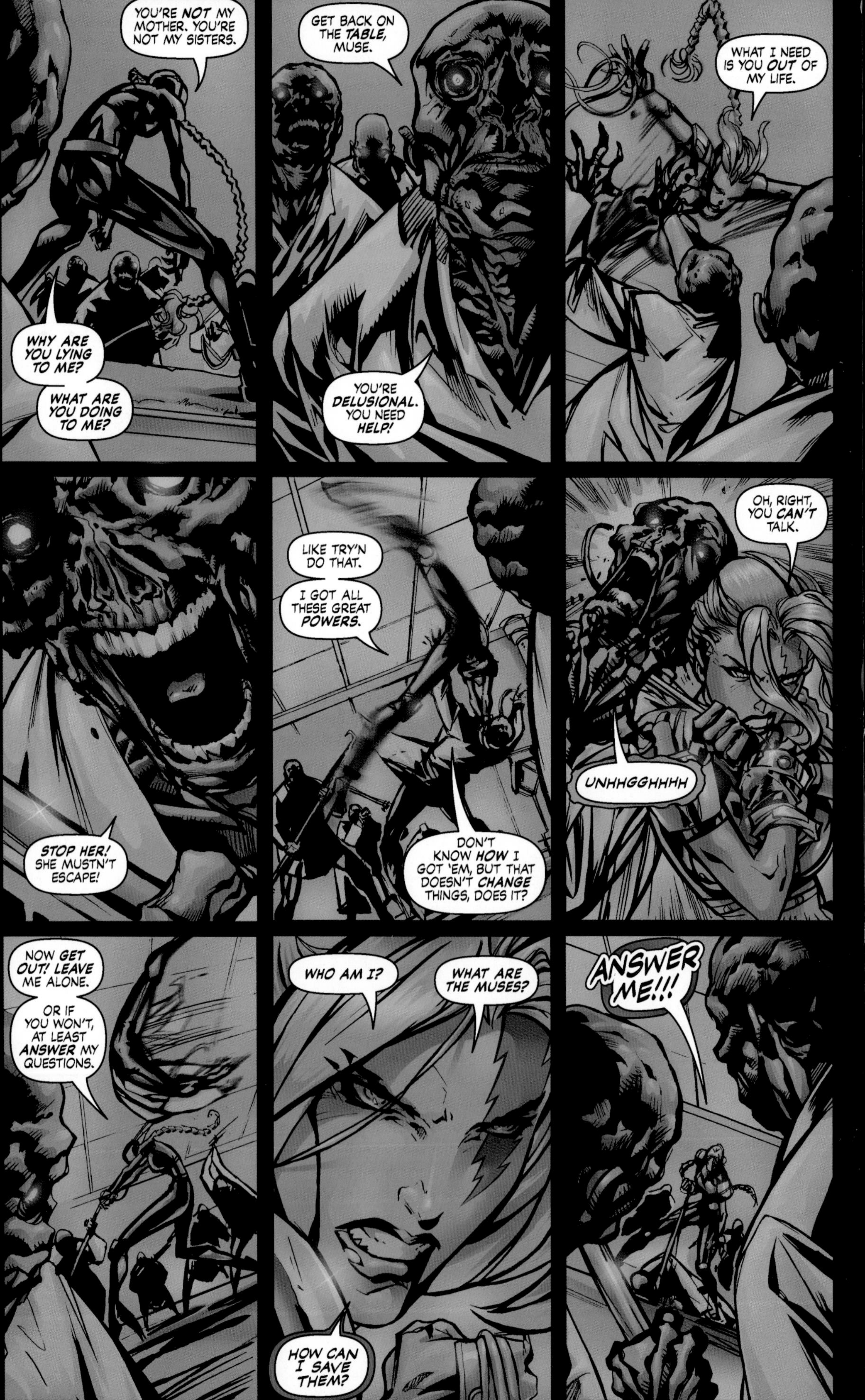

YOU'RE NOT MY MOTHER. YOU'RE NOT MY SISTERS.
WHY ARE YOU LYING TO ME?
WHAT ARE YOU DOING TO ME?
GET BACK ON THE TABLE, MUSE.
YOU'RE DELUSIONAL. YOU NEED HELP!
WHAT I NEED IS YOU OUT OF MY LIFE.
STOP HER! SHE MUSTN'T ESCAPE!
LIKE TRY'N DO THAT.
I GOT ALL THESE GREAT POWERS.
DON'T KNOW HOW I GOT 'EM, BUT THAT DOESN'T CHANGE THINGS, DOES IT?
OH, RIGHT, YOU CAN'T TALK.
UNHHGGHHHH
NOW GET OUT! LEAVE ME ALONE.
OR IF YOU WON'T, AT LEAST ANSWER MY QUESTIONS.
WHO AM I?
WHAT ARE THE MUSES?
HOW CAN I SAVE THEM?
ANSWER ME!!!

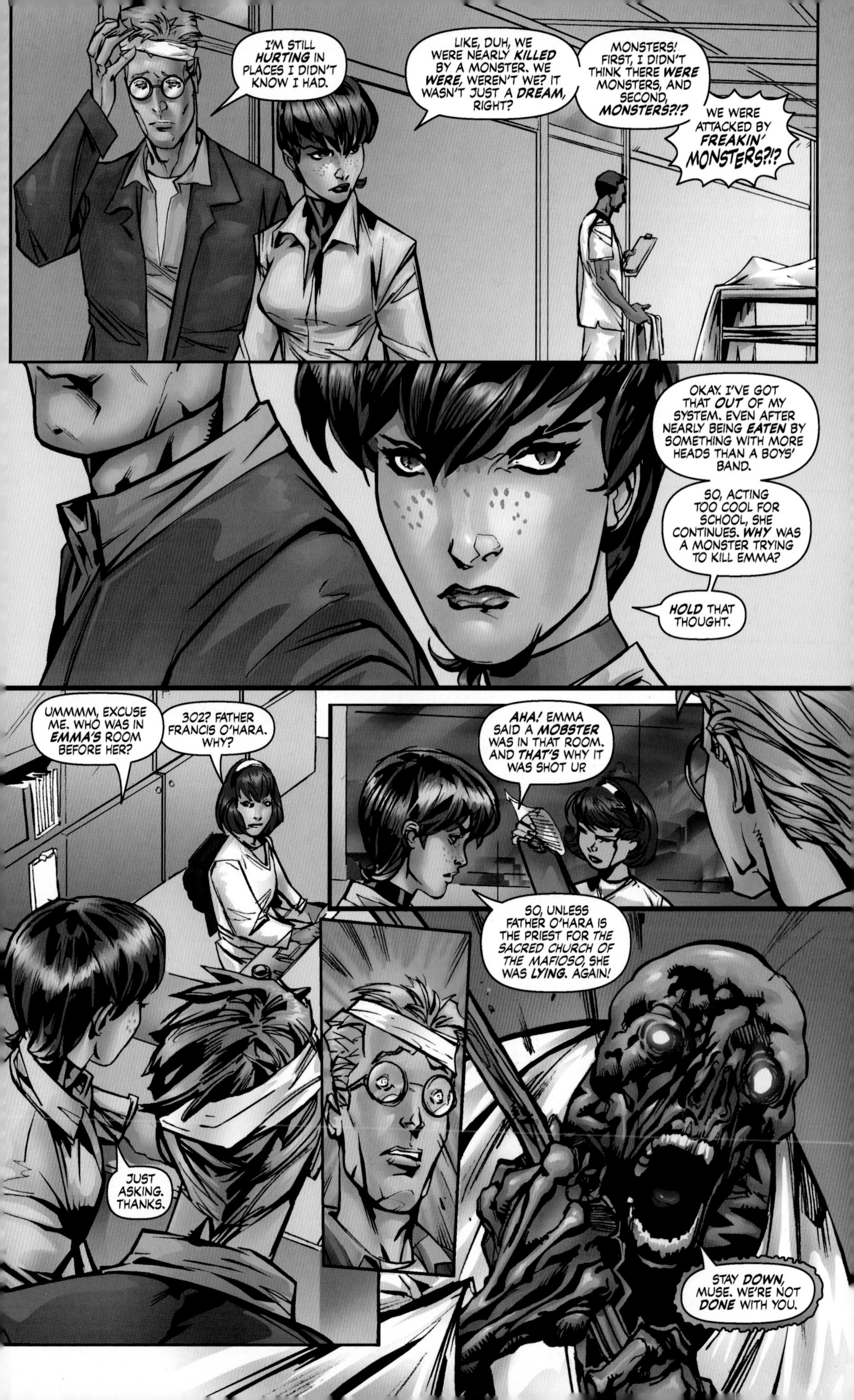
I'M STILL HURTING IN PLACES I DIDN'T KNOW I HAD.
LIKE, DUH, WE WERE NEARLY KILLED BY A MONSTER. WE WERE, WEREN'T WE? IT WASN'T JUST A DREAM, RIGHT?
MONSTERS! FIRST, I DIDN'T THINK THERE WERE MONSTERS, AND SECOND, MONSTERS?!?
WE WERE ATTACKED BY FREAKIN' MONSTERS?!?
OKAY. I'VE GOT THAT OUT OF MY SYSTEM. EVEN AFTER NEARLY BEING EATEN BY SOMETHING WITH MORE HEADS THAN A BOYS' BAND.
SO, ACTING TOO COOL FOR SCHOOL, SHE CONTINUES. WHY WAS A MONSTER TRYING TO KILL EMMA?
HOLD THAT THOUGHT.
UMMMM, EXCUSE ME. WHO WAS IN EMMA'S ROOM BEFORE HER?
302? FATHER FRANCIS O'HARA. WHY?
AHA! EMMA SAID A MOBSTER WAS IN THAT ROOM. AND THAT'S WHY IT WAS SHOT UP.
JUST ASKING. THANKS.
SO, UNLESS FATHER O'HARA IS THE PRIEST FOR THE SACRED CHURCH OF THE MAFIOSO, SHE WAS LYING. AGAIN!
STAY DOWN, MUSE. WE'RE NOT DONE WITH YOU.

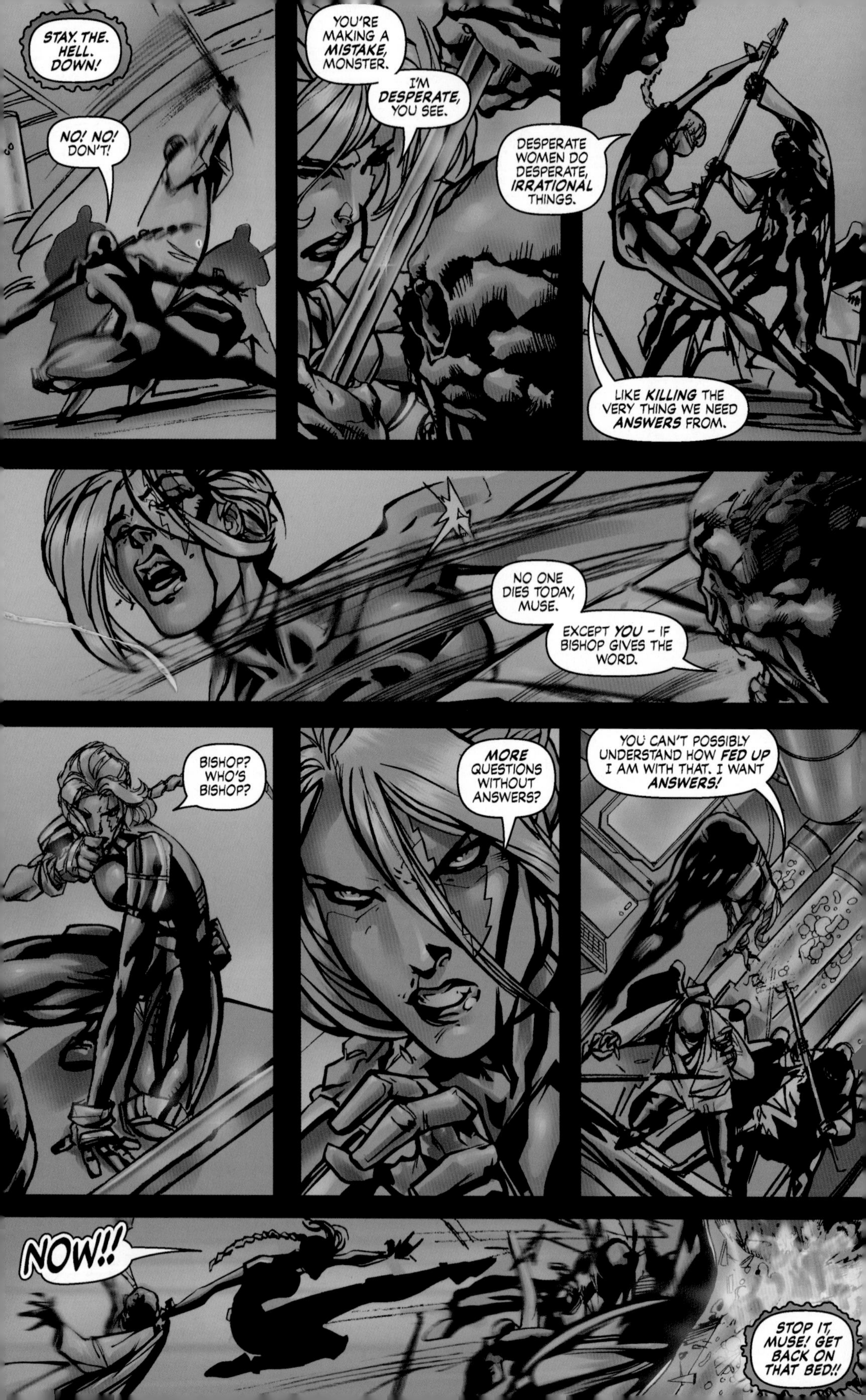
STAY. THE. HELL. DOWN!
NO! NO! DON'T!
YOU'RE MAKING A MISTAKE, MONSTER.
I'M DESPERATE, YOU SEE.
DESPERATE WOMEN DO DESPERATE, IRRATIONAL THINGS.
LIKE KILLING THE VERY THING WE NEED ANSWERS FROM.
NO ONE DIES TODAY, MUSE.
EXCEPT YOU - IF BISHOP GIVES THE WORD.
BISHOP? WHO'S BISHOP?
MORE QUESTIONS WITHOUT ANSWERS?
YOU CAN'T POSSIBLY UNDERSTAND HOW FED UP I AM WITH THAT. I WANT ANSWERS!
NOW!!
STOP IT, MUSE! GET BACK ON THAT BED!!

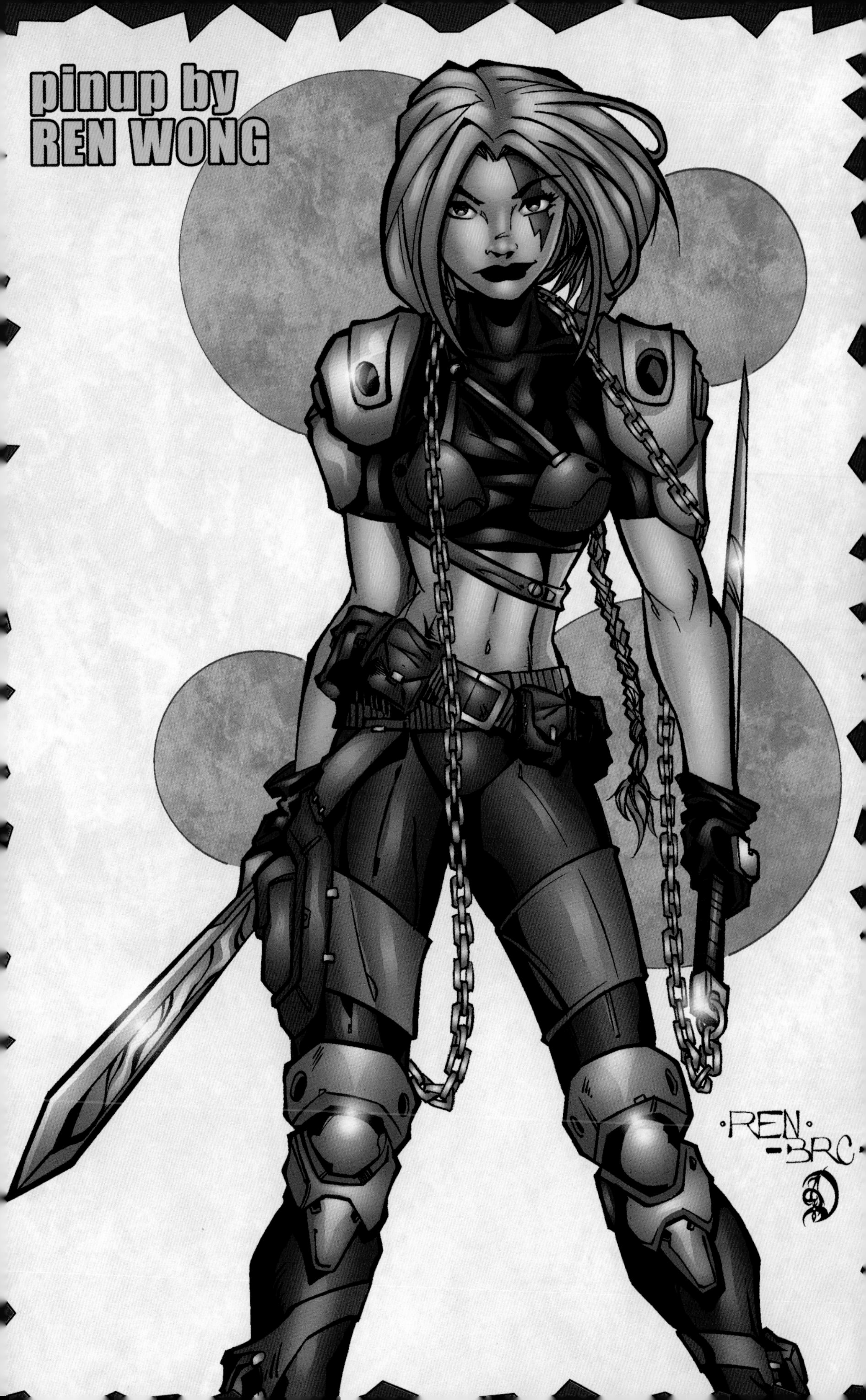
pinup by
REN WONG
·REN·
-BRC·

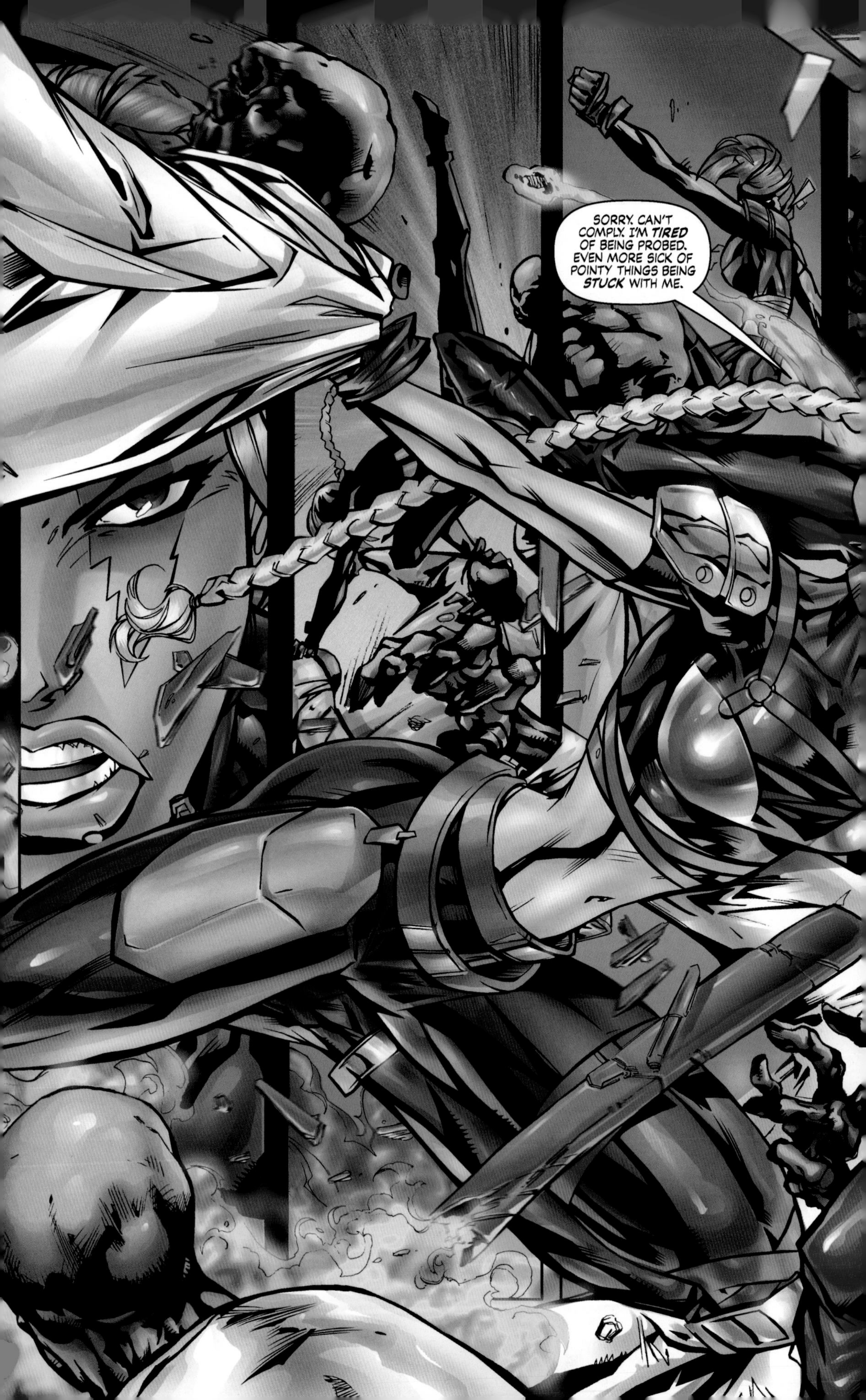
SORRY. CAN'T COMPLY. I'M *TIRED* OF BEING PROBED. EVEN MORE SICK OF POINTY THINGS BEING *STUCK* WITH ME.

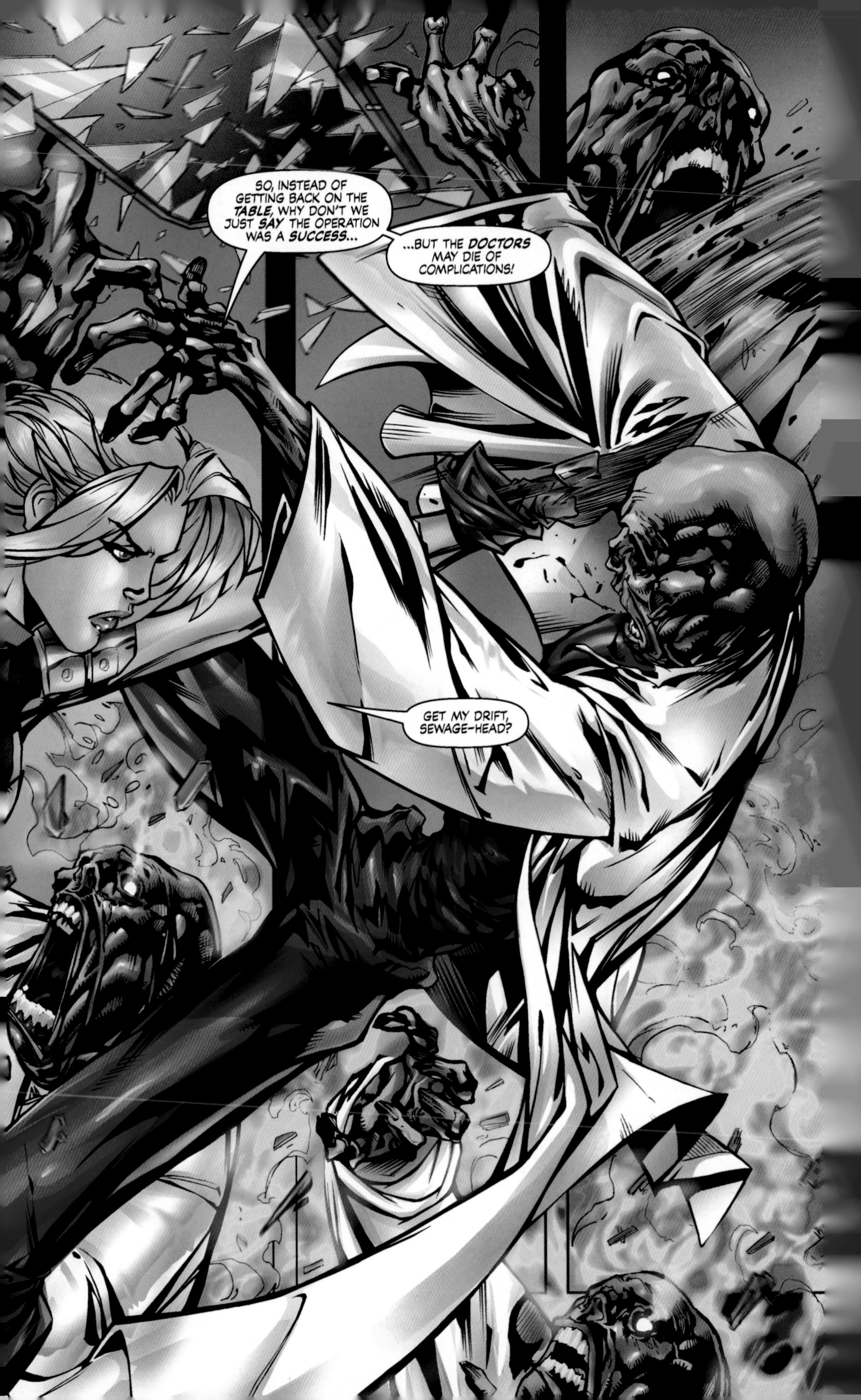
SO, INSTEAD OF GETTING BACK ON THE TABLE, WHY DON'T WE JUST SAY THE OPERATION WAS A SUCCESS...
...BUT THE DOCTORS MAY DIE OF COMPLICATIONS!
GET MY DRIFT, SEWAGE-HEAD?

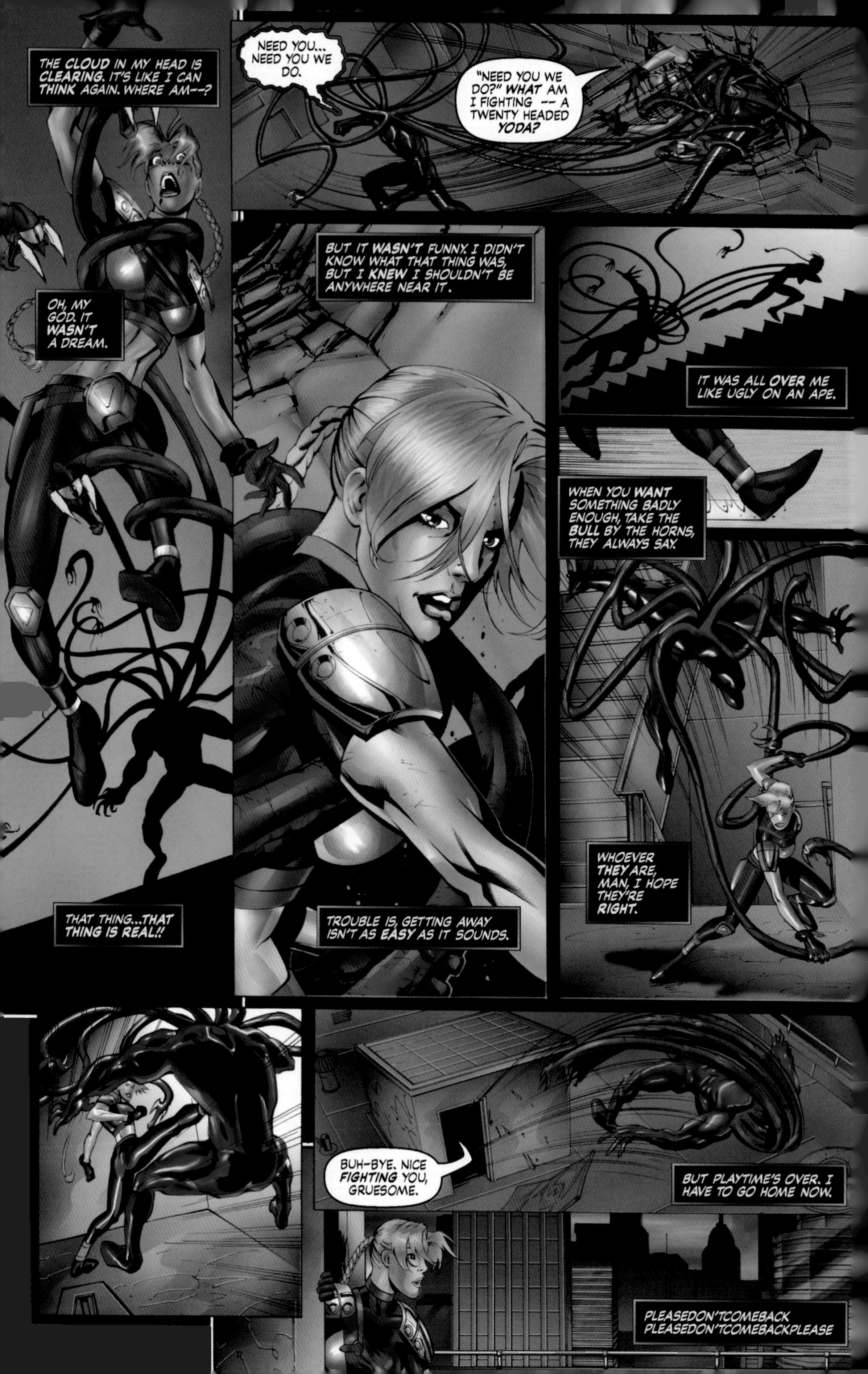
THE CLOUD IN MY HEAD IS CLEARING. IT'S LIKE I CAN THINK AGAIN. WHERE AM--?
OH, MY GOD. IT WASN'T A DREAM.
THAT THING...THAT THING IS REAL!!
NEED YOU... NEED YOU WE DO.
"NEED YOU WE DO?" WHAT AM I FIGHTING -- A TWENTY HEADED YODA?
BUT IT WASN'T FUNNY. I DIDN'T KNOW WHAT THAT THING WAS, BUT I KNEW I SHOULDN'T BE ANYWHERE NEAR IT.
TROUBLE IS, GETTING AWAY ISN'T AS EASY AS IT SOUNDS.
IT WAS ALL OVER ME LIKE UGLY ON AN APE.
WHEN YOU WANT SOMETHING BADLY ENOUGH, TAKE THE BULL BY THE HORNS, THEY ALWAYS SAY.
WHOEVER THEY ARE, MAN, I HOPE THEY'RE RIGHT.
BUH-BYE. NICE FIGHTING YOU, GRUESOME.
BUT PLAYTIME'S OVER. I HAVE TO GO HOME NOW.
PLEASEDON'TCOMEBACK PLEASEDON'TCOMEBACKPLEASE

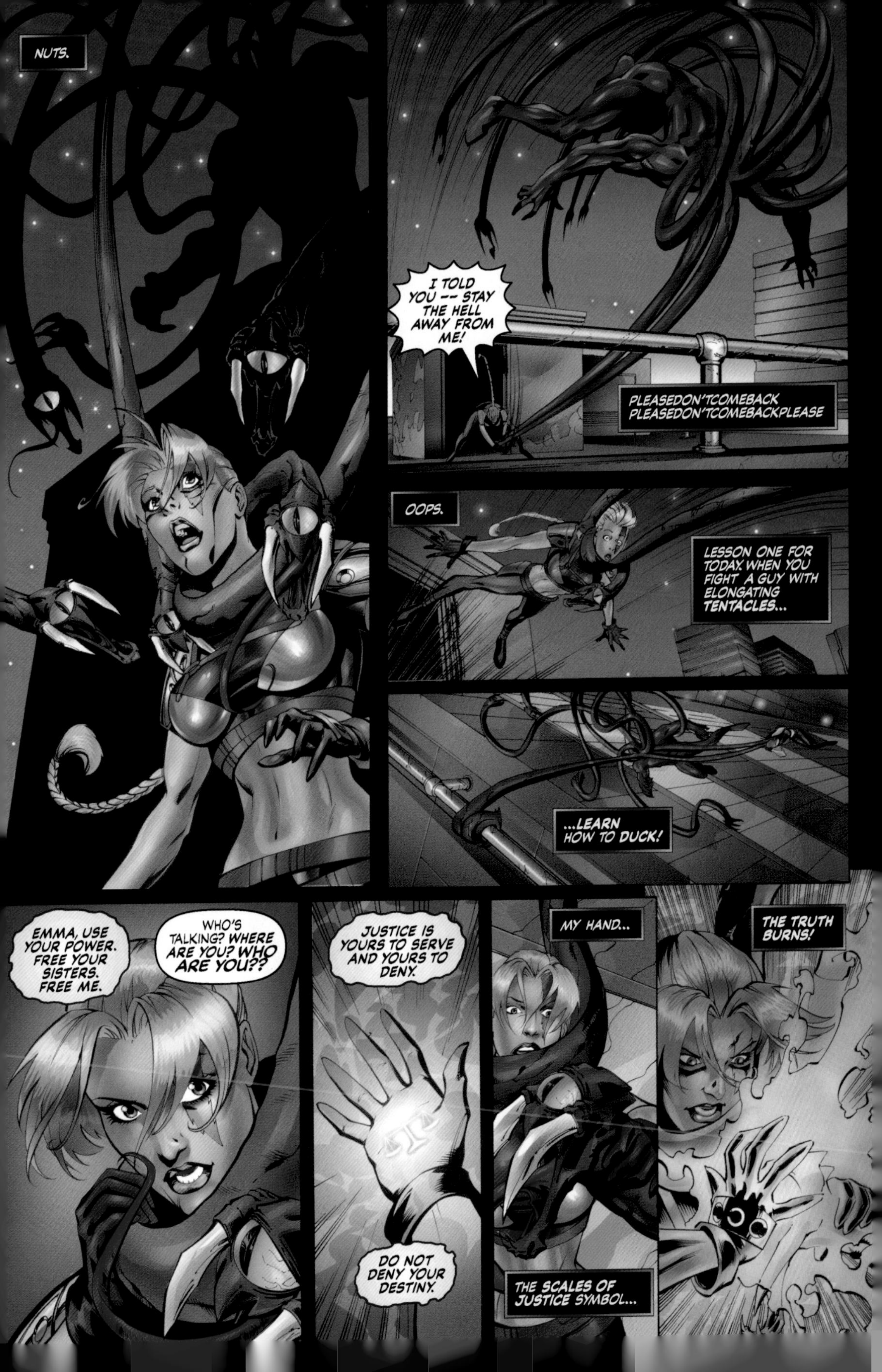
NUTS.
I TOLD YOU -- STAY THE HELL AWAY FROM ME!
PLEASEDON'TCOMEBACK PLEASEDON'TCOMEBACKPLEASE
OOPS.
LESSON ONE FOR TODAY. WHEN YOU FIGHT A GUY WITH ELONGATING TENTACLES...
...LEARN HOW TO DUCK!
EMMA, USE YOUR POWER. FREE YOUR SISTERS. FREE ME.
WHO'S TALKING? WHERE ARE YOU? WHO ARE YOU??
JUSTICE IS YOURS TO SERVE AND YOURS TO DENY.
DO NOT DENY YOUR DESTINY.
MY HAND...
THE SCALES OF JUSTICE SYMBOL...
THE TRUTH BURNS!

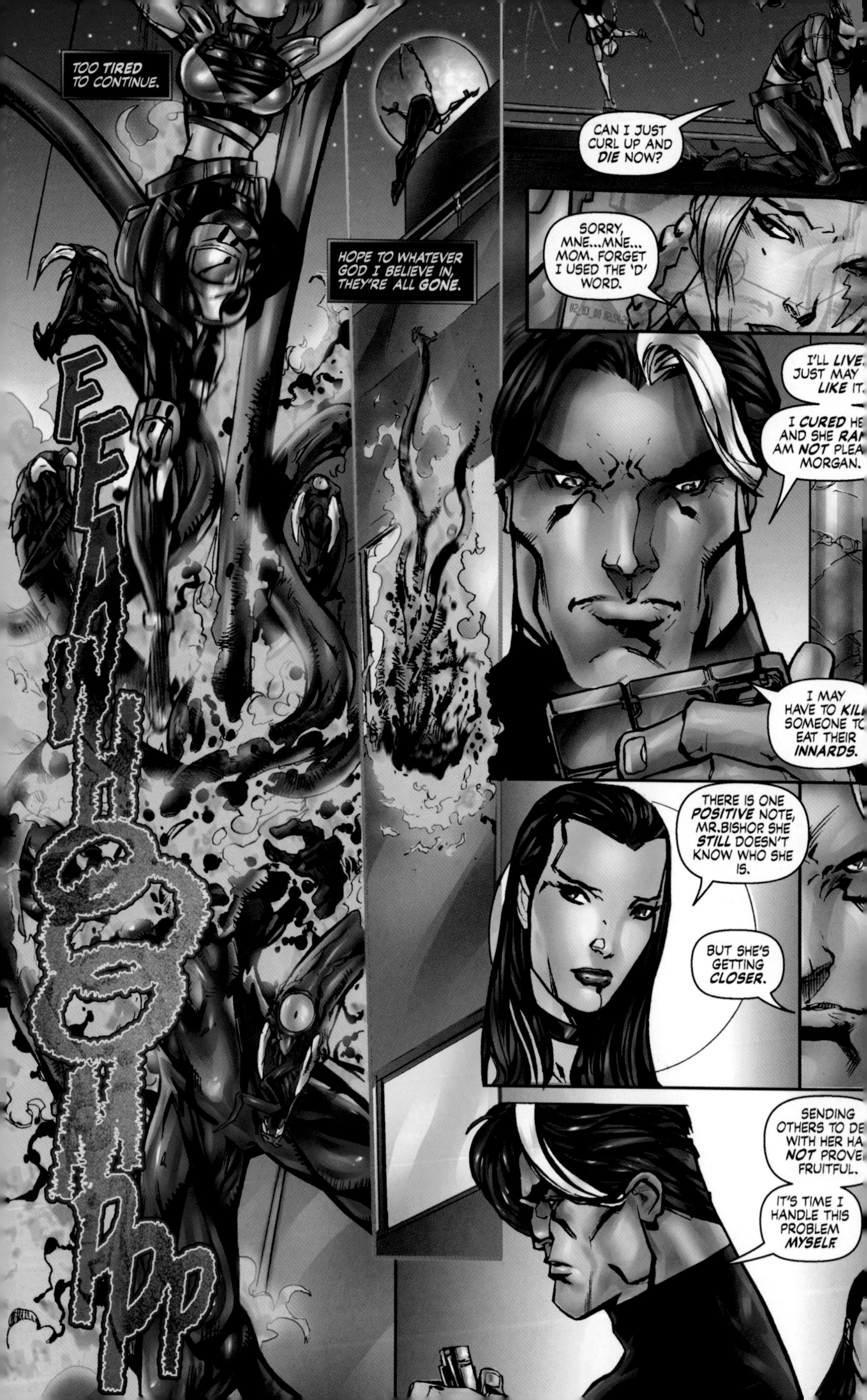
TOO TIRED TO CONTINUE.
FFAAWHOOSHAPP
HOPE TO WHATEVER GOD I BELIEVE IN, THEY'RE ALL GONE.
CAN I JUST CURL UP AND DIE NOW?
SORRY, MNE...MNE... MOM. FORGET I USED THE 'D' WORD.
I'LL LIVE. JUST MAY LIKE IT.
I CURED HE AND SHE RAN AM NOT PLEA MORGAN.
I MAY HAVE TO KIL SOMEONE TO EAT THEIR INNARDS.
THERE IS ONE POSITIVE NOTE, MR.BISHOR SHE STILL DOESN'T KNOW WHO SHE IS.
BUT SHE'S GETTING CLOSER.
SENDING OTHERS TO DE WITH HER HA NOT PROVE FRUITFUL.
IT'S TIME I HANDLE THIS PROBLEM MYSELF.

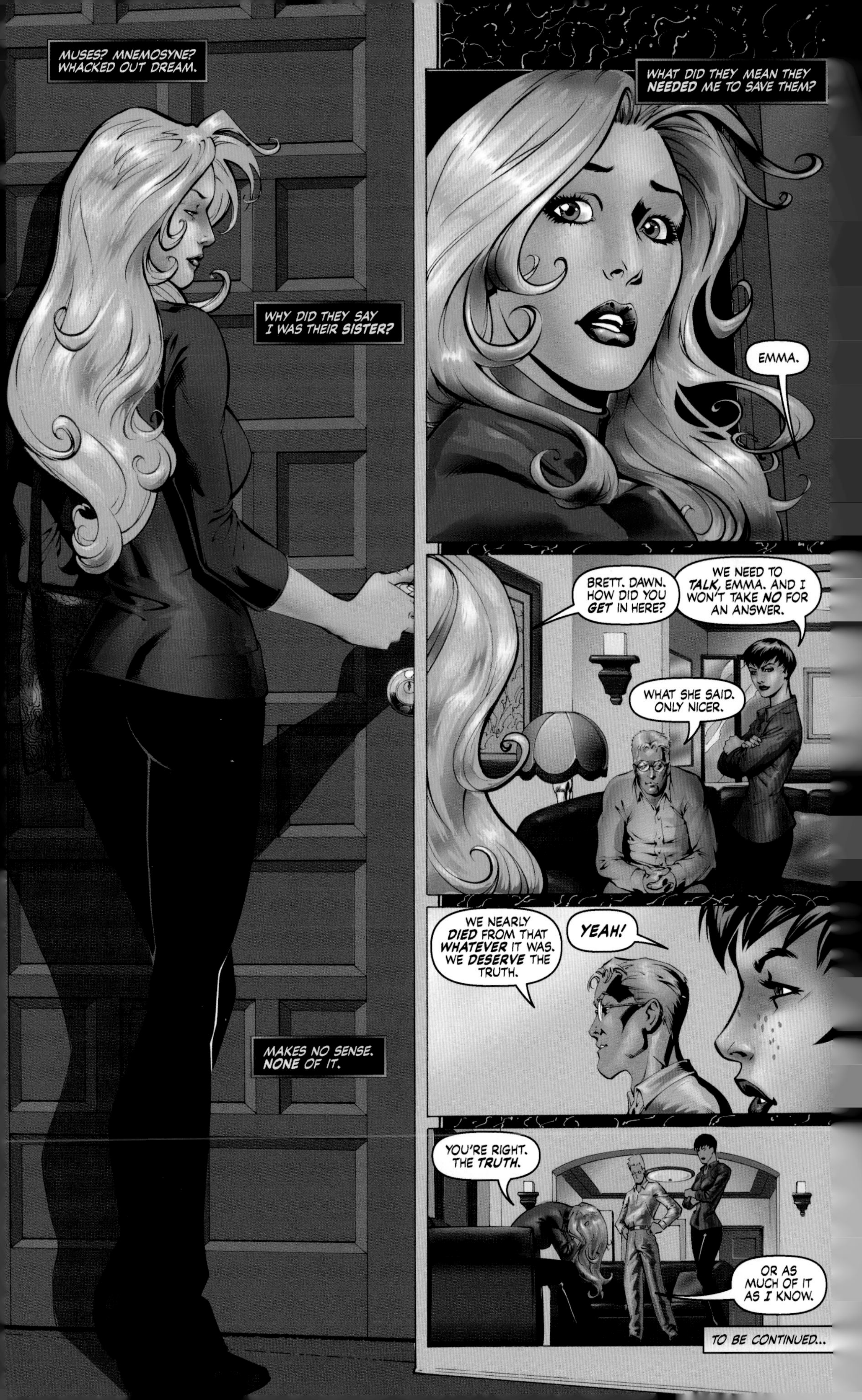
MUSES? MNEMOSYNE? WHACKED OUT DREAM.
WHY DID THEY SAY I WAS THEIR SISTER?
MAKES NO SENSE. NONE OF IT.
WHAT DID THEY MEAN THEY NEEDED ME TO SAVE THEM?
EMMA.
BRETT. DAWN. HOW DID YOU GET IN HERE?
WE NEED TO TALK, EMMA. AND I WON'T TAKE NO FOR AN ANSWER.
WHAT SHE SAID. ONLY NICER.
WE NEARLY DIED FROM THAT WHATEVER IT WAS. WE DESERVE THE TRUTH.
YEAH!
YOU'RE RIGHT. THE TRUTH.
OR AS MUCH OF IT AS I KNOW.
TO BE CONTINUED...

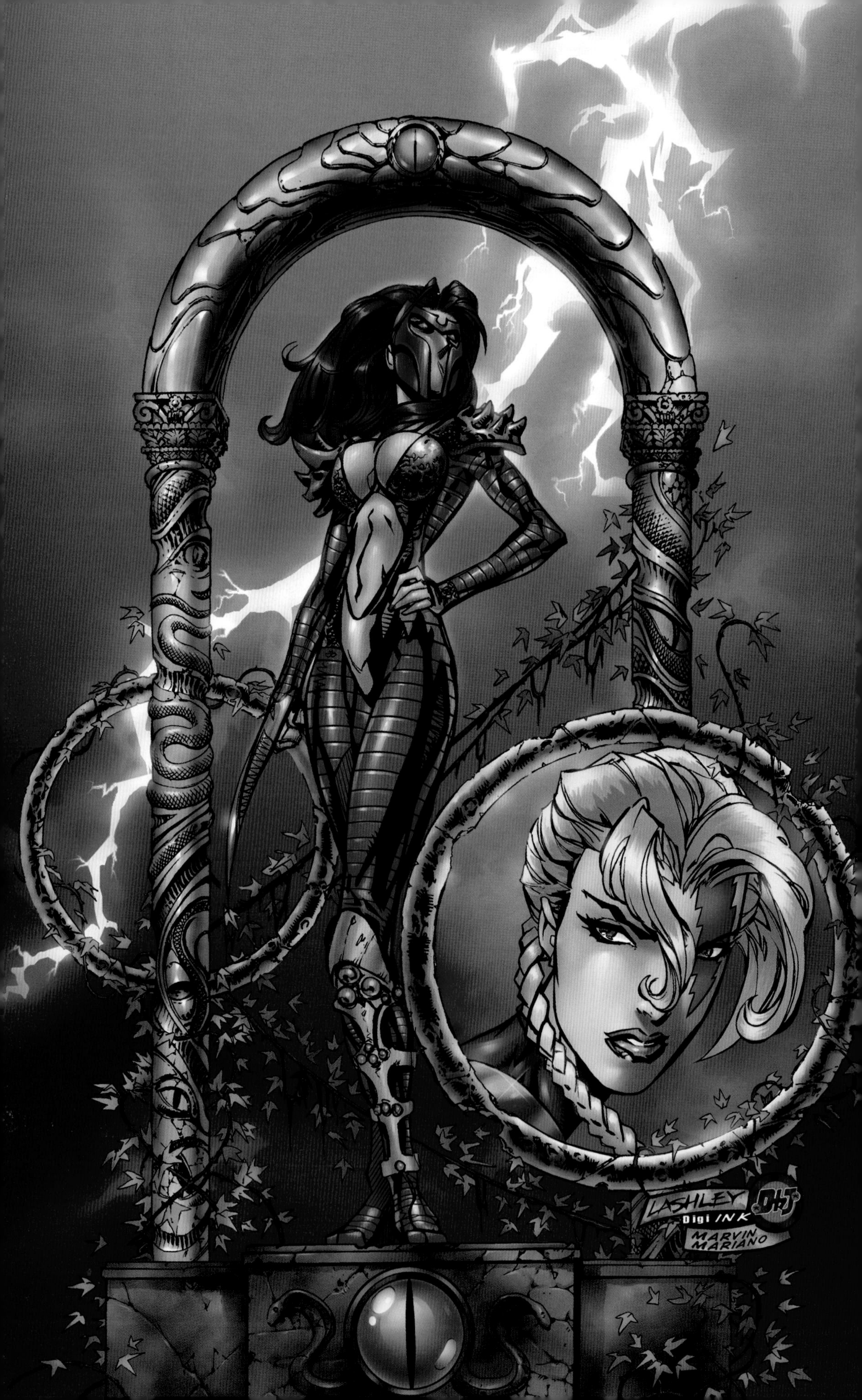
LASHLEY
DHJ
Digi INK
MARVIN MARIANO

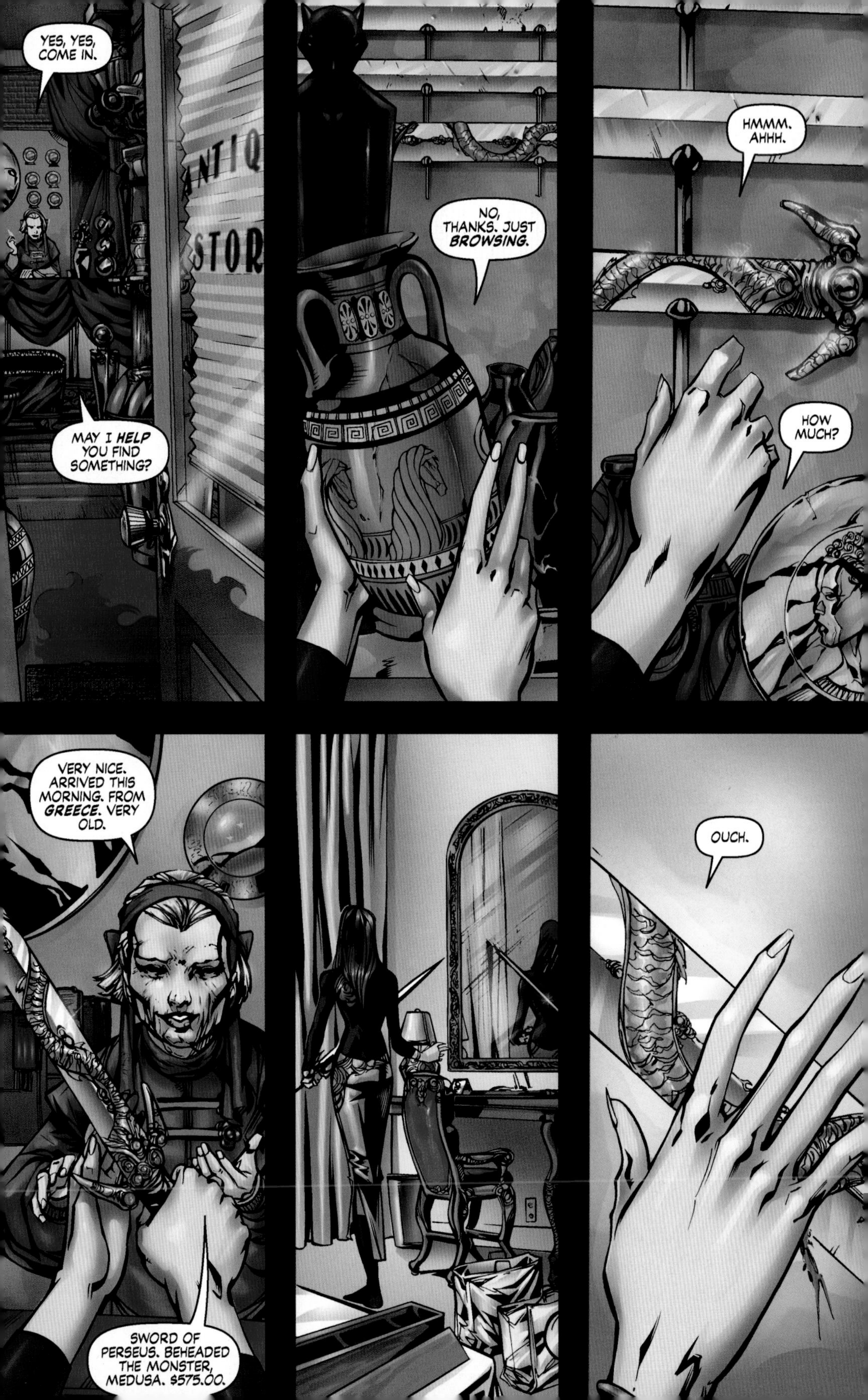
YES, YES, COME IN.
ANTIQ
STOR
MAY I HELP YOU FIND SOMETHING?
NO, THANKS. JUST BROWSING.
HMMM. AHHH.
HOW MUCH?
VERY NICE. ARRIVED THIS MORNING. FROM GREECE. VERY OLD.
SWORD OF PERSEUS. BEHEADED THE MONSTER, MEDUSA. $575.00.
OUCH.

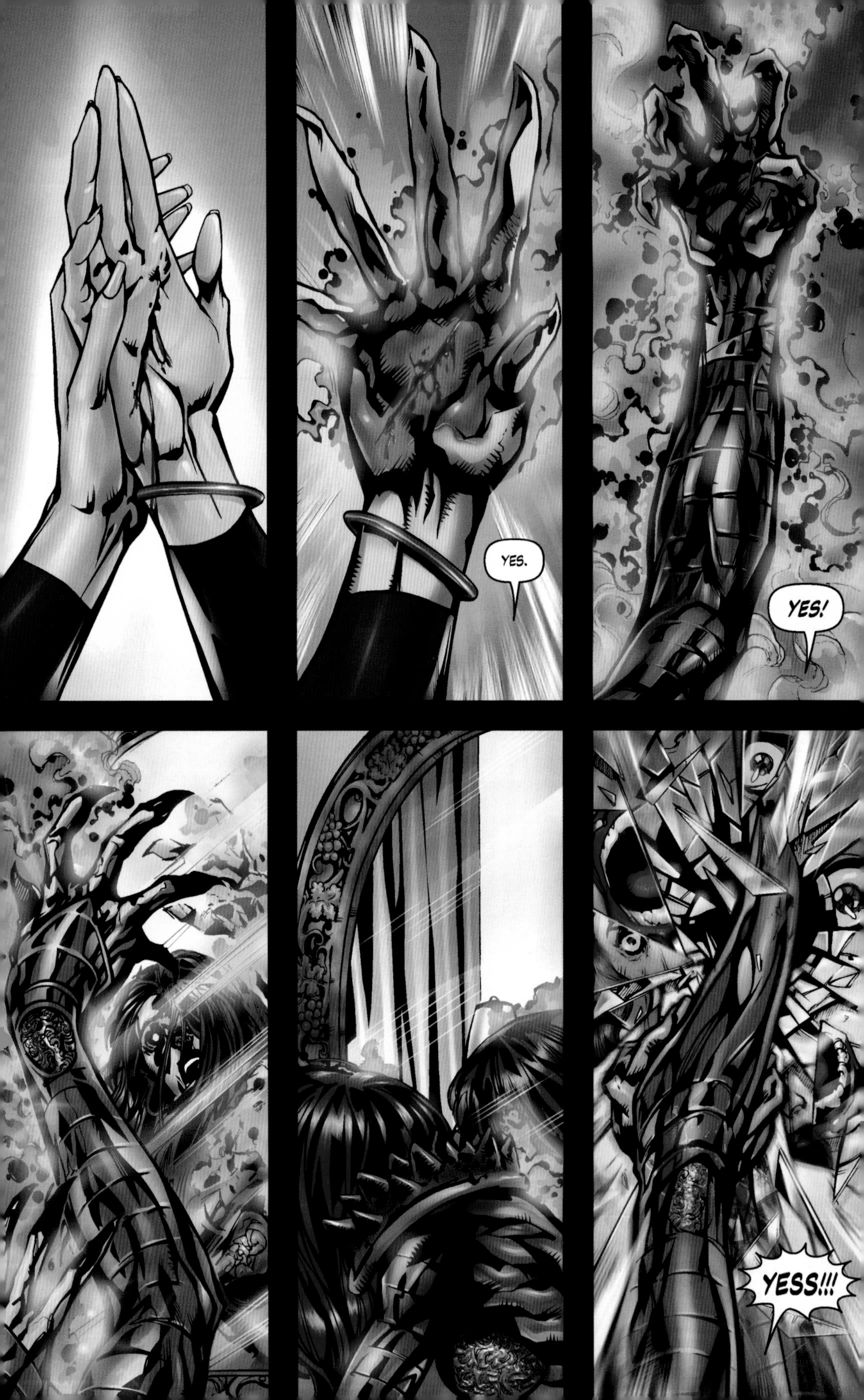
YES.
YES!
YESS!!!

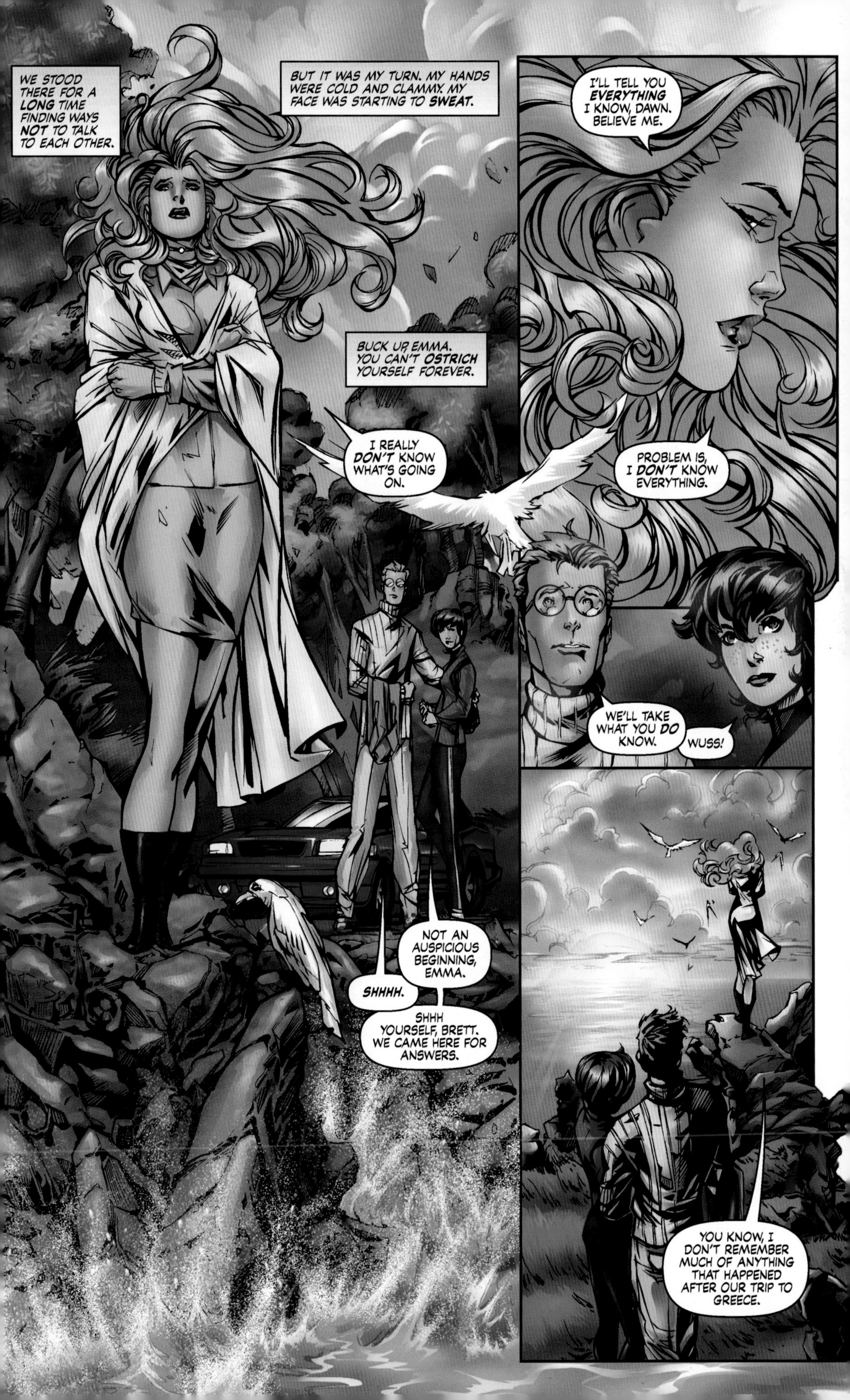
WE STOOD THERE FOR A LONG TIME FINDING WAYS NOT TO TALK TO EACH OTHER.
BUT IT WAS MY TURN. MY HANDS WERE COLD AND CLAMMY. MY FACE WAS STARTING TO SWEAT.
BUCK UP, EMMA. YOU CAN'T OSTRICH YOURSELF FOREVER.
I REALLY DON'T KNOW WHAT'S GOING ON.
NOT AN AUSPICIOUS BEGINNING, EMMA.
SHHHH.
SHHH YOURSELF, BRETT. WE CAME HERE FOR ANSWERS.
I'LL TELL YOU EVERYTHING I KNOW, DAWN. BELIEVE ME.
PROBLEM IS, I DON'T KNOW EVERYTHING.
WE'LL TAKE WHAT YOU DO KNOW.
WUSS!
YOU KNOW, I DON'T REMEMBER MUCH OF ANYTHING THAT HAPPENED AFTER OUR TRIP TO GREECE.

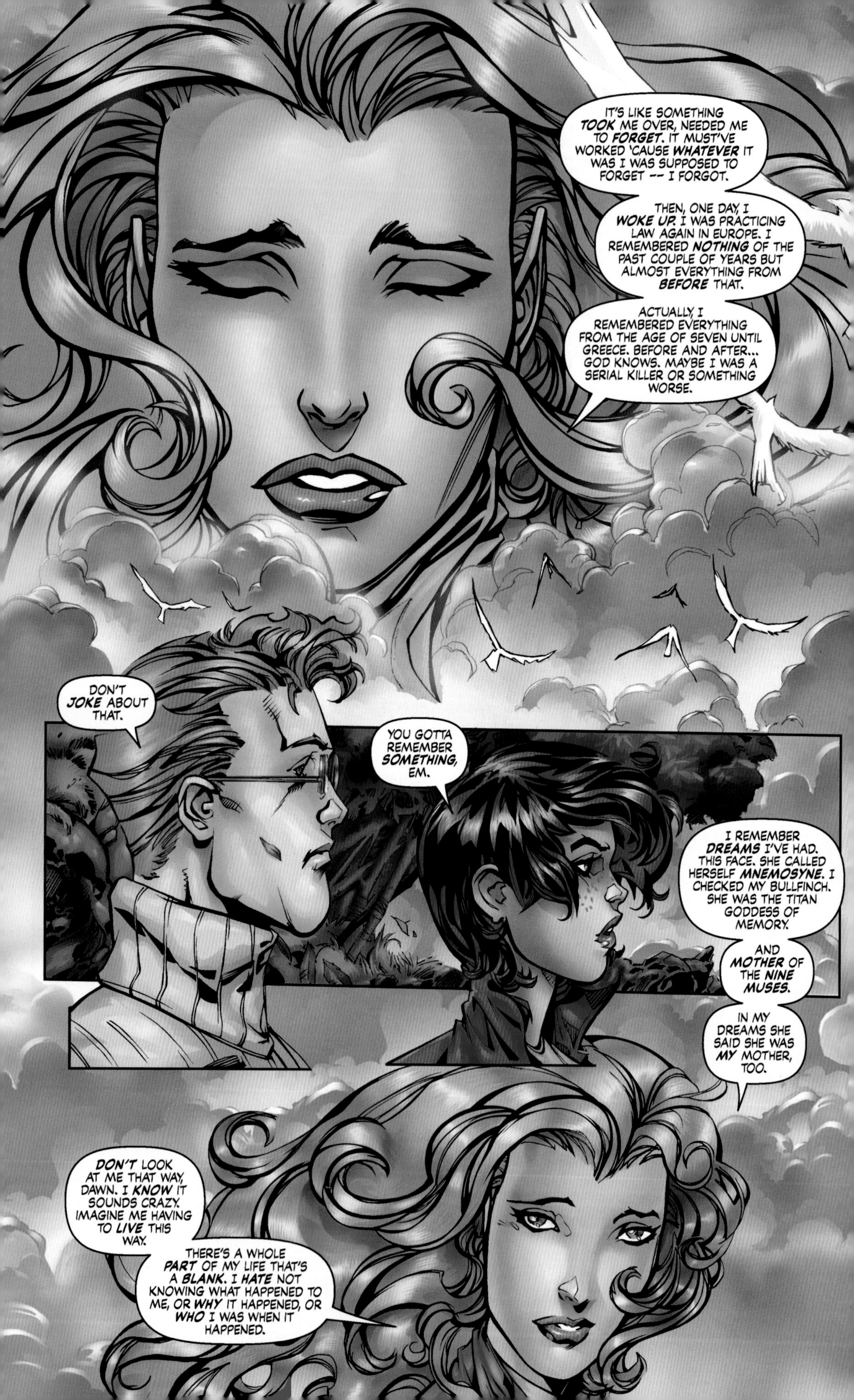
IT'S LIKE SOMETHING TOOK ME OVER, NEEDED ME TO FORGET. IT MUST'VE WORKED 'CAUSE WHATEVER IT WAS I WAS SUPPOSED TO FORGET -- I FORGOT.
THEN, ONE DAY, I WOKE UP. I WAS PRACTICING LAW AGAIN IN EUROPE. I REMEMBERED NOTHING OF THE PAST COUPLE OF YEARS BUT ALMOST EVERYTHING FROM BEFORE THAT.
ACTUALLY, I REMEMBERED EVERYTHING FROM THE AGE OF SEVEN UNTIL GREECE. BEFORE AND AFTER... GOD KNOWS. MAYBE I WAS A SERIAL KILLER OR SOMETHING WORSE.
DON'T JOKE ABOUT THAT.
YOU GOTTA REMEMBER SOMETHING, EM.
I REMEMBER DREAMS I'VE HAD. THIS FACE. SHE CALLED HERSELF MNEMOSYNE. I CHECKED MY BULLFINCH. SHE WAS THE TITAN GODDESS OF MEMORY.
AND MOTHER OF THE NINE MUSES.
IN MY DREAMS SHE SAID SHE WAS MY MOTHER, TOO.
DON'T LOOK AT ME THAT WAY, DAWN. I KNOW IT SOUNDS CRAZY. IMAGINE ME HAVING TO LIVE THIS WAY.
THERE'S A WHOLE PART OF MY LIFE THAT'S A BLANK. I HATE NOT KNOWING WHAT HAPPENED TO ME, OR WHY IT HAPPENED, OR WHO I WAS WHEN IT HAPPENED.

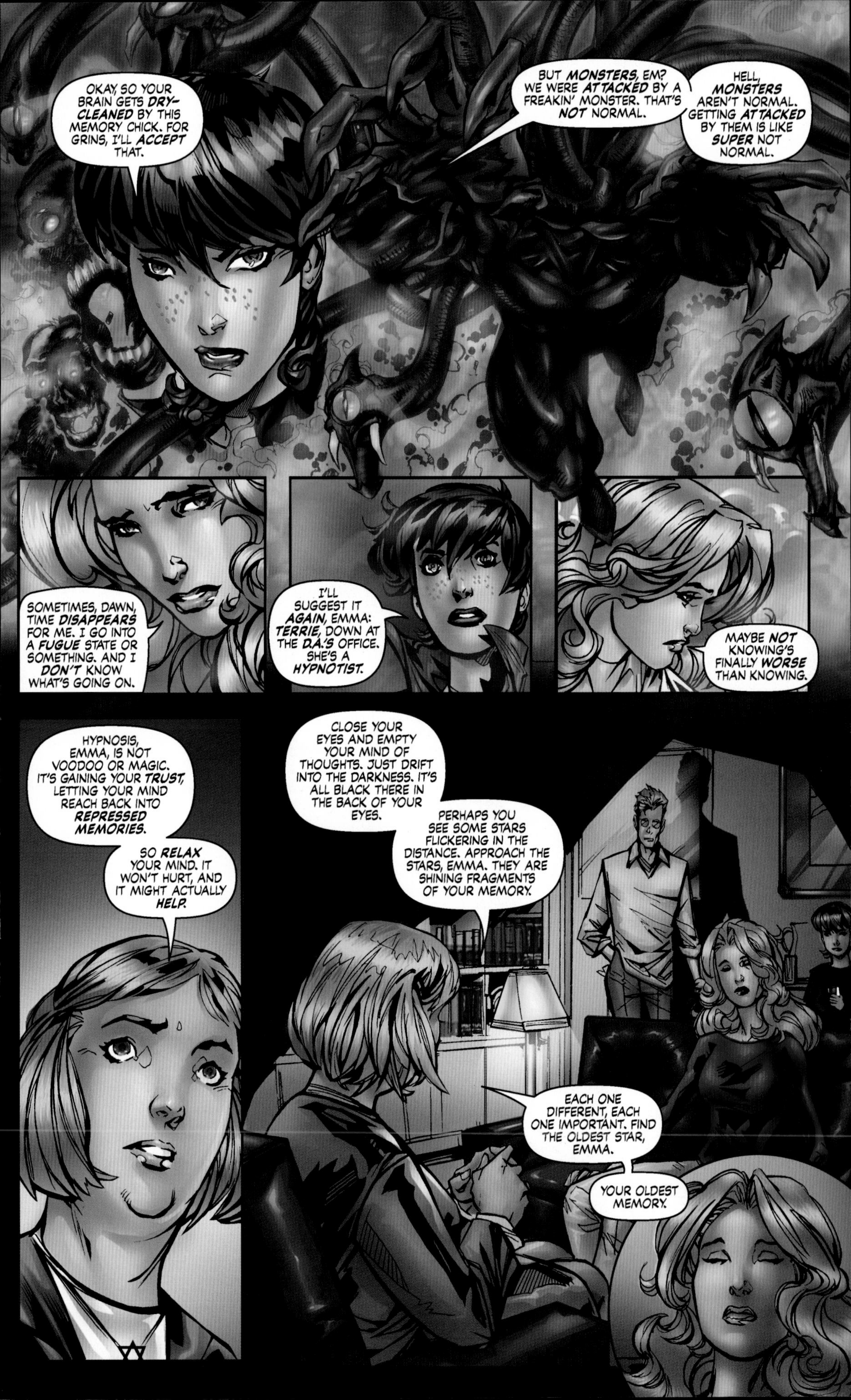
OKAY, SO YOUR BRAIN GETS DRY-CLEANED BY THIS MEMORY CHICK. FOR GRINS, I'LL ACCEPT THAT.
BUT MONSTERS, EM? WE WERE ATTACKED BY A FREAKIN' MONSTER. THAT'S NOT NORMAL.
HELL, MONSTERS AREN'T NORMAL. GETTING ATTACKED BY THEM IS LIKE SUPER NOT NORMAL.
SOMETIMES, DAWN, TIME DISAPPEARS FOR ME. I GO INTO A FUGUE STATE OR SOMETHING. AND I DON'T KNOW WHAT'S GOING ON.
I'LL SUGGEST IT AGAIN, EMMA: TERRIE, DOWN AT THE D.A.'S OFFICE. SHE'S A HYPNOTIST.
MAYBE NOT KNOWING'S FINALLY WORSE THAN KNOWING.
HYPNOSIS, EMMA, IS NOT VOODOO OR MAGIC. IT'S GAINING YOUR TRUST, LETTING YOUR MIND REACH BACK INTO REPRESSED MEMORIES.
SO RELAX YOUR MIND. IT WON'T HURT, AND IT MIGHT ACTUALLY HELP.
CLOSE YOUR EYES AND EMPTY YOUR MIND OF THOUGHTS. JUST DRIFT INTO THE DARKNESS. IT'S ALL BLACK THERE IN THE BACK OF YOUR EYES.
PERHAPS YOU SEE SOME STARS FLICKERING IN THE DISTANCE. APPROACH THE STARS, EMMA. THEY ARE SHINING FRAGMENTS OF YOUR MEMORY.
EACH ONE DIFFERENT, EACH ONE IMPORTANT. FIND THE OLDEST STAR, EMMA.
YOUR OLDEST MEMORY.

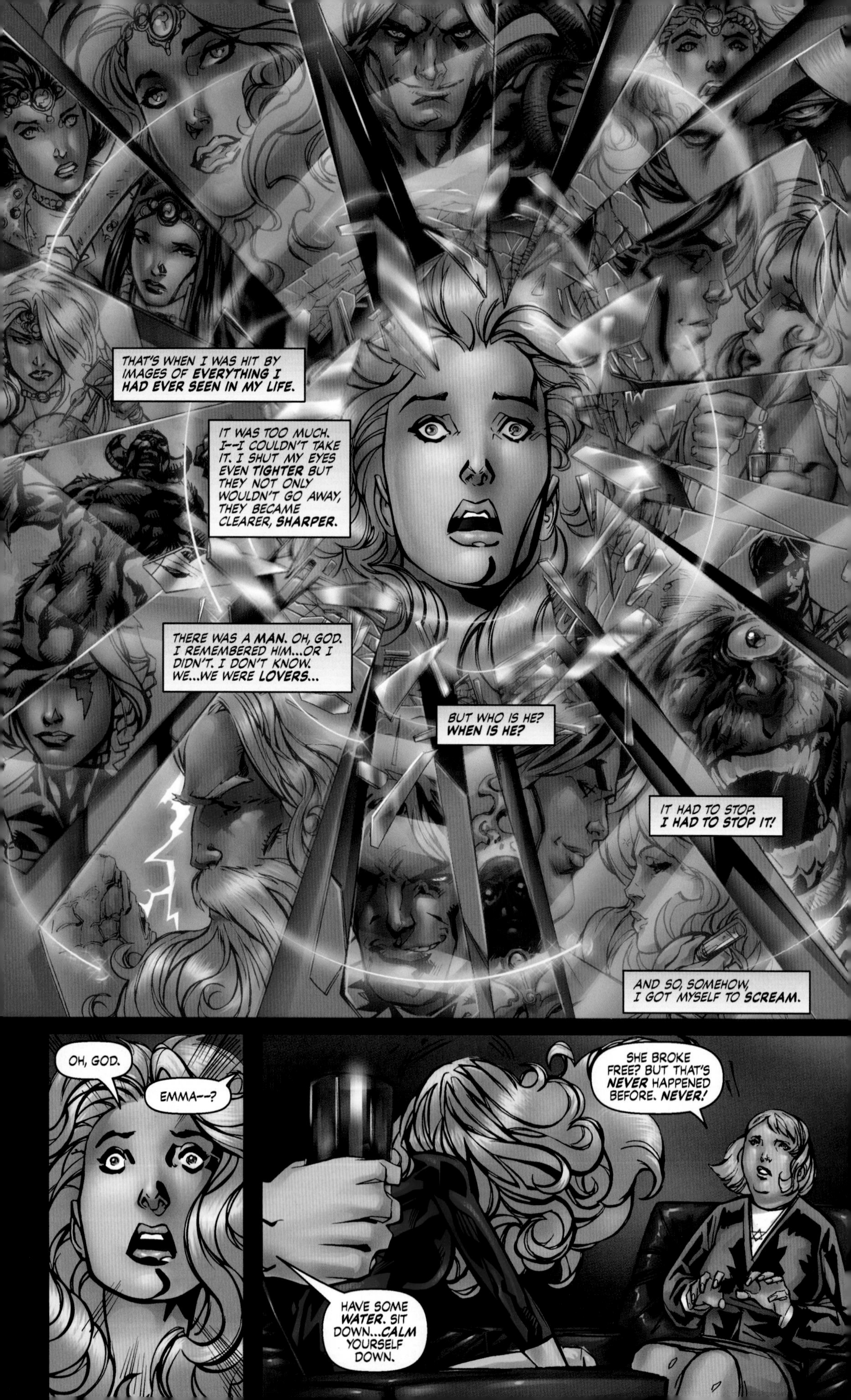

THAT'S WHEN I WAS HIT BY IMAGES OF EVERYTHING I HAD EVER SEEN IN MY LIFE.
IT WAS TOO MUCH. I--I COULDN'T TAKE IT. I SHUT MY EYES EVEN TIGHTER BUT THEY NOT ONLY WOULDN'T GO AWAY, THEY BECAME CLEARER, SHARPER.
THERE WAS A MAN. OH, GOD. I REMEMBERED HIM...OR I DIDN'T. I DON'T KNOW. WE...WE WERE LOVERS...
BUT WHO IS HE? WHEN IS HE?
IT HAD TO STOP. I HAD TO STOP IT!
AND SO, SOMEHOW, I GOT MYSELF TO SCREAM.
OH, GOD.
EMMA--?
SHE BROKE FREE? BUT THAT'S NEVER HAPPENED BEFORE. NEVER!
HAVE SOME WATER. SIT DOWN...CALM YOURSELF DOWN.

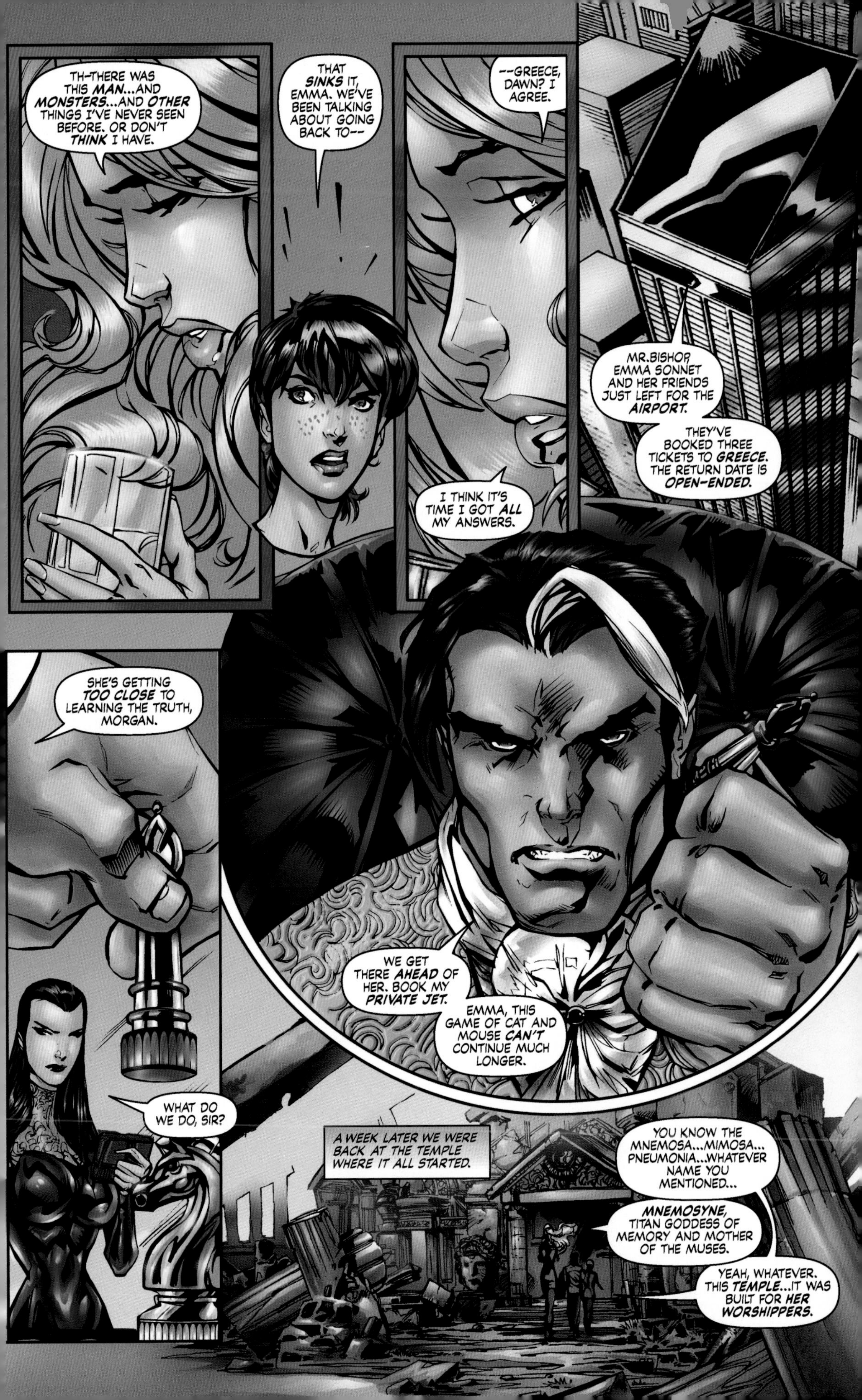

TH-THERE WAS THIS MAN...AND MONSTERS...AND OTHER THINGS I'VE NEVER SEEN BEFORE. OR DON'T THINK I HAVE.
THAT SINKS IT, EMMA. WE'VE BEEN TALKING ABOUT GOING BACK TO--
--GREECE, DAWN? I AGREE.
I THINK IT'S TIME I GOT ALL MY ANSWERS.
MR.BISHOP, EMMA SONNET AND HER FRIENDS JUST LEFT FOR THE AIRPORT.
THEY'VE BOOKED THREE TICKETS TO GREECE. THE RETURN DATE IS OPEN-ENDED.
SHE'S GETTING TOO CLOSE TO LEARNING THE TRUTH, MORGAN.
WHAT DO WE DO, SIR?
WE GET THERE AHEAD OF HER. BOOK MY PRIVATE JET.
EMMA, THIS GAME OF CAT AND MOUSE CAN'T CONTINUE MUCH LONGER.
A WEEK LATER WE WERE BACK AT THE TEMPLE WHERE IT ALL STARTED.
YOU KNOW THE MNEMOSA...MIMOSA... PNEUMONIA...WHATEVER NAME YOU MENTIONED...
MNEMOSYNE, TITAN GODDESS OF MEMORY AND MOTHER OF THE MUSES.
YEAH, WHATEVER. THIS TEMPLE...IT WAS BUILT FOR HER WORSHIPPERS.

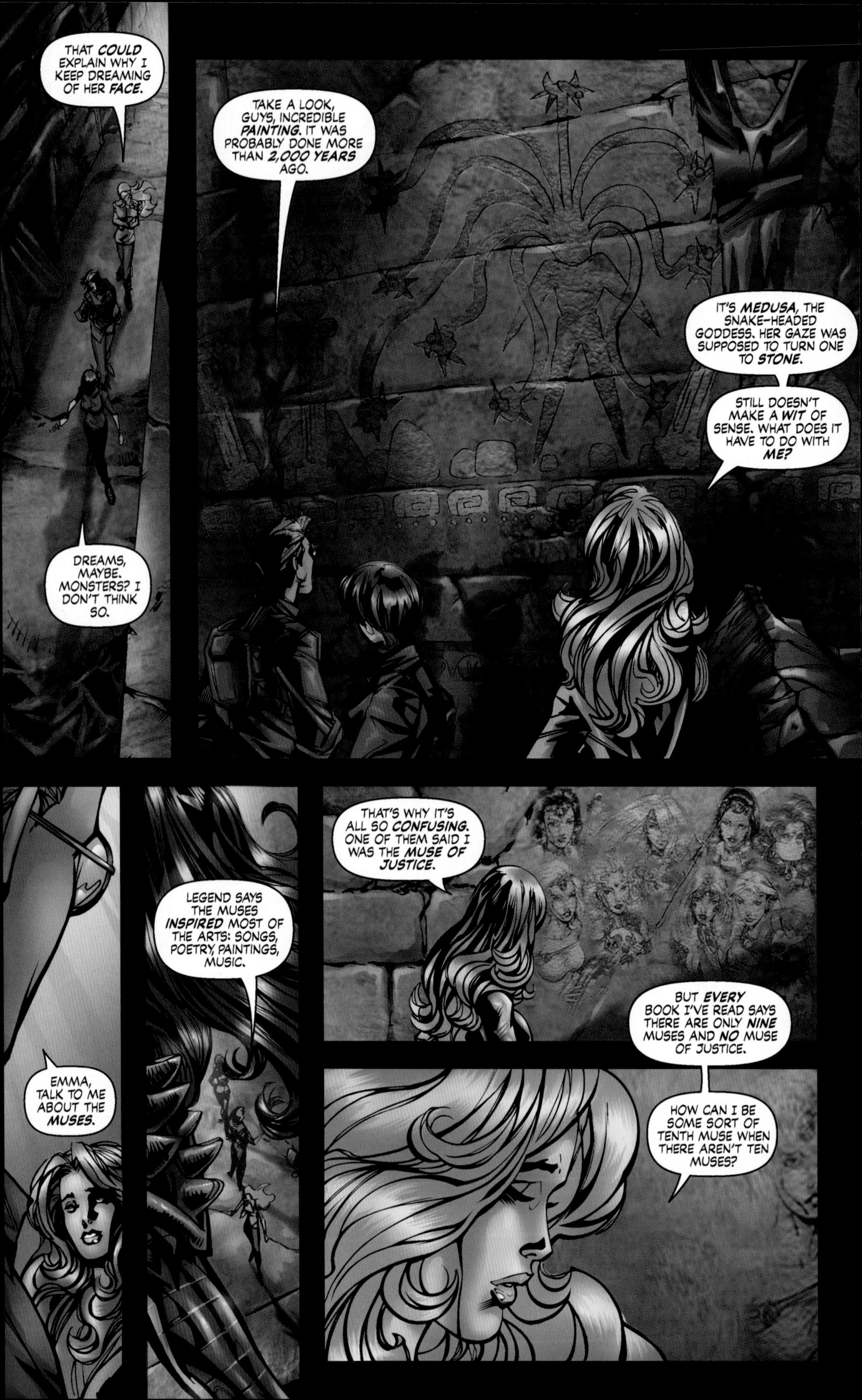
THAT COULD EXPLAIN WHY I KEEP DREAMING OF HER FACE.
TAKE A LOOK, GUYS, INCREDIBLE PAINTING. IT WAS PROBABLY DONE MORE THAN 2,000 YEARS AGO.
DREAMS, MAYBE. MONSTERS? I DON'T THINK SO.
IT'S MEDUSA, THE SNAKE-HEADED GODDESS. HER GAZE WAS SUPPOSED TO TURN ONE TO STONE.
STILL DOESN'T MAKE A WIT OF SENSE. WHAT DOES IT HAVE TO DO WITH ME?
EMMA, TALK TO ME ABOUT THE MUSES.
LEGEND SAYS THE MUSES INSPIRED MOST OF THE ARTS: SONGS, POETRY, PAINTINGS, MUSIC.
THAT'S WHY IT'S ALL SO CONFUSING. ONE OF THEM SAID I WAS THE MUSE OF JUSTICE.
BUT EVERY BOOK I'VE READ SAYS THERE ARE ONLY NINE MUSES AND NO MUSE OF JUSTICE.
HOW CAN I BE SOME SORT OF TENTH MUSE WHEN THERE AREN'T TEN MUSES?

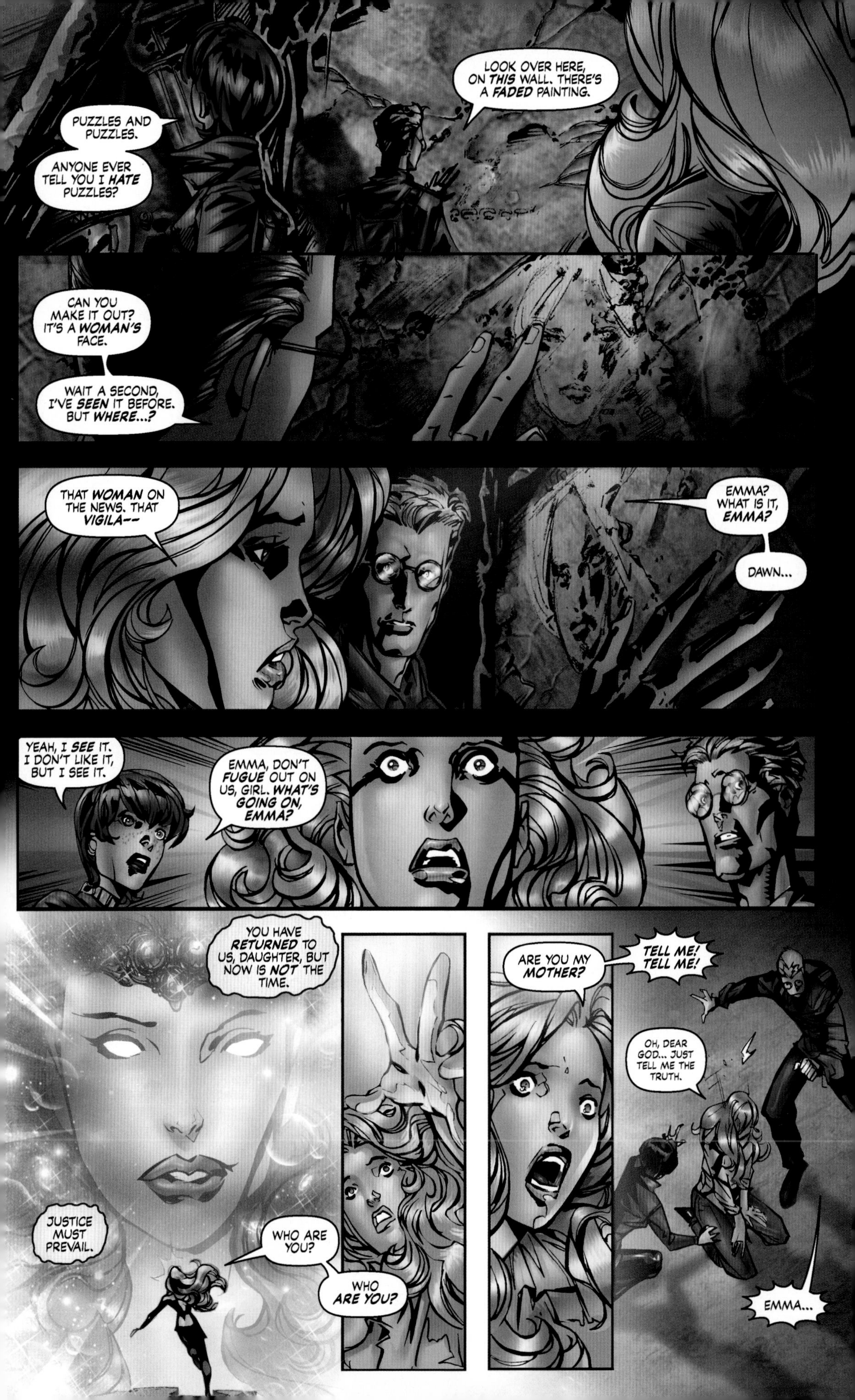
PUZZLES AND PUZZLES.
ANYONE EVER TELL YOU I HATE PUZZLES?
LOOK OVER HERE, ON THIS WALL. THERE'S A FADED PAINTING.
CAN YOU MAKE IT OUT? IT'S A WOMAN'S FACE.
WAIT A SECOND, I'VE SEEN IT BEFORE. BUT WHERE...?
THAT WOMAN ON THE NEWS. THAT VIGILA--
EMMA? WHAT IS IT, EMMA?
DAWN...
YEAH, I SEE IT. I DON'T LIKE IT, BUT I SEE IT.
EMMA, DON'T FUGUE OUT ON US, GIRL. WHAT'S GOING ON, EMMA?
YOU HAVE RETURNED TO US, DAUGHTER, BUT NOW IS NOT THE TIME.
JUSTICE MUST PREVAIL.
WHO ARE YOU?
WHO ARE YOU?
ARE YOU MY MOTHER?
TELL ME! TELL ME!
OH, DEAR GOD... JUST TELL ME THE TRUTH.
EMMA...

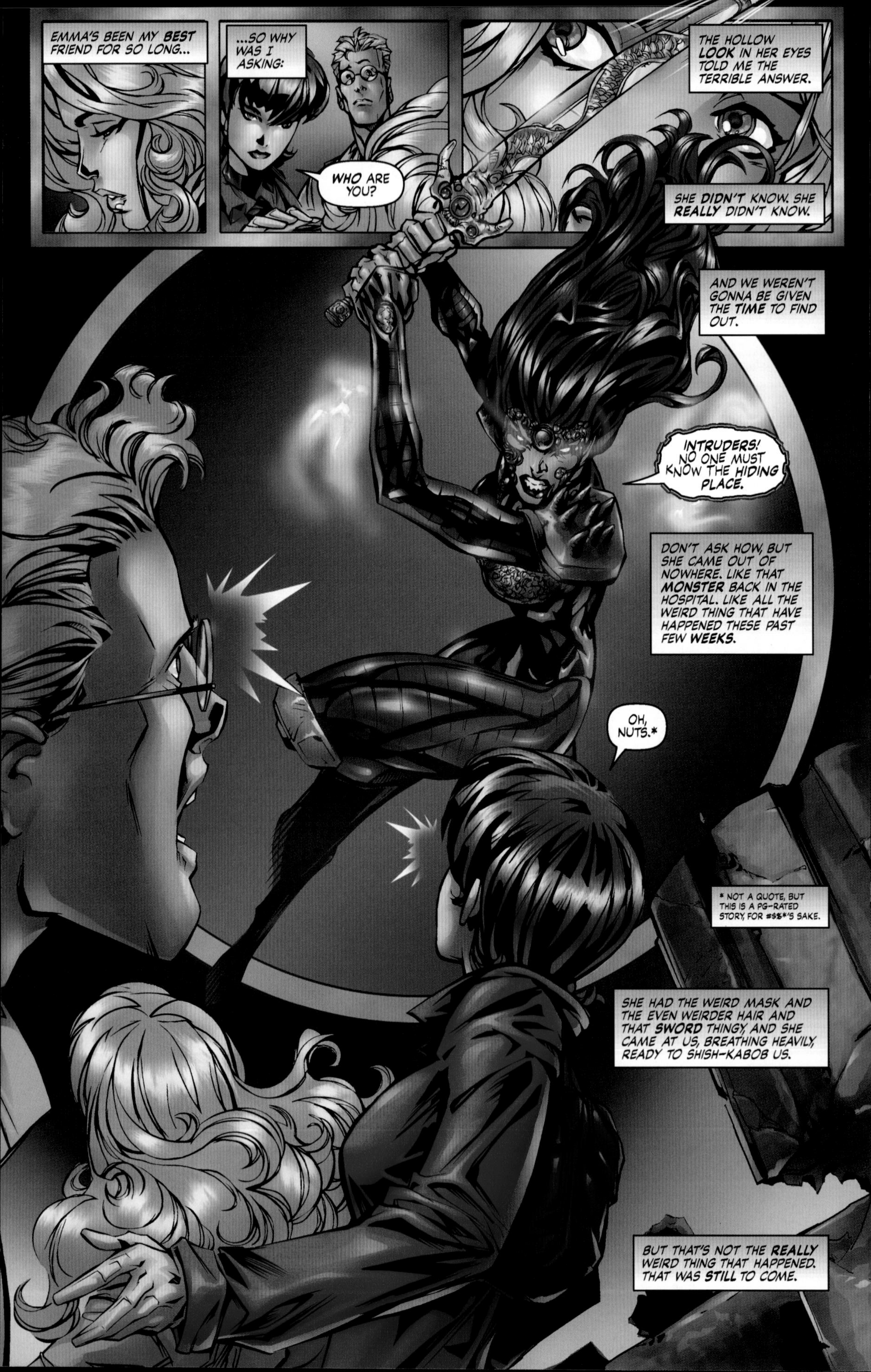
EMMA'S BEEN MY BEST FRIEND FOR SO LONG...
...SO WHY WAS I ASKING:
WHO ARE YOU?
THE HOLLOW LOOK IN HER EYES TOLD ME THE TERRIBLE ANSWER.
SHE DIDN'T KNOW. SHE REALLY DIDN'T KNOW.
AND WE WEREN'T GONNA BE GIVEN THE TIME TO FIND OUT.
INTRUDERS! NO ONE MUST KNOW THE HIDING PLACE.
DON'T ASK HOW, BUT SHE CAME OUT OF NOWHERE. LIKE THAT MONSTER BACK IN THE HOSPITAL. LIKE ALL THE WEIRD THING THAT HAVE HAPPENED THESE PAST FEW WEEKS.
OH, NUTS.*
* NOT A QUOTE, BUT THIS IS A PG-RATED STORY, FOR #$%*'S SAKE.
SHE HAD THE WEIRD MASK AND THE EVEN WEIRDER HAIR AND THAT SWORD THINGY, AND SHE CAME AT US, BREATHING HEAVILY, READY TO SHISH-KABOB US.
BUT THAT'S NOT THE REALLY WEIRD THING THAT HAPPENED. THAT WAS STILL TO COME.

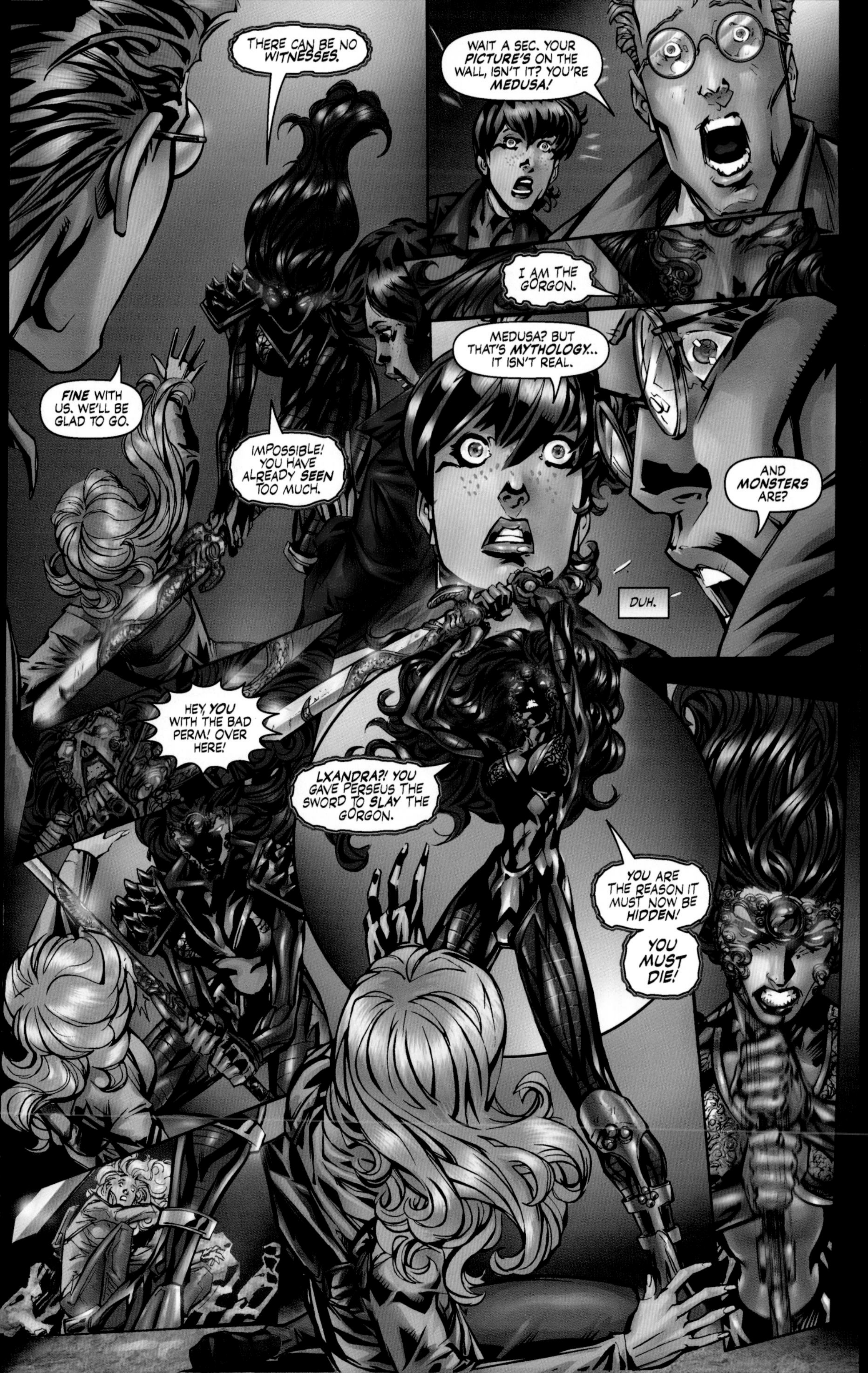
THERE CAN BE NO WITNESSES.
WAIT A SEC. YOUR PICTURE'S ON THE WALL, ISN'T IT? YOU'RE MEDUSA!
I AM THE GORGON.
MEDUSA? BUT THAT'S MYTHOLOGY... IT ISN'T REAL.
FINE WITH US. WE'LL BE GLAD TO GO.
IMPOSSIBLE! YOU HAVE ALREADY SEEN TOO MUCH.
AND MONSTERS ARE?
DUH.
HEY, YOU WITH THE BAD PERM! OVER HERE!
LXANDRA?! YOU GAVE PERSEUS THE SWORD TO SLAY THE GORGON.
YOU ARE THE REASON IT MUST NOW BE HIDDEN!
YOU MUST DIE!

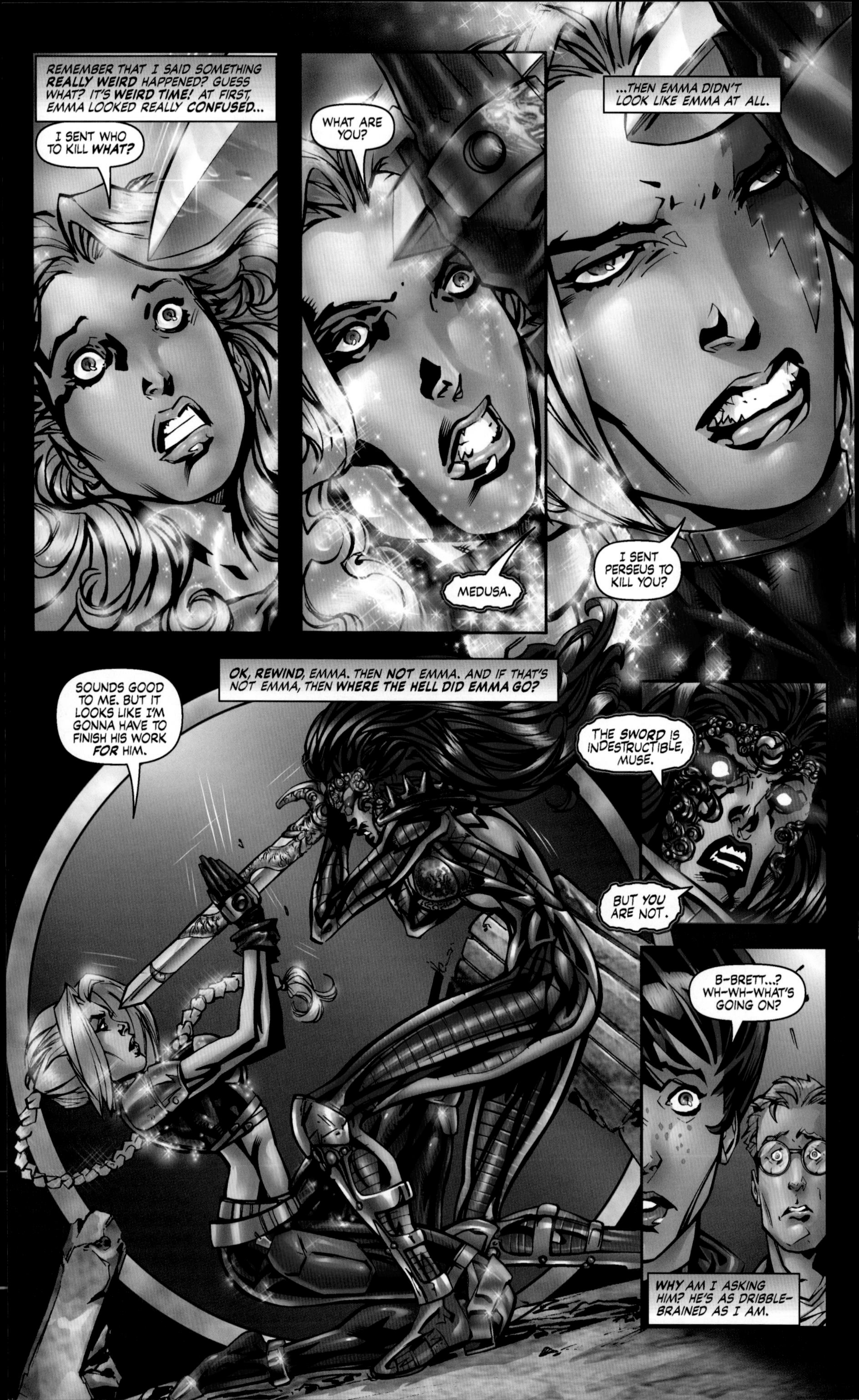

REMEMBER THAT I SAID SOMETHING REALLY WEIRD HAPPENED? GUESS WHAT? IT'S WEIRD TIME! AT FIRST, EMMA LOOKED REALLY CONFUSED...
I SENT WHO TO KILL WHAT?
WHAT ARE YOU?
MEDUSA.
...THEN EMMA DIDN'T LOOK LIKE EMMA AT ALL.
I SENT PERSEUS TO KILL YOU?
OK, REWIND, EMMA. THEN NOT EMMA. AND IF THAT'S NOT EMMA, THEN WHERE THE HELL DID EMMA GO?
SOUNDS GOOD TO ME. BUT IT LOOKS LIKE I'M GONNA HAVE TO FINISH HIS WORK FOR HIM.
THE SWORD IS INDESTRUCTIBLE, MUSE.
BUT YOU ARE NOT.
B-BRETT...? WH-WH-WHAT'S GOING ON?
WHY AM I ASKING HIM? HE'S AS DRIBBLE-BRAINED AS I AM.

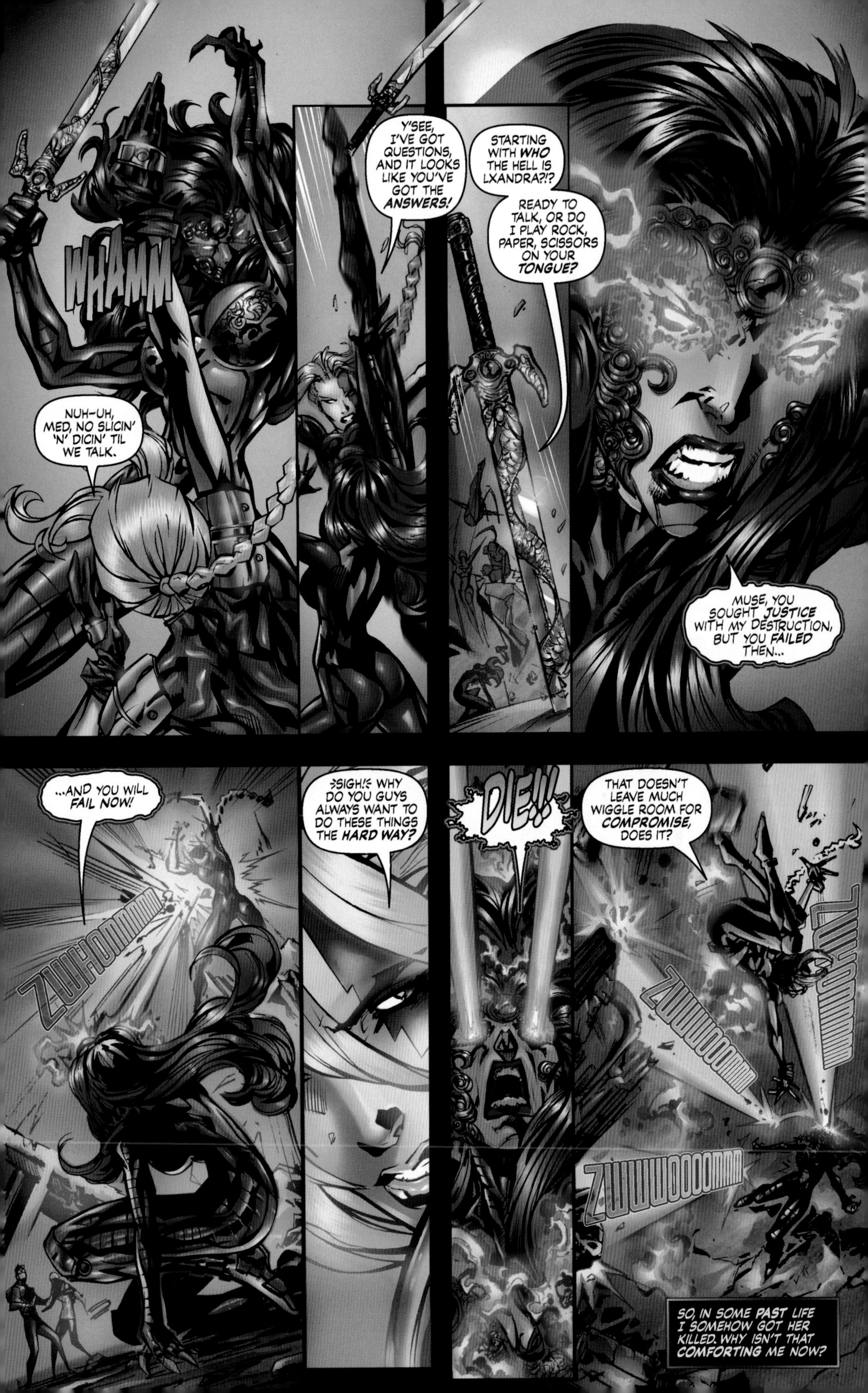
WHAMM
NUH-UH, MED, NO SLICIN' 'N' DICIN' TIL WE TALK.
Y'SEE, I'VE GOT QUESTIONS, AND IT LOOKS LIKE YOU'VE GOT THE ANSWERS!
STARTING WITH WHO THE HELL IS LXANDRA?!?
READY TO TALK, OR DO I PLAY ROCK, PAPER, SCISSORS ON YOUR TONGUE?
MUSE, YOU SOUGHT JUSTICE WITH MY DESTRUCTION, BUT YOU FAILED THEN...
...AND YOU WILL FAIL NOW!
>SIGH!< WHY DO YOU GUYS ALWAYS WANT TO DO THESE THINGS THE HARD WAY?
DIE!!
THAT DOESN'T LEAVE MUCH WIGGLE ROOM FOR COMPROMISE, DOES IT?
SO, IN SOME PAST LIFE I SOMEHOW GOT HER KILLED. WHY ISN'T THAT COMFORTING ME NOW?

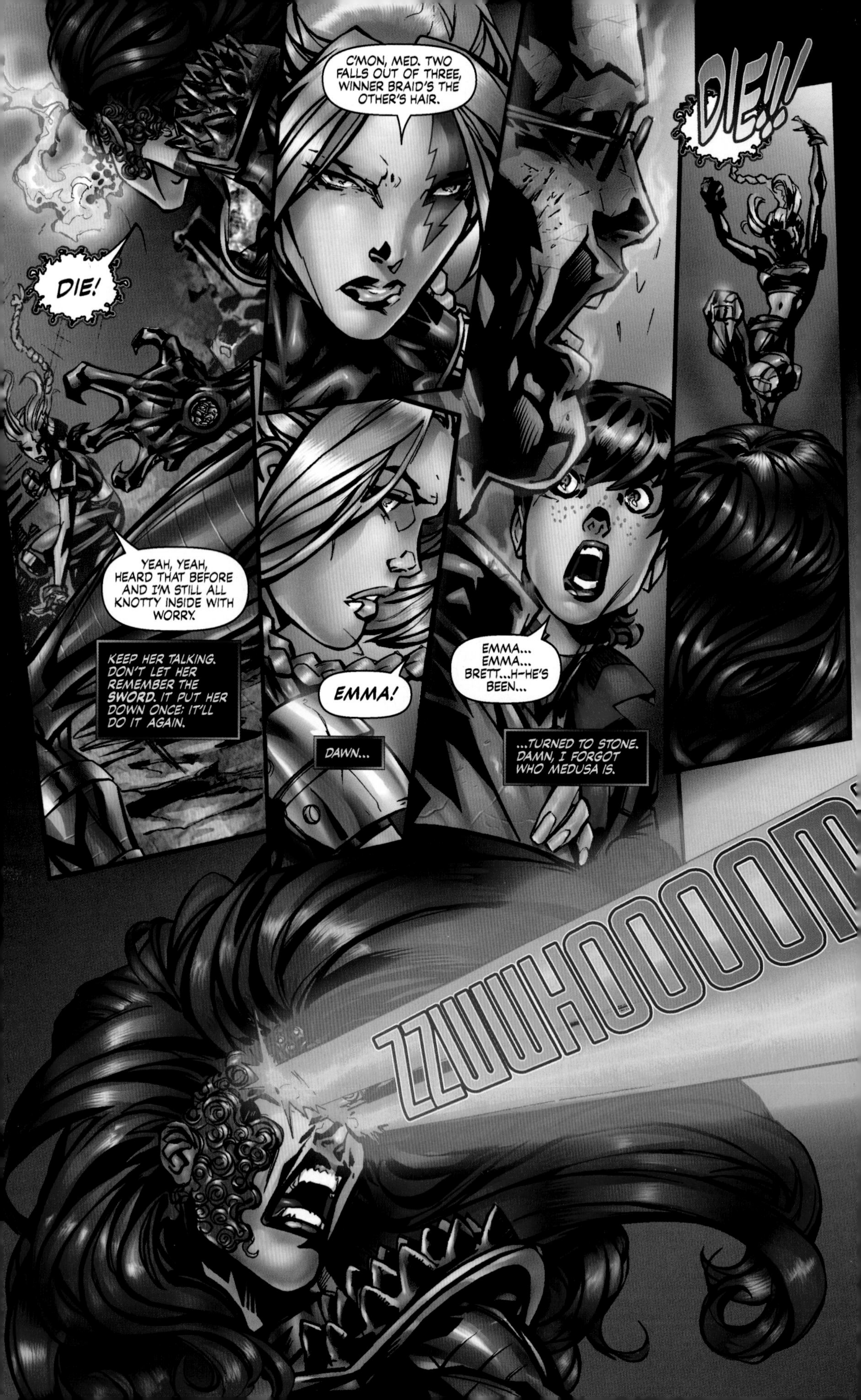
C'MON, MED. TWO FALLS OUT OF THREE, WINNER BRAID'S THE OTHER'S HAIR.
DIE!
DIE!!!
YEAH, YEAH, HEARD THAT BEFORE AND I'M STILL ALL KNOTTY INSIDE WITH WORRY.
KEEP HER TALKING. DON'T LET HER REMEMBER THE SWORD. IT PUT HER DOWN ONCE: IT'LL DO IT AGAIN.
EMMA!
DAWN...
EMMA... EMMA... BRETT...H-HE'S BEEN...
...TURNED TO STONE. DAMN, I FORGOT WHO MEDUSA IS.
ZZWWHOOOOM

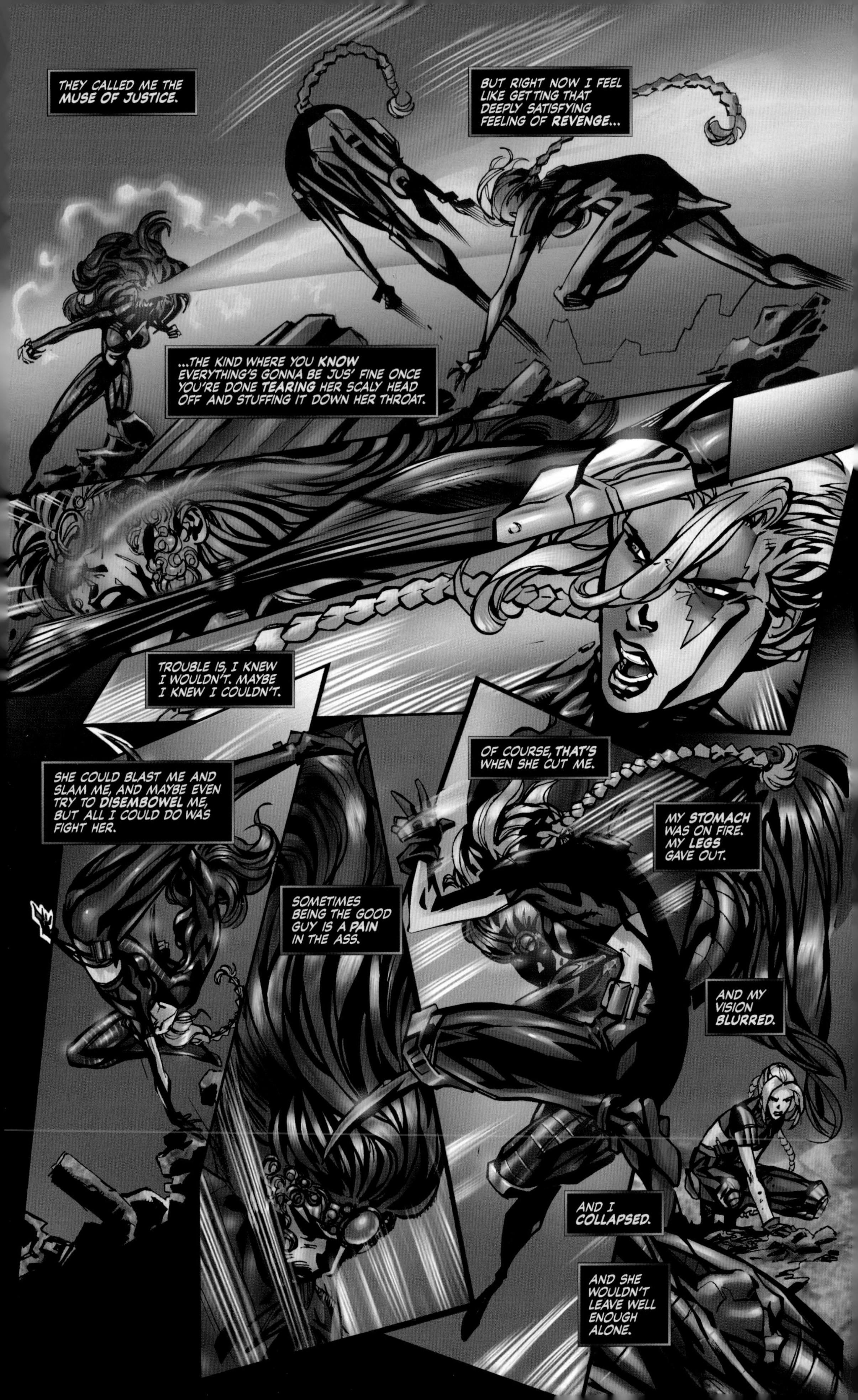
THEY CALLED ME THE MUSE OF JUSTICE.
BUT RIGHT NOW I FEEL LIKE GETTING THAT DEEPLY SATISFYING FEELING OF REVENGE...
...THE KIND WHERE YOU KNOW EVERYTHING'S GONNA BE JUS' FINE ONCE YOU'RE DONE TEARING HER SCALY HEAD OFF AND STUFFING IT DOWN HER THROAT.
TROUBLE IS, I KNEW I WOULDN'T. MAYBE I KNEW I COULDN'T.
SHE COULD BLAST ME AND SLAM ME, AND MAYBE EVEN TRY TO DISEMBOWEL ME, BUT ALL I COULD DO WAS FIGHT HER.
SOMETIMES BEING THE GOOD GUY IS A PAIN IN THE ASS.
OF COURSE, THAT'S WHEN SHE CUT ME.
MY STOMACH WAS ON FIRE. MY LEGS GAVE OUT.
AND MY VISION BLURRED.
AND I COLLAPSED.
AND SHE WOULDN'T LEAVE WELL ENOUGH ALONE.

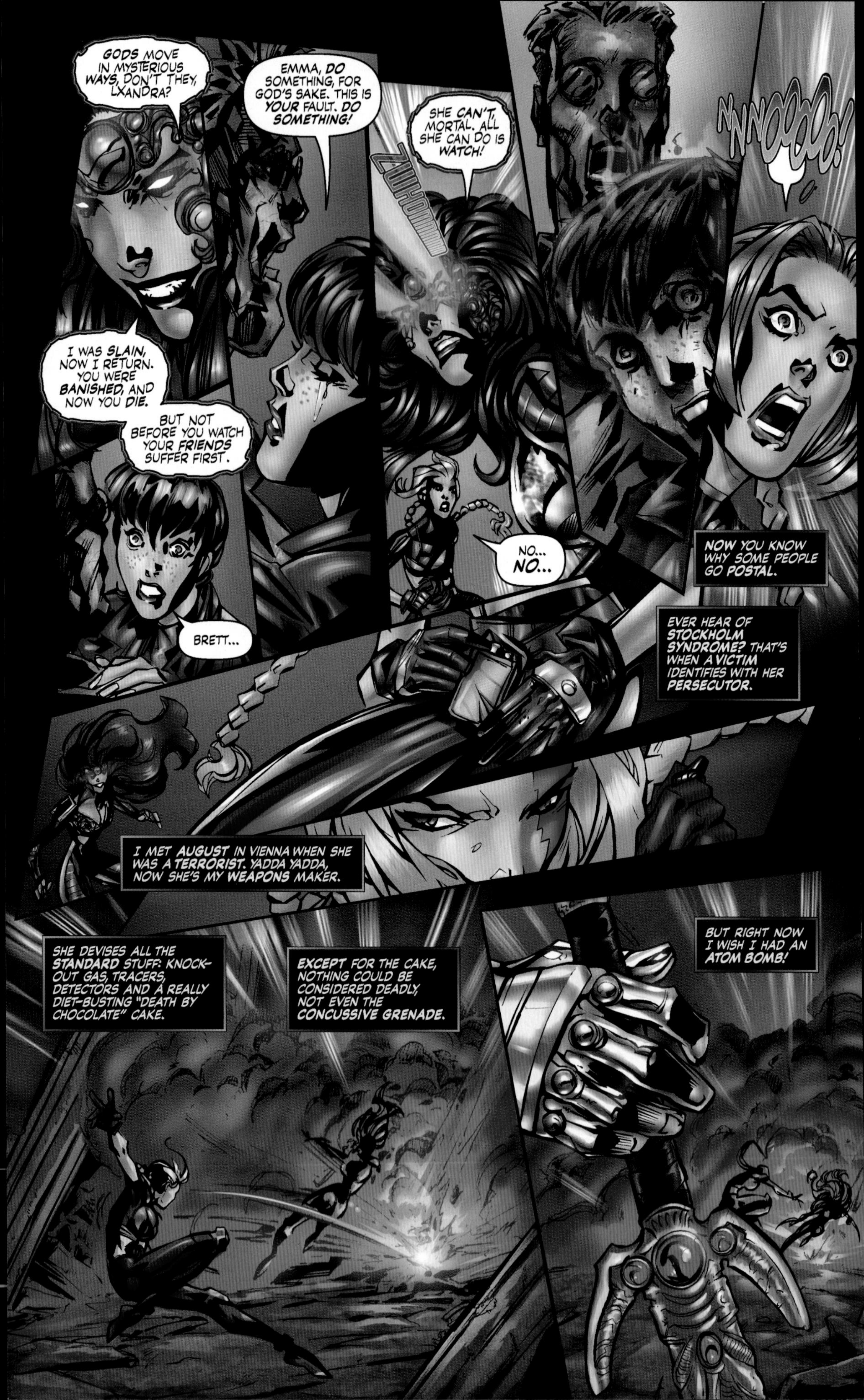
GODS MOVE IN MYSTERIOUS WAYS, DON'T THEY, LXANDRA?
I WAS SLAIN, NOW I RETURN. YOU WERE BANISHED, AND NOW YOU DIE.
BUT NOT BEFORE YOU WATCH YOUR FRIENDS SUFFER FIRST.
BRETT...
EMMA, DO SOMETHING, FOR GOD'S SAKE. THIS IS YOUR FAULT. DO SOMETHING!
SHE CAN'T, MORTAL. ALL SHE CAN DO IS WATCH!
ZUHOMMM
NO... NO...
NNNOOOOO!
NOW YOU KNOW WHY SOME PEOPLE GO POSTAL.
EVER HEAR OF STOCKHOLM SYNDROME? THAT'S WHEN A VICTIM IDENTIFIES WITH HER PERSECUTOR.
I MET AUGUST IN VIENNA WHEN SHE WAS A TERRORIST. YADDA YADDA, NOW SHE'S MY WEAPONS MAKER.
SHE DEVISES ALL THE STANDARD STUFF: KNOCK-OUT GAS, TRACERS, DETECTORS AND A REALLY DIET-BUSTING "DEATH BY CHOCOLATE" CAKE.
EXCEPT FOR THE CAKE, NOTHING COULD BE CONSIDERED DEADLY, NOT EVEN THE CONCUSSIVE GRENADE.
BUT RIGHT NOW I WISH I HAD AN ATOM BOMB!

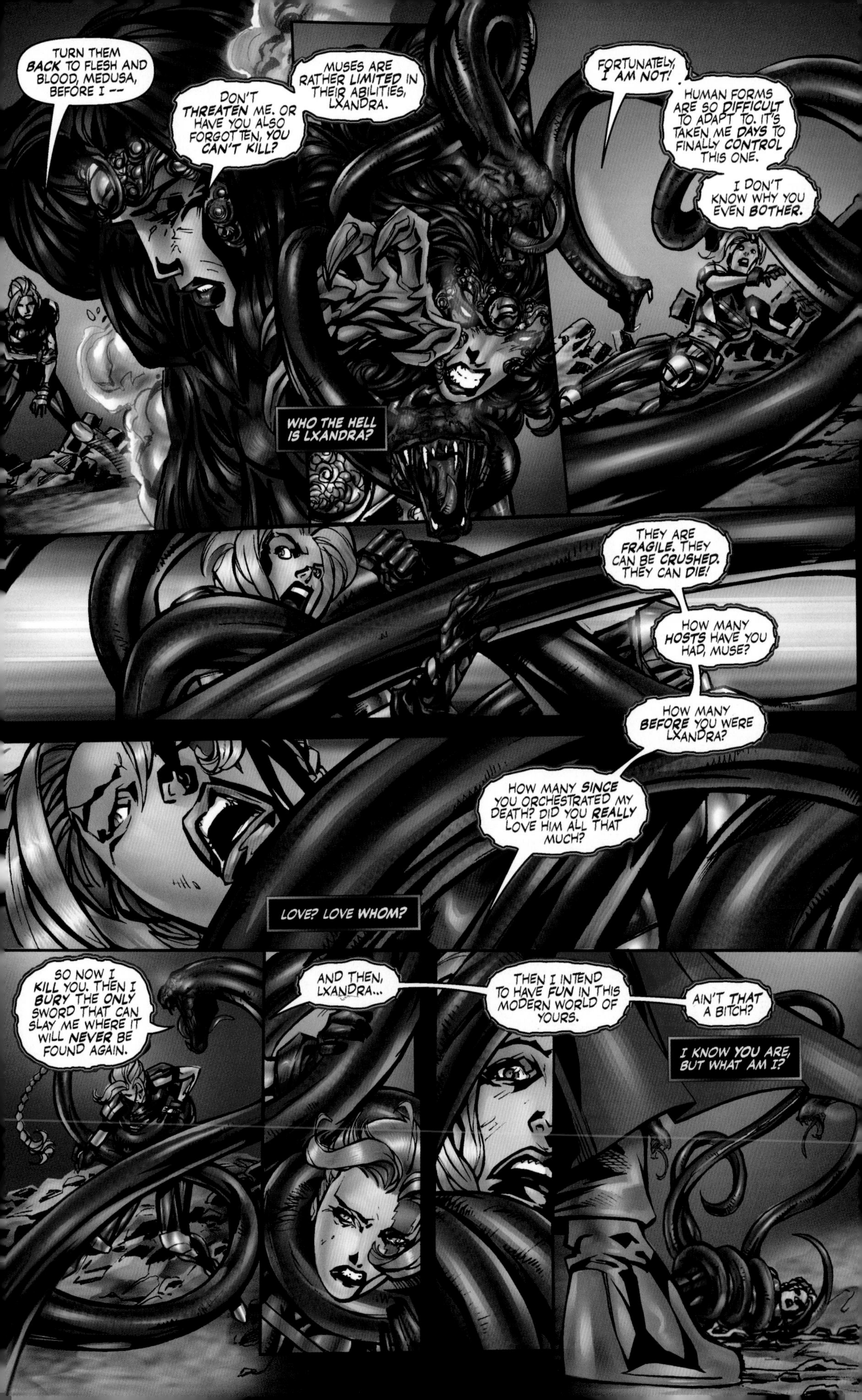
TURN THEM BACK TO FLESH AND BLOOD, MEDUSA, BEFORE I --
DON'T THREATEN ME. OR HAVE YOU ALSO FORGOTTEN, YOU CAN'T KILL?
MUSES ARE RATHER LIMITED IN THEIR ABILITIES, LXANDRA.
WHO THE HELL IS LXANDRA?
FORTUNATELY, I AM NOT!
HUMAN FORMS ARE SO DIFFICULT TO ADAPT TO. IT'S TAKEN ME DAYS TO FINALLY CONTROL THIS ONE.
I DON'T KNOW WHY YOU EVEN BOTHER.
THEY ARE FRAGILE. THEY CAN BE CRUSHED. THEY CAN DIE!
HOW MANY HOSTS HAVE YOU HAD, MUSE?
HOW MANY BEFORE YOU WERE LXANDRA?
HOW MANY SINCE YOU ORCHESTRATED MY DEATH? DID YOU REALLY LOVE HIM ALL THAT MUCH?
LOVE? LOVE WHOM?
SO NOW I KILL YOU. THEN I BURY THE ONLY SWORD THAT CAN SLAY ME WHERE IT WILL NEVER BE FOUND AGAIN.
AND THEN, LXANDRA...
THEN I INTEND TO HAVE FUN IN THIS MODERN WORLD OF YOURS.
AIN'T THAT A BITCH?
I KNOW YOU ARE, BUT WHAT AM I?

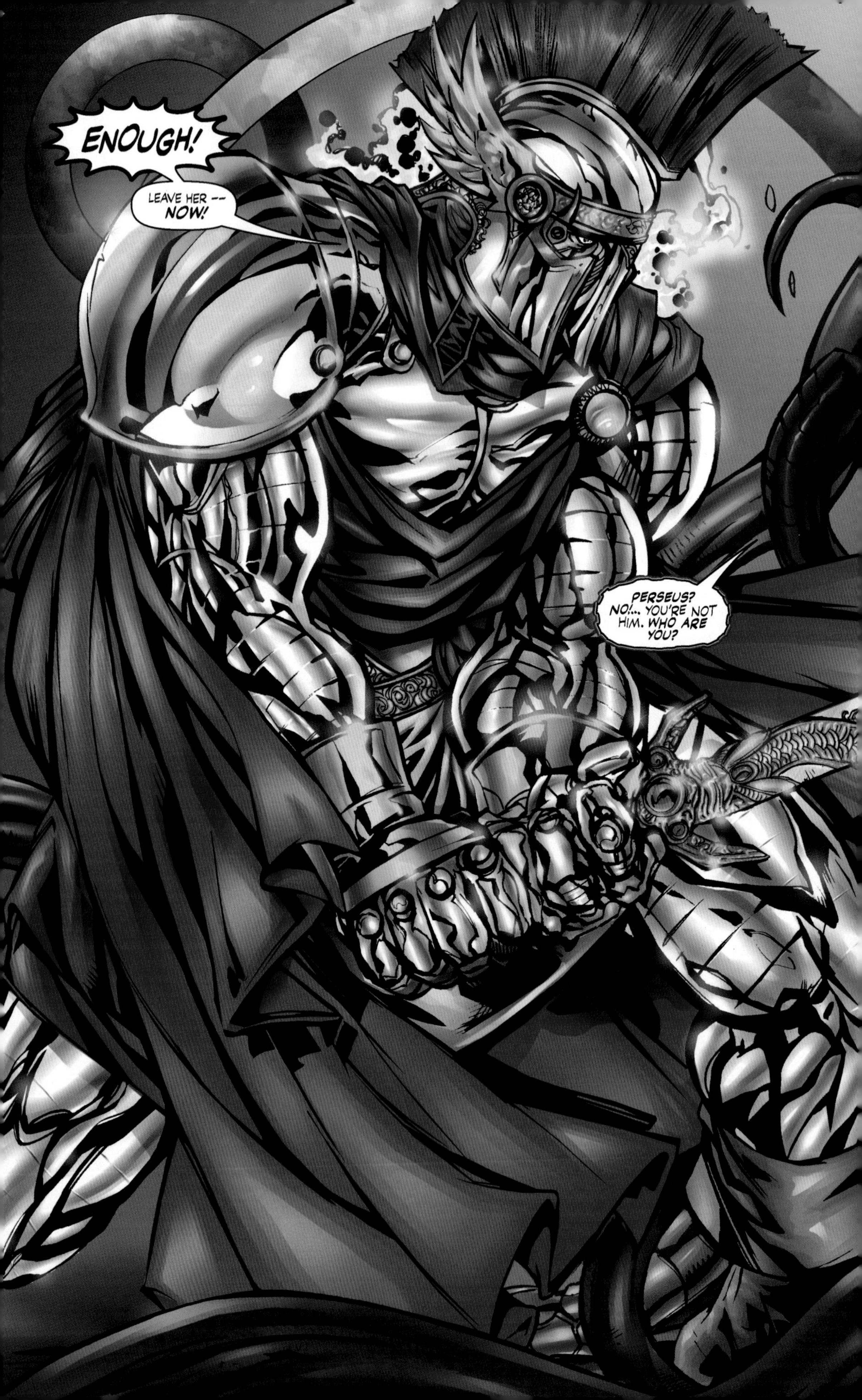
ENOUGH!
LEAVE HER -- NOW!
PERSEUS? NO!... YOU'RE NOT HIM. WHO ARE YOU?

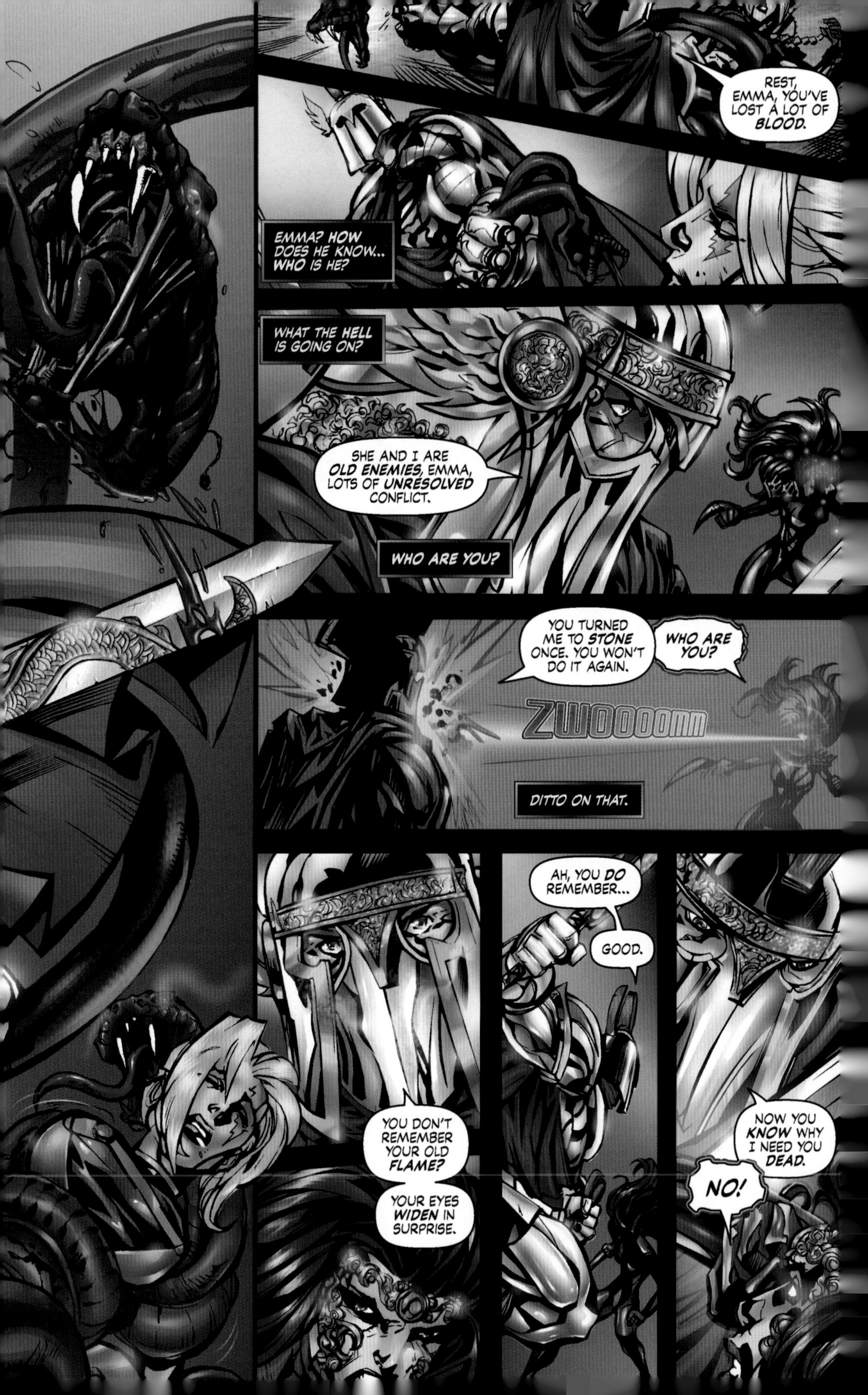
REST, EMMA, YOU'VE LOST A LOT OF BLOOD.
EMMA? HOW DOES HE KNOW... WHO IS HE?
WHAT THE HELL IS GOING ON?
SHE AND I ARE OLD ENEMIES, EMMA, LOTS OF UNRESOLVED CONFLICT.
WHO ARE YOU?
YOU TURNED ME TO STONE ONCE. YOU WON'T DO IT AGAIN.
WHO ARE YOU?
ZWOOOOMM
DITTO ON THAT.
YOU DON'T REMEMBER YOUR OLD FLAME?
YOUR EYES WIDEN IN SURPRISE.
AH, YOU DO REMEMBER...
GOOD.
NOW YOU KNOW WHY I NEED YOU DEAD.
NO!

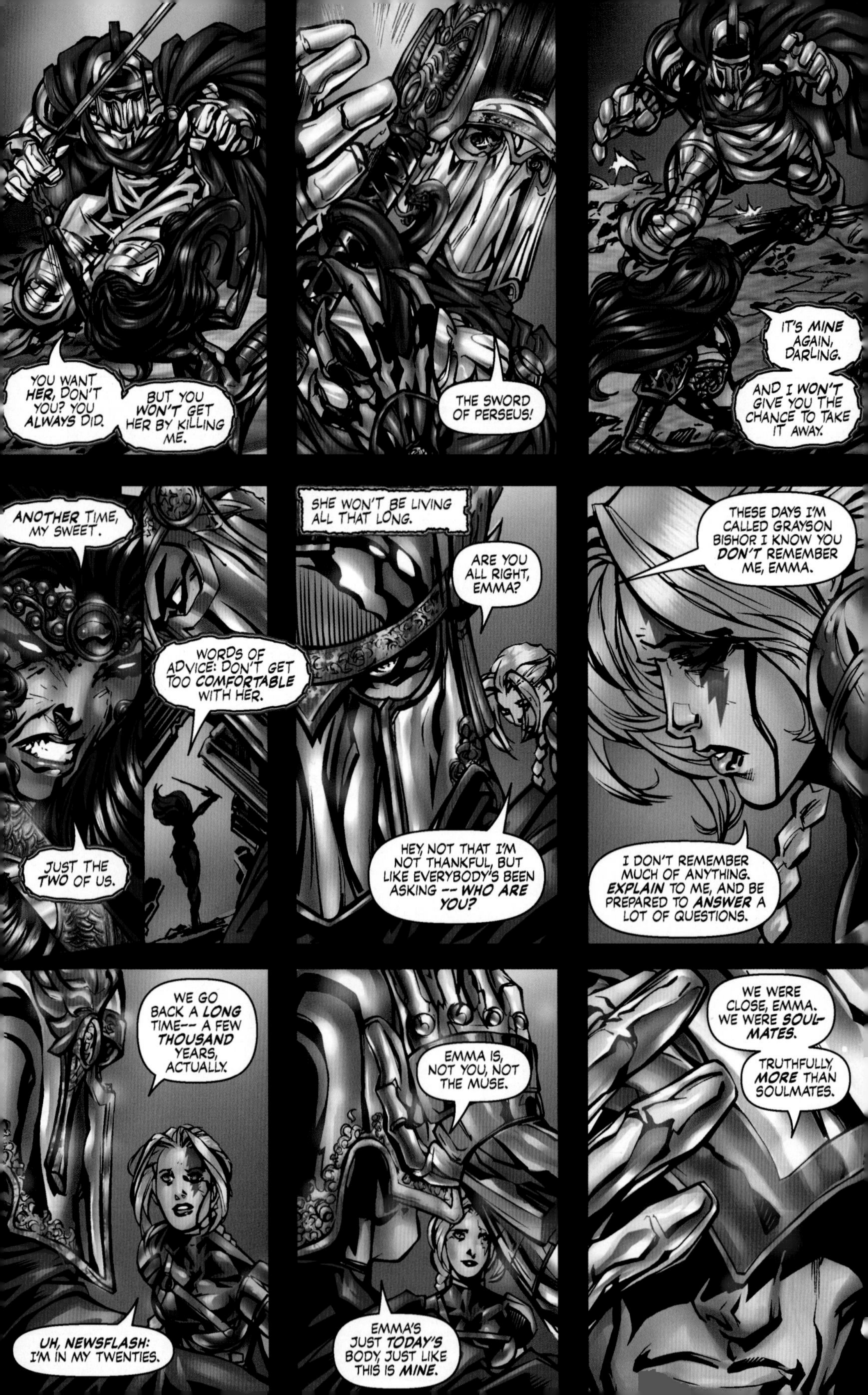

YOU WANT HER, DON'T YOU? YOU ALWAYS DID.
BUT YOU WON'T GET HER BY KILLING ME.
THE SWORD OF PERSEUS!
IT'S MINE AGAIN, DARLING.
AND I WON'T GIVE YOU THE CHANCE TO TAKE IT AWAY.
ANOTHER TIME, MY SWEET.
WORDS OF ADVICE: DON'T GET TOO COMFORTABLE WITH HER.
JUST THE TWO OF US.
SHE WON'T BE LIVING ALL THAT LONG.
ARE YOU ALL RIGHT, EMMA?
HEY, NOT THAT I'M NOT THANKFUL, BUT LIKE EVERYBODY'S BEEN ASKING -- WHO ARE YOU?
THESE DAYS I'M CALLED GRAYSON BISHOP. I KNOW YOU DON'T REMEMBER ME, EMMA.
I DON'T REMEMBER MUCH OF ANYTHING. EXPLAIN TO ME, AND BE PREPARED TO ANSWER A LOT OF QUESTIONS.
WE GO BACK A LONG TIME-- A FEW THOUSAND YEARS, ACTUALLY.
UH, NEWSFLASH: I'M IN MY TWENTIES.
EMMA IS, NOT YOU, NOT THE MUSE.
EMMA'S JUST TODAY'S BODY, JUST LIKE THIS IS MINE.
WE WERE CLOSE, EMMA. WE WERE SOUL-MATES.
TRUTHFULLY, MORE THAN SOULMATES.

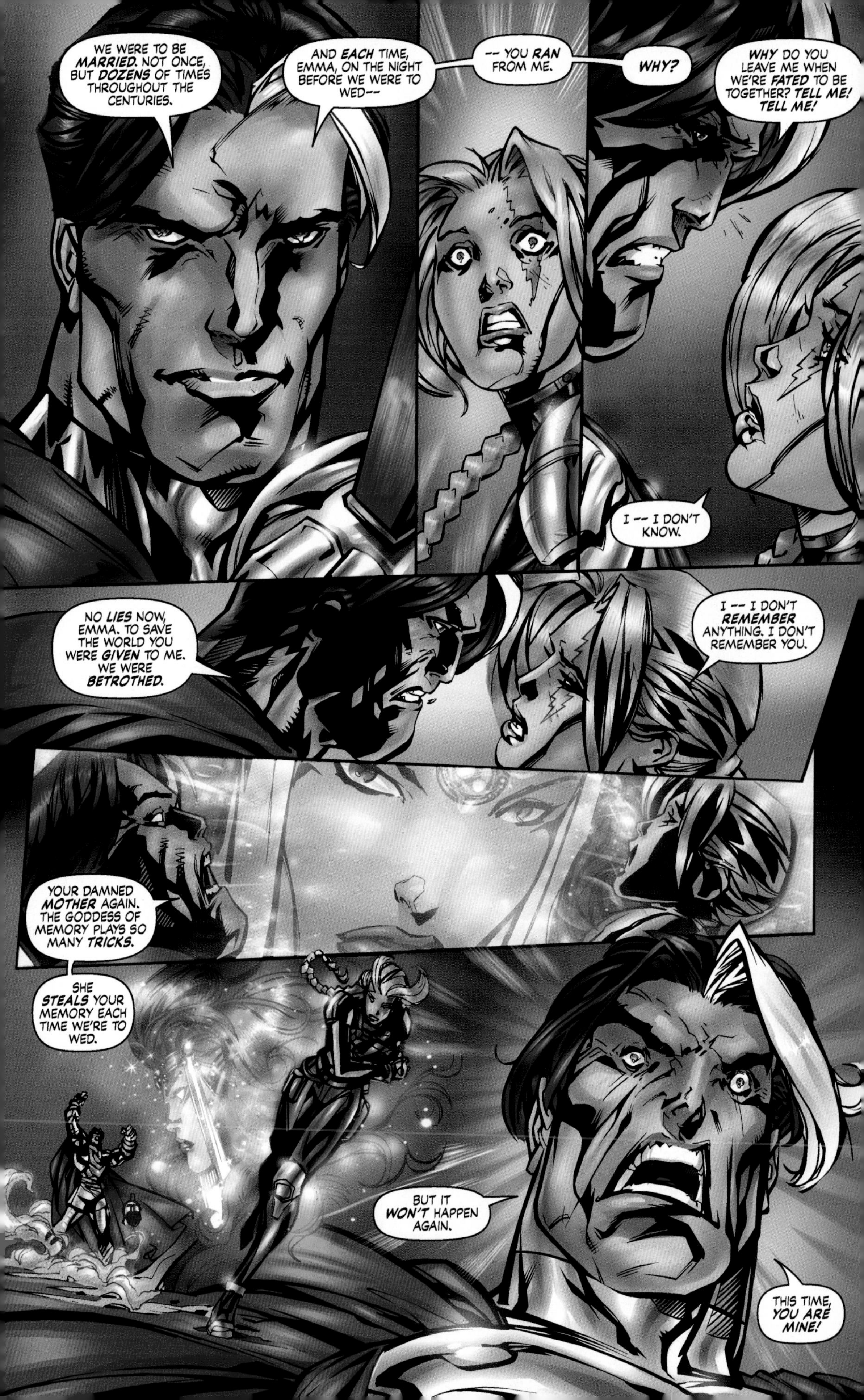
WE WERE TO BE MARRIED. NOT ONCE, BUT DOZENS OF TIMES THROUGHOUT THE CENTURIES.
AND EACH TIME, EMMA, ON THE NIGHT BEFORE WE WERE TO WED--
-- YOU RAN FROM ME.
WHY?
WHY DO YOU LEAVE ME WHEN WE'RE FATED TO BE TOGETHER? TELL ME! TELL ME!
I -- I DON'T KNOW.
NO LIES NOW, EMMA. TO SAVE THE WORLD YOU WERE GIVEN TO ME. WE WERE BETROTHED.
I -- I DON'T REMEMBER ANYTHING. I DON'T REMEMBER YOU.
YOUR DAMNED MOTHER AGAIN. THE GODDESS OF MEMORY PLAYS SO MANY TRICKS.
SHE STEALS YOUR MEMORY EACH TIME WE'RE TO WED.
BUT IT WON'T HAPPEN AGAIN.
THIS TIME, YOU ARE MINE!

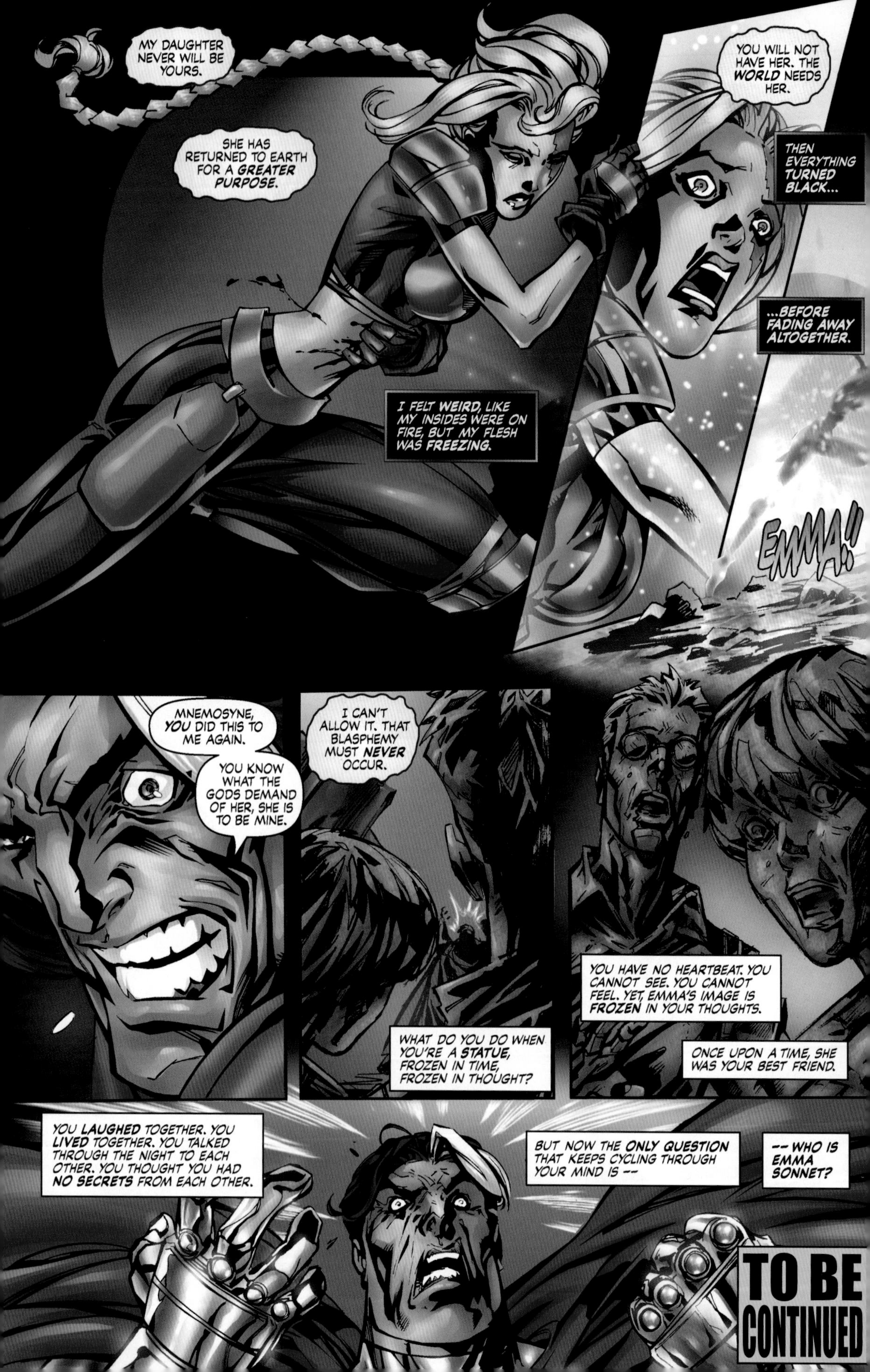
MY DAUGHTER NEVER WILL BE YOURS.
SHE HAS RETURNED TO EARTH FOR A GREATER PURPOSE.
YOU WILL NOT HAVE HER. THE WORLD NEEDS HER.
THEN EVERYTHING TURNED BLACK...
...BEFORE FADING AWAY ALTOGETHER.
I FELT WEIRD, LIKE MY INSIDES WERE ON FIRE, BUT MY FLESH WAS FREEZING.
EMMA!!
MNEMOSYNE, YOU DID THIS TO ME AGAIN.
YOU KNOW WHAT THE GODS DEMAND OF HER, SHE IS TO BE MINE.
I CAN'T ALLOW IT. THAT BLASPHEMY MUST NEVER OCCUR.
WHAT DO YOU DO WHEN YOU'RE A STATUE, FROZEN IN TIME, FROZEN IN THOUGHT?
YOU HAVE NO HEARTBEAT. YOU CANNOT SEE. YOU CANNOT FEEL. YET, EMMA'S IMAGE IS FROZEN IN YOUR THOUGHTS.
ONCE UPON A TIME, SHE WAS YOUR BEST FRIEND.
YOU LAUGHED TOGETHER. YOU LIVED TOGETHER. YOU TALKED THROUGH THE NIGHT TO EACH OTHER. YOU THOUGHT YOU HAD NO SECRETS FROM EACH OTHER.
BUT NOW THE ONLY QUESTION THAT KEEPS CYCLING THROUGH YOUR MIND IS --
-- WHO IS EMMA SONNET?
TO BE CONTINUED

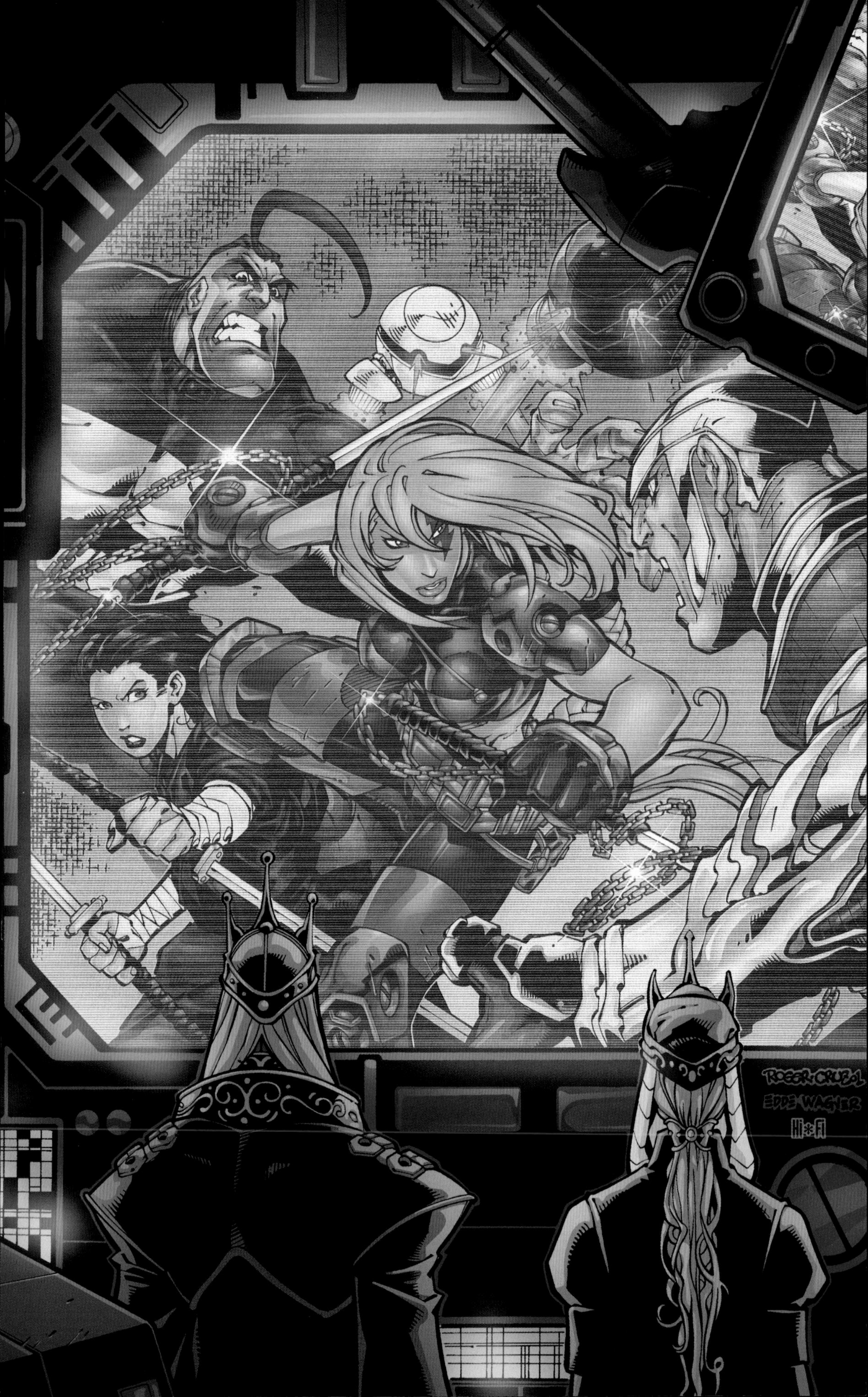
ROGER CRUZ 01
EDDE WAGNER
Hi*Fi

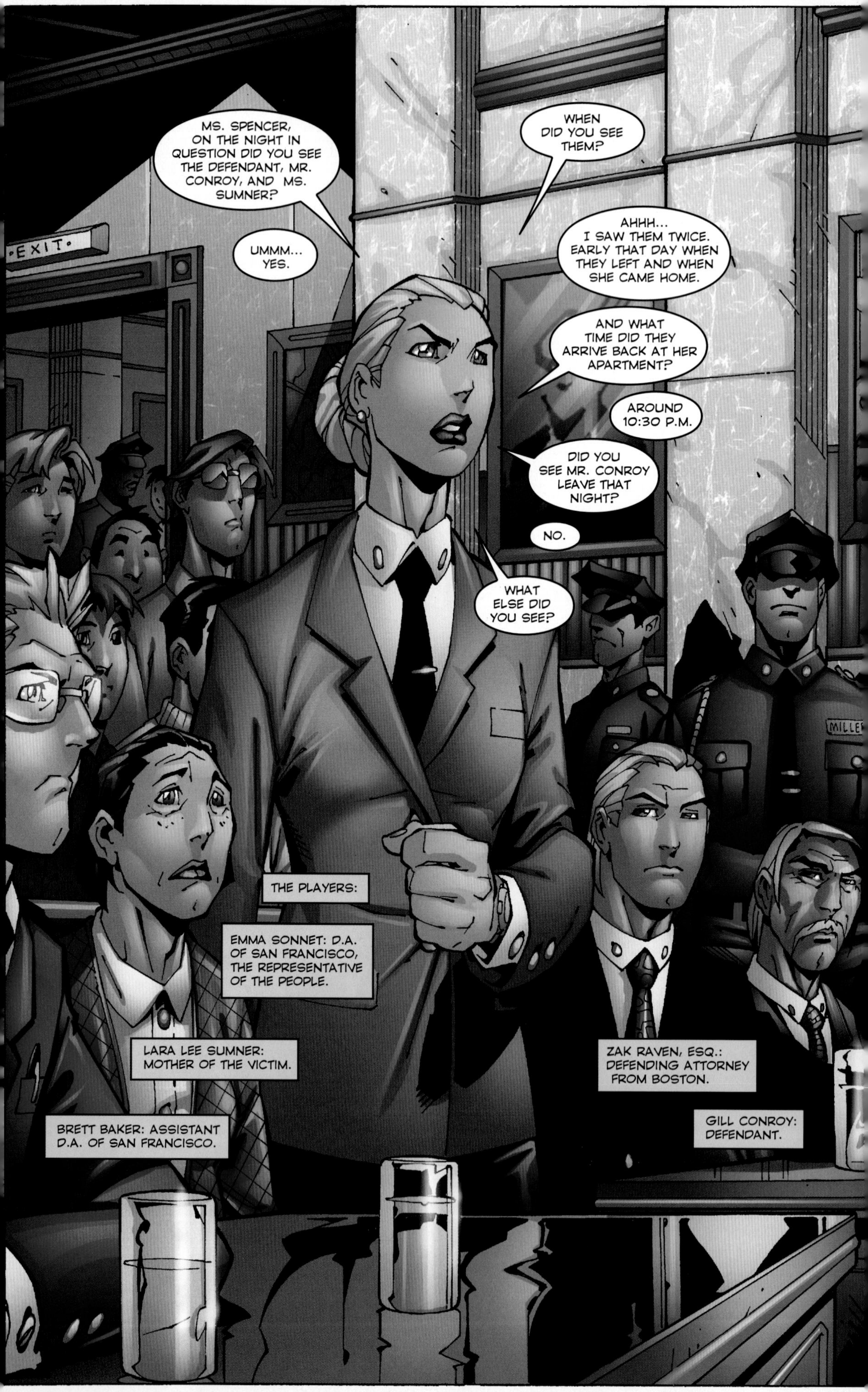
EXIT
MS. SPENCER, ON THE NIGHT IN QUESTION DID YOU SEE THE DEFENDANT, MR. CONROY, AND MS. SUMNER?
UMMM... YES.
WHEN DID YOU SEE THEM?
AHHH... I SAW THEM TWICE. EARLY THAT DAY WHEN THEY LEFT AND WHEN SHE CAME HOME.
AND WHAT TIME DID THEY ARRIVE BACK AT HER APARTMENT?
AROUND 10:30 P.M.
DID YOU SEE MR. CONROY LEAVE THAT NIGHT?
NO.
WHAT ELSE DID YOU SEE?
THE PLAYERS:
EMMA SONNET: D.A. OF SAN FRANCISCO, THE REPRESENTATIVE OF THE PEOPLE.
LARA LEE SUMNER: MOTHER OF THE VICTIM.
BRETT BAKER: ASSISTANT D.A. OF SAN FRANCISCO.
ZAK RAVEN, ESQ.: DEFENDING ATTORNEY FROM BOSTON.
GILL CONROY: DEFENDANT.

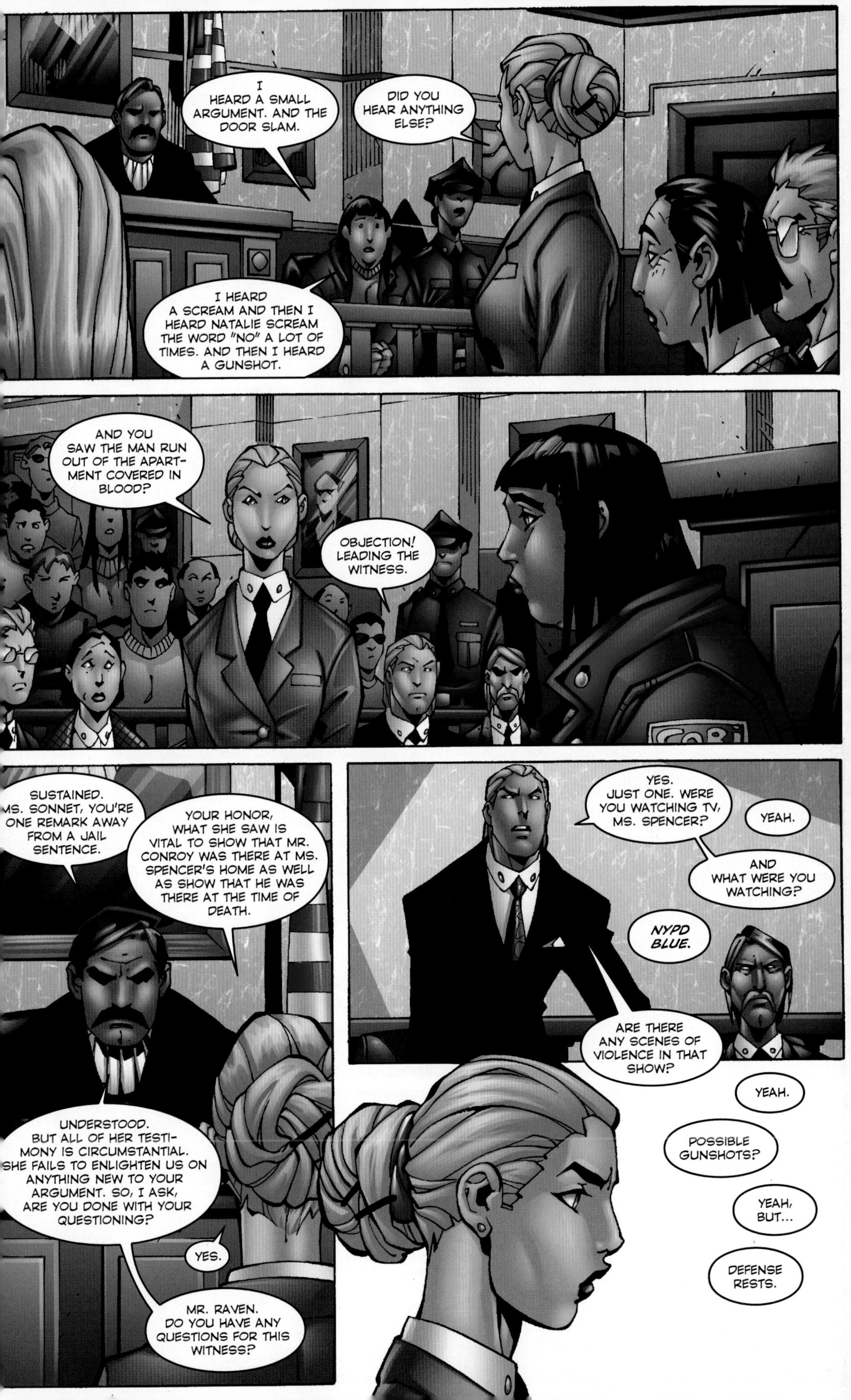
I HEARD A SMALL ARGUMENT. AND THE DOOR SLAM.
DID YOU HEAR ANYTHING ELSE?
I HEARD A SCREAM AND THEN I HEARD NATALIE SCREAM THE WORD "NO" A LOT OF TIMES. AND THEN I HEARD A GUNSHOT.
AND YOU SAW THE MAN RUN OUT OF THE APARTMENT COVERED IN BLOOD?
OBJECTION! LEADING THE WITNESS.
SUSTAINED. MS. SONNET, YOU'RE ONE REMARK AWAY FROM A JAIL SENTENCE.
YOUR HONOR, WHAT SHE SAW IS VITAL TO SHOW THAT MR. CONROY WAS THERE AT MS. SPENCER'S HOME AS WELL AS SHOW THAT HE WAS THERE AT THE TIME OF DEATH.
UNDERSTOOD. BUT ALL OF HER TESTIMONY IS CIRCUMSTANTIAL. SHE FAILS TO ENLIGHTEN US ON ANYTHING NEW TO YOUR ARGUMENT. SO, I ASK, ARE YOU DONE WITH YOUR QUESTIONING?
YES.
MR. RAVEN. DO YOU HAVE ANY QUESTIONS FOR THIS WITNESS?
YES. JUST ONE. WERE YOU WATCHING TV, MS. SPENCER?
YEAH.
AND WHAT WERE YOU WATCHING?
NYPD BLUE.
ARE THERE ANY SCENES OF VIOLENCE IN THAT SHOW?
YEAH.
POSSIBLE GUNSHOTS?
YEAH, BUT...
DEFENSE RESTS.

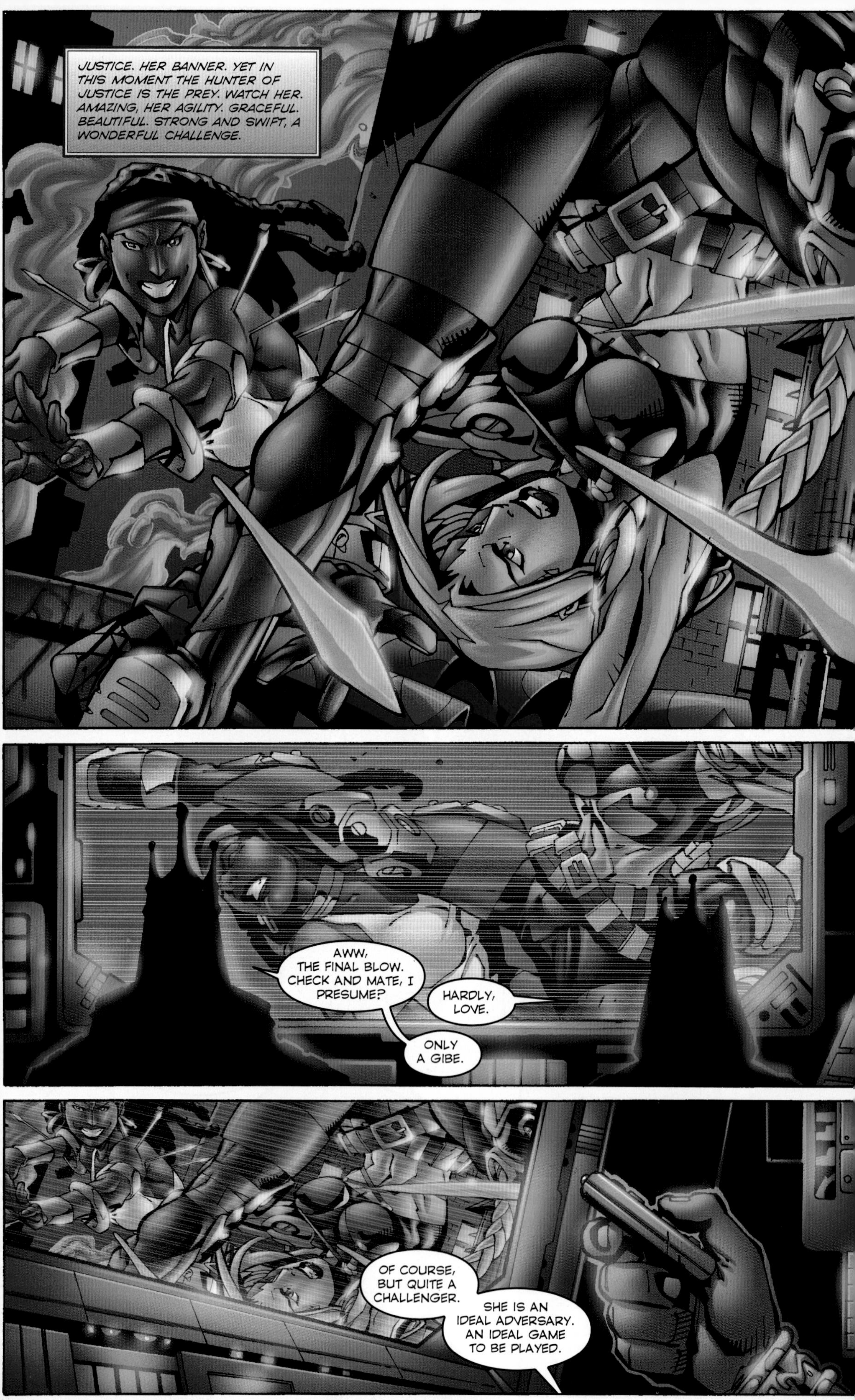
JUSTICE. HER BANNER. YET IN THIS MOMENT THE HUNTER OF JUSTICE IS THE PREY. WATCH HER. AMAZING, HER AGILITY. GRACEFUL. BEAUTIFUL. STRONG AND SWIFT, A WONDERFUL CHALLENGE.
AWW, THE FINAL BLOW. CHECK AND MATE, I PRESUME?
HARDLY, LOVE.
ONLY A GIBE.
OF COURSE, BUT QUITE A CHALLENGER.
SHE IS AN IDEAL ADVERSARY. AN IDEAL GAME TO BE PLAYED.

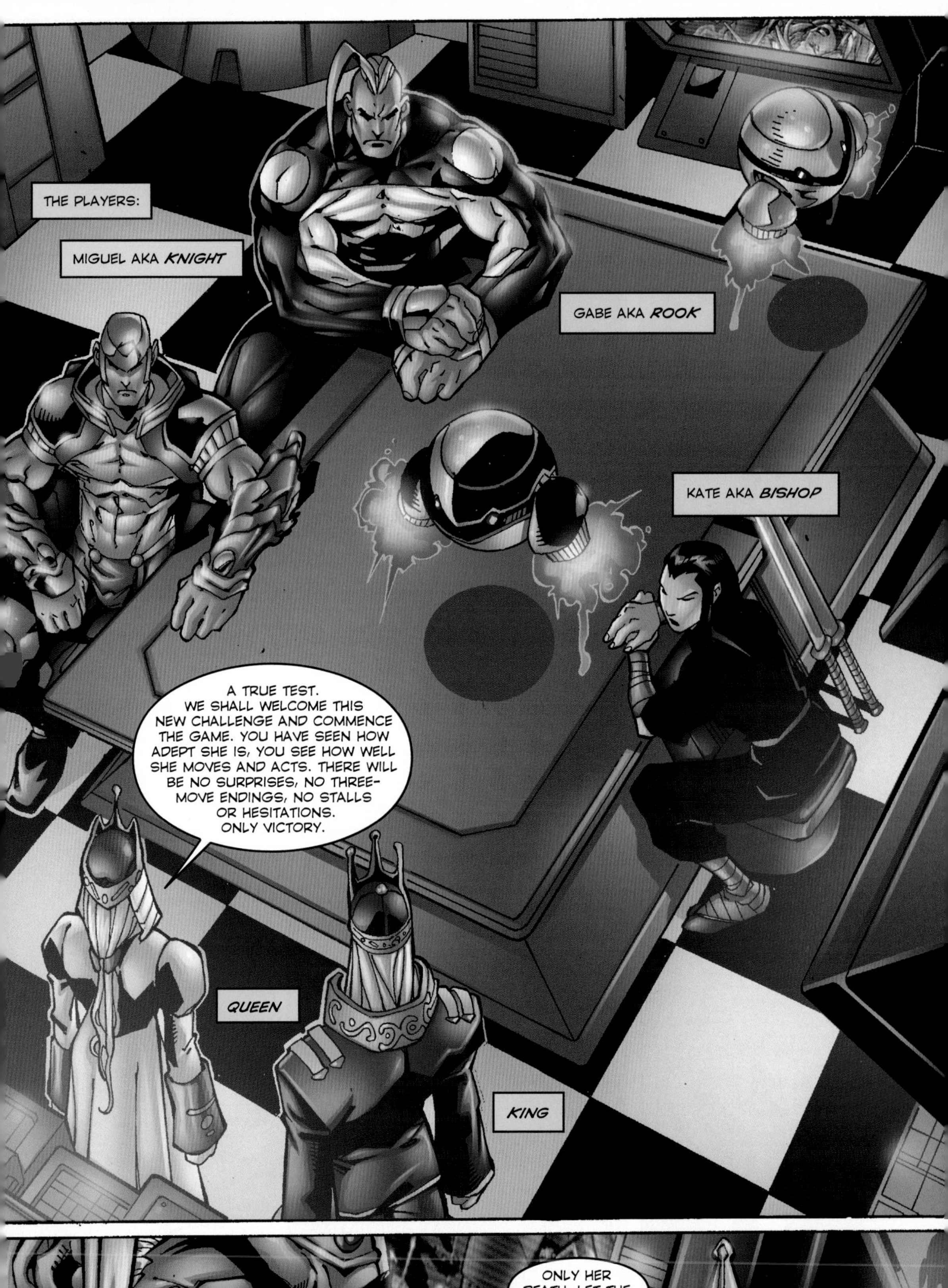
THE PLAYERS:
MIGUEL AKA KNIGHT
GABE AKA ROOK
KATE AKA BISHOP
A TRUE TEST. WE SHALL WELCOME THIS NEW CHALLENGE AND COMMENCE THE GAME. YOU HAVE SEEN HOW ADEPT SHE IS, YOU SEE HOW WELL SHE MOVES AND ACTS. THERE WILL BE NO SURPRISES, NO THREE-MOVE ENDINGS, NO STALLS OR HESITATIONS. ONLY VICTORY.
QUEEN
KING

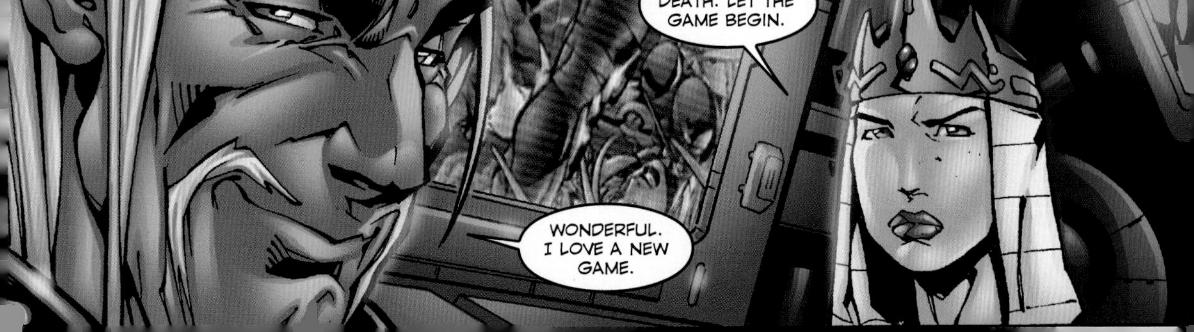
ONLY HER DEATH. LET THE GAME BEGIN.
WONDERFUL. I LOVE A NEW GAME.

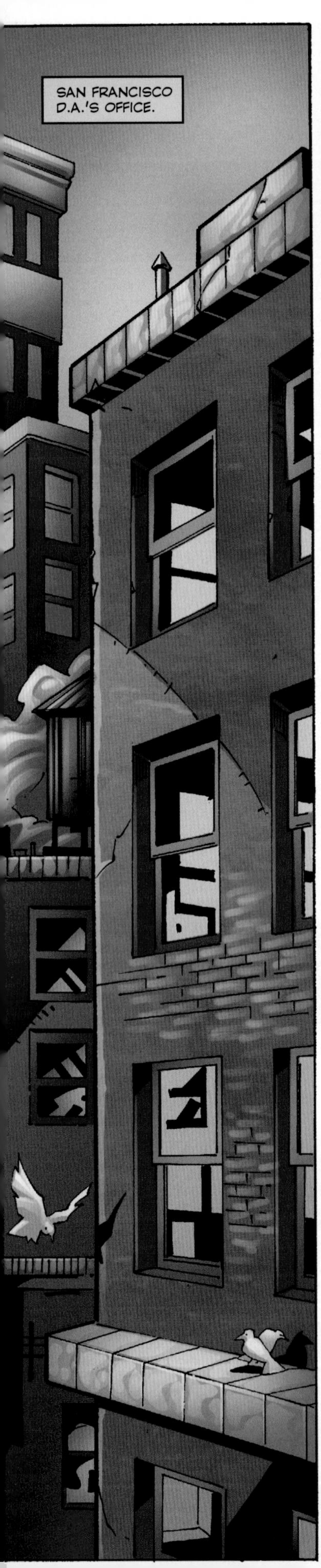
SAN FRANCISCO D.A.'S OFFICE.

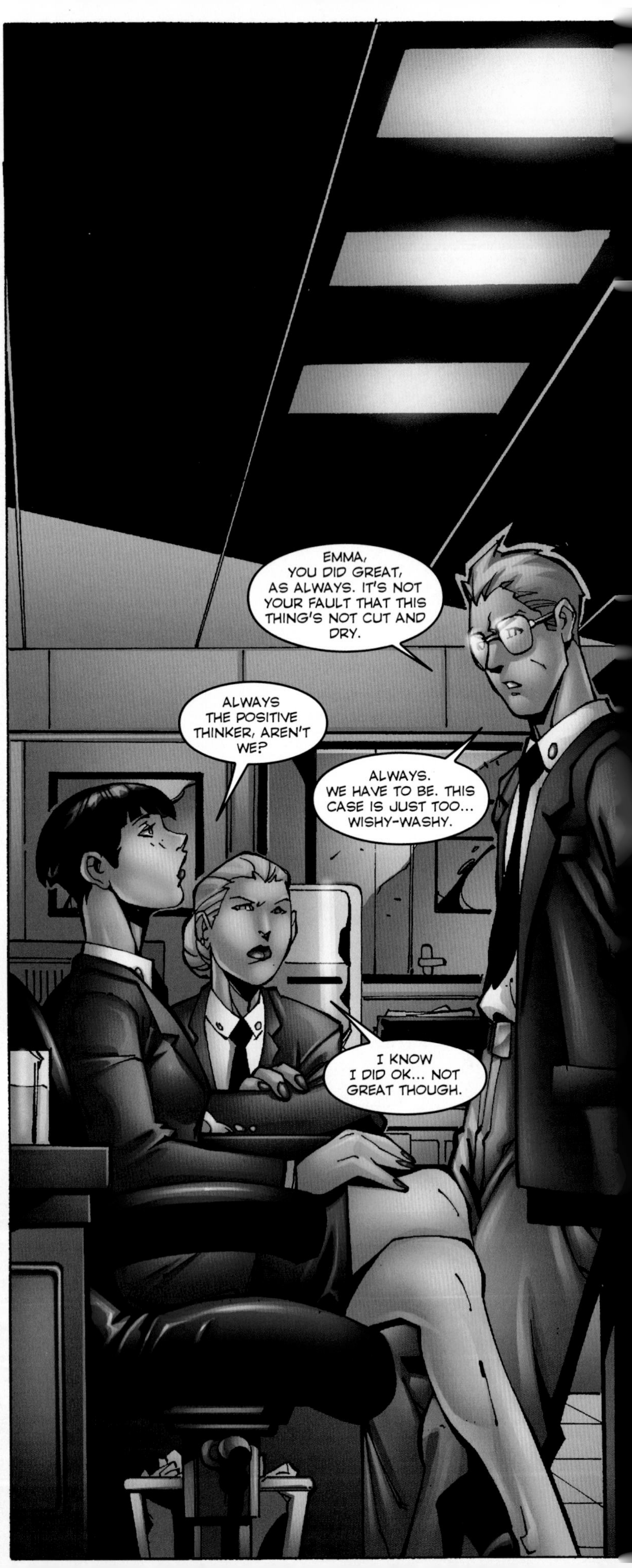
EMMA, YOU DID GREAT, AS ALWAYS. IT'S NOT YOUR FAULT THAT THIS THING'S NOT CUT AND DRY.
ALWAYS THE POSITIVE THINKER, AREN'T WE?
ALWAYS. WE HAVE TO BE. THIS CASE IS JUST TOO... WISHY-WASHY.
I KNOW I DID OK... NOT GREAT THOUGH.

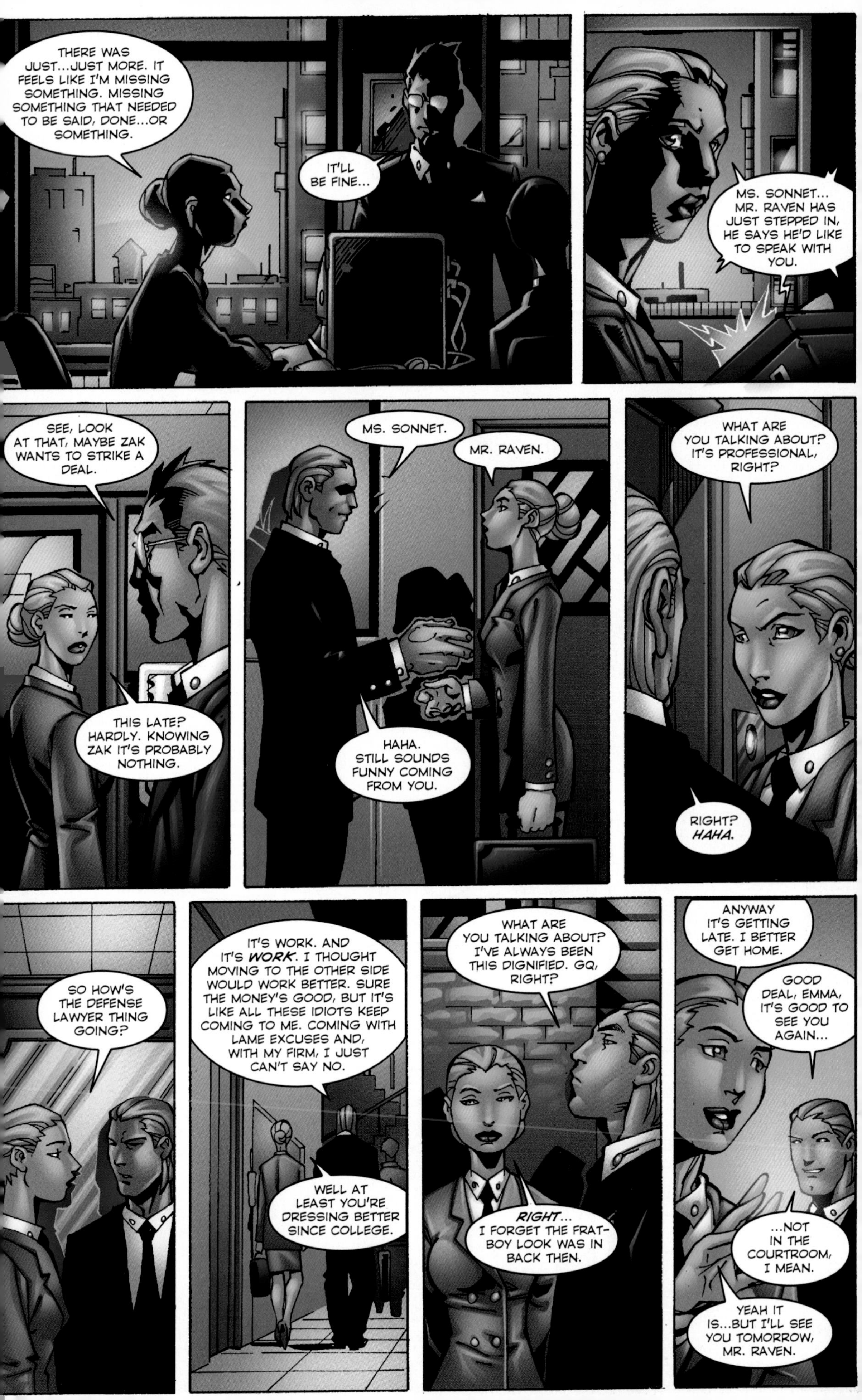
THERE WAS JUST...JUST MORE. IT FEELS LIKE I'M MISSING SOMETHING. MISSING SOMETHING THAT NEEDED TO BE SAID, DONE...OR SOMETHING.
IT'LL BE FINE...
MS. SONNET... MR. RAVEN HAS JUST STEPPED IN, HE SAYS HE'D LIKE TO SPEAK WITH YOU.
SEE, LOOK AT THAT, MAYBE ZAK WANTS TO STRIKE A DEAL.
THIS LATE? HARDLY. KNOWING ZAK IT'S PROBABLY NOTHING.
MS. SONNET.
MR. RAVEN.
HAHA. STILL SOUNDS FUNNY COMING FROM YOU.
WHAT ARE YOU TALKING ABOUT? IT'S PROFESSIONAL, RIGHT?
RIGHT? *HAHA*.
SO HOW'S THE DEFENSE LAWYER THING GOING?
IT'S WORK. AND IT'S *WORK*. I THOUGHT MOVING TO THE OTHER SIDE WOULD WORK BETTER. SURE THE MONEY'S GOOD, BUT IT'S LIKE ALL THESE IDIOTS KEEP COMING TO ME. COMING WITH LAME EXCUSES AND, WITH MY FIRM, I JUST CAN'T SAY NO.
WELL AT LEAST YOU'RE DRESSING BETTER SINCE COLLEGE.
WHAT ARE YOU TALKING ABOUT? I'VE ALWAYS BEEN THIS DIGNIFIED. GQ, RIGHT?
RIGHT... I FORGET THE FRAT-BOY LOOK WAS IN BACK THEN.
ANYWAY IT'S GETTING LATE. I BETTER GET HOME.
GOOD DEAL, EMMA, IT'S GOOD TO SEE YOU AGAIN...
...NOT IN THE COURTROOM, I MEAN.
YEAH IT IS...BUT I'LL SEE YOU TOMORROW, MR. RAVEN.

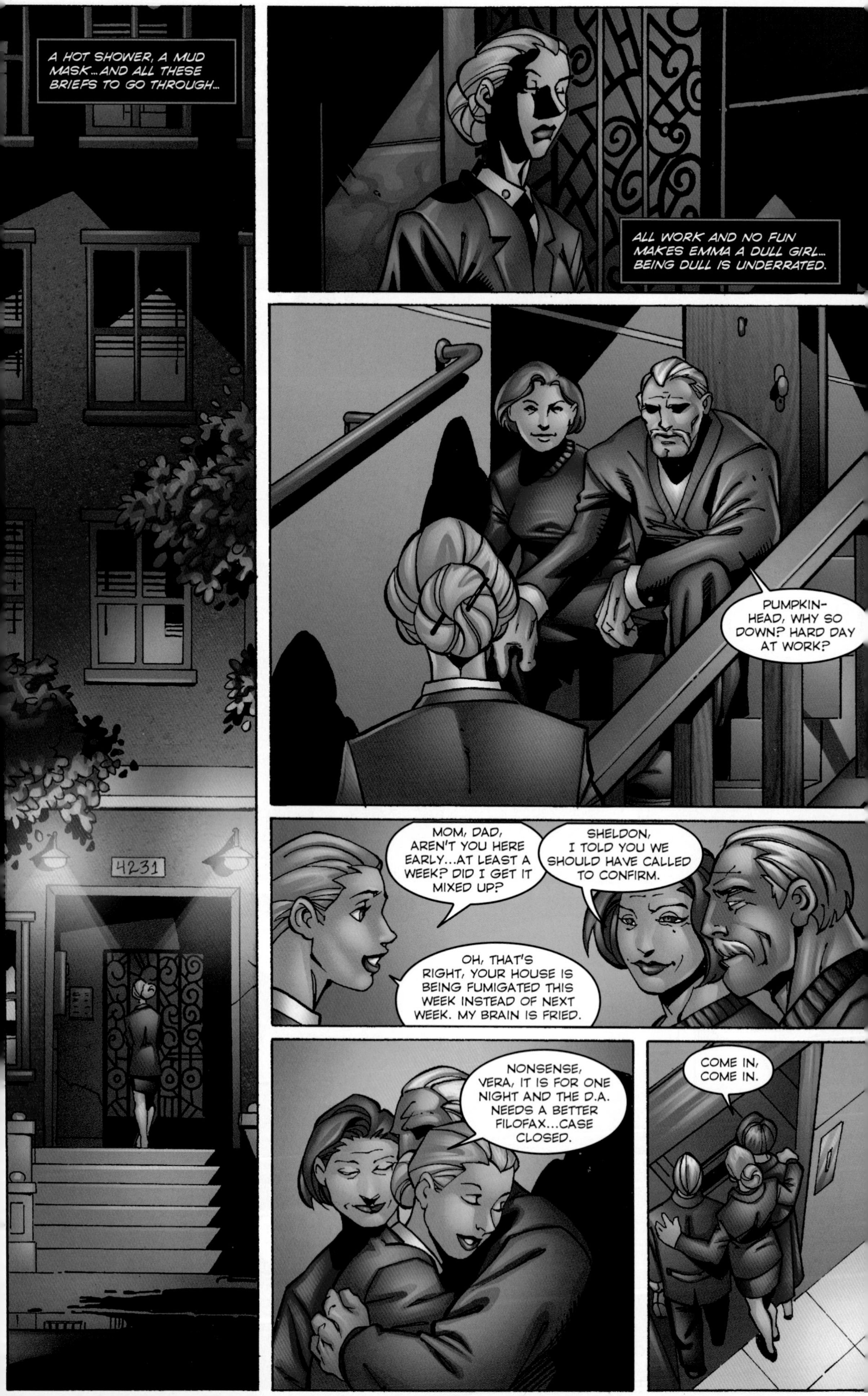
A HOT SHOWER, A MUD MASK...AND ALL THESE BRIEFS TO GO THROUGH...
4231
ALL WORK AND NO FUN MAKES EMMA A DULL GIRL... BEING DULL IS UNDERRATED.
PUMPKIN-HEAD, WHY SO DOWN? HARD DAY AT WORK?
MOM, DAD, AREN'T YOU HERE EARLY...AT LEAST A WEEK? DID I GET IT MIXED UP?
SHELDON, I TOLD YOU WE SHOULD HAVE CALLED TO CONFIRM.
OH, THAT'S RIGHT, YOUR HOUSE IS BEING FUMIGATED THIS WEEK INSTEAD OF NEXT WEEK. MY BRAIN IS FRIED.
NONSENSE, VERA, IT IS FOR ONE NIGHT AND THE D.A. NEEDS A BETTER FILOFAX...CASE CLOSED.
COME IN, COME IN.

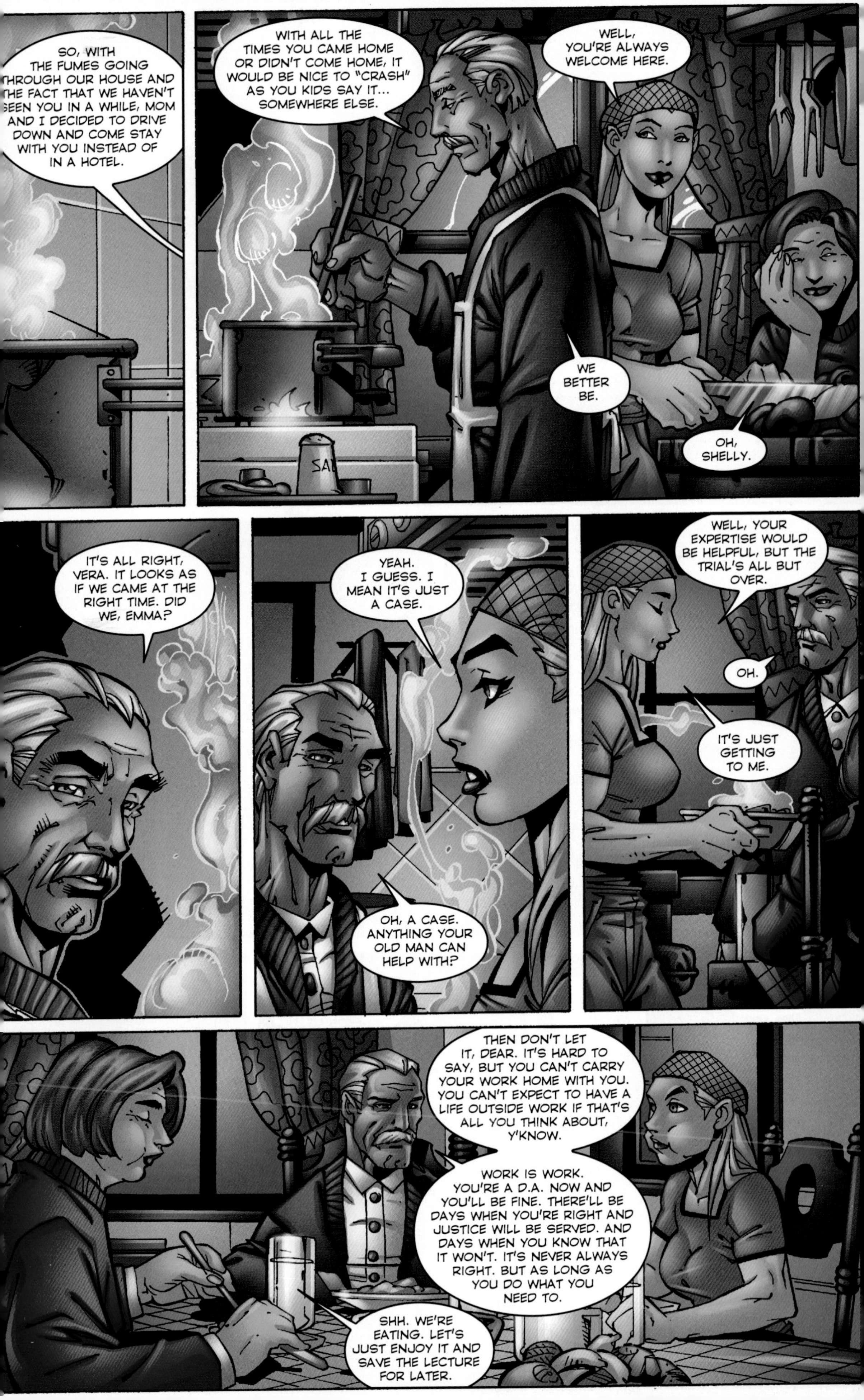

SO, WITH THE FUMES GOING THROUGH OUR HOUSE AND THE FACT THAT WE HAVEN'T SEEN YOU IN A WHILE, MOM AND I DECIDED TO DRIVE DOWN AND COME STAY WITH YOU INSTEAD OF IN A HOTEL.
WITH ALL THE TIMES YOU CAME HOME OR DIDN'T COME HOME, IT WOULD BE NICE TO "CRASH" AS YOU KIDS SAY IT... SOMEWHERE ELSE.
WELL, YOU'RE ALWAYS WELCOME HERE.
WE BETTER BE.
OH, SHELLY.
IT'S ALL RIGHT, VERA. IT LOOKS AS IF WE CAME AT THE RIGHT TIME. DID WE, EMMA?
YEAH. I GUESS. I MEAN IT'S JUST A CASE.
OH, A CASE. ANYTHING YOUR OLD MAN CAN HELP WITH?
WELL, YOUR EXPERTISE WOULD BE HELPFUL, BUT THE TRIAL'S ALL BUT OVER.
OH.
IT'S JUST GETTING TO ME.
THEN DON'T LET IT, DEAR. IT'S HARD TO SAY, BUT YOU CAN'T CARRY YOUR WORK HOME WITH YOU. YOU CAN'T EXPECT TO HAVE A LIFE OUTSIDE WORK IF THAT'S ALL YOU THINK ABOUT, Y'KNOW.
WORK IS WORK. YOU'RE A D.A. NOW AND YOU'LL BE FINE. THERE'LL BE DAYS WHEN YOU'RE RIGHT AND JUSTICE WILL BE SERVED. AND DAYS WHEN YOU KNOW THAT IT WON'T. IT'S NEVER ALWAYS RIGHT. BUT AS LONG AS YOU DO WHAT YOU NEED TO.
SHH. WE'RE EATING. LET'S JUST ENJOY IT AND SAVE THE LECTURE FOR LATER.

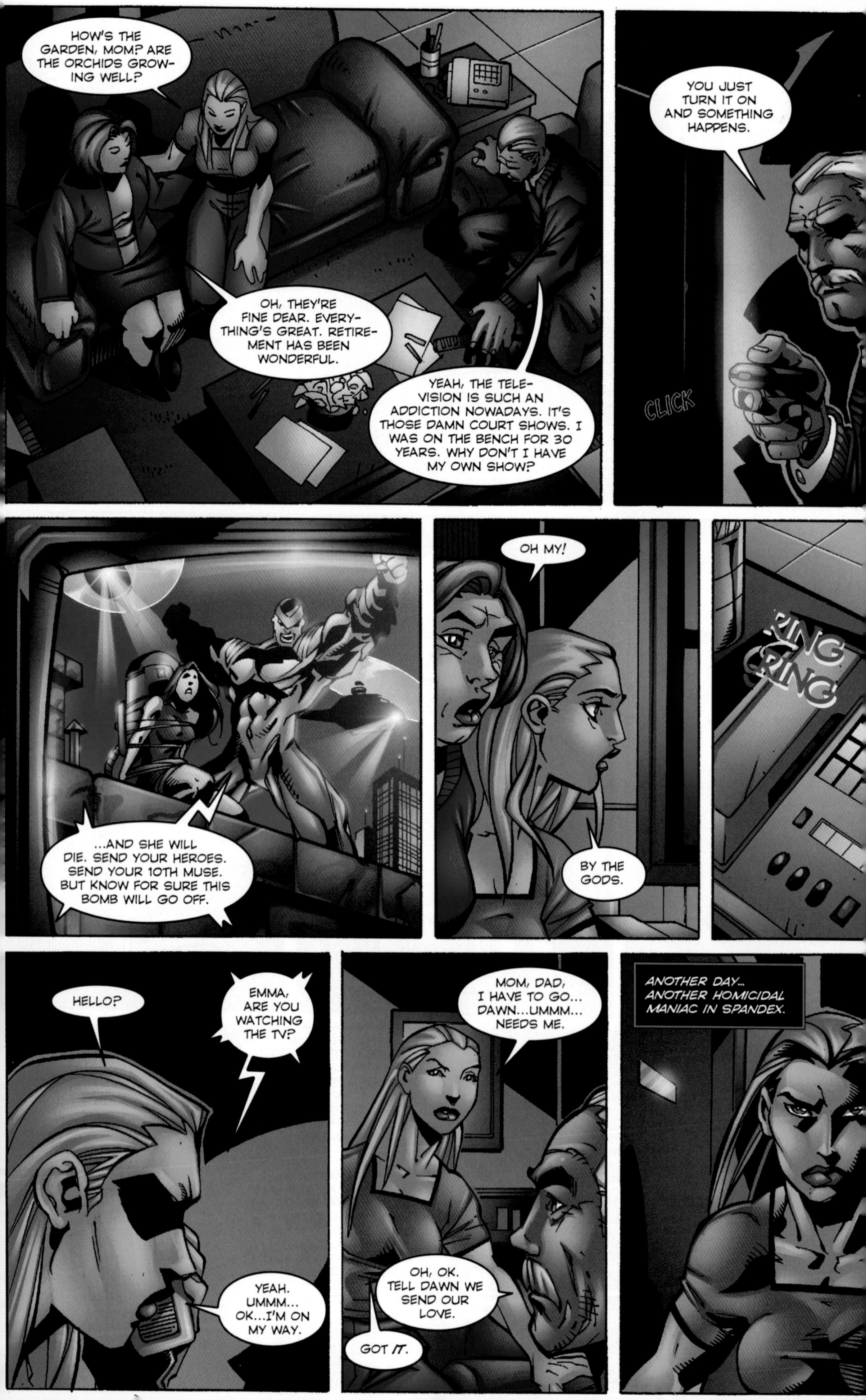
HOW'S THE GARDEN, MOM? ARE THE ORCHIDS GROWING WELL?
OH, THEY'RE FINE DEAR. EVERYTHING'S GREAT. RETIREMENT HAS BEEN WONDERFUL.
YEAH, THE TELEVISION IS SUCH AN ADDICTION NOWADAYS. IT'S THOSE DAMN COURT SHOWS. I WAS ON THE BENCH FOR 30 YEARS. WHY DON'T I HAVE MY OWN SHOW?
YOU JUST TURN IT ON AND SOMETHING HAPPENS.
CLICK
...AND SHE WILL DIE. SEND YOUR HEROES. SEND YOUR 10TH MUSE. BUT KNOW FOR SURE THIS BOMB WILL GO OFF.
OH MY!
BY THE GODS.
RING RING
HELLO?
EMMA, ARE YOU WATCHING THE TV?
YEAH. UMMM... OK...I'M ON MY WAY.
MOM, DAD, I HAVE TO GO... DAWN...UMMM... NEEDS ME.
OH, OK. TELL DAWN WE SEND OUR LOVE.
GOT IT.
ANOTHER DAY... ANOTHER HOMICIDAL MANIAC IN SPANDEX.

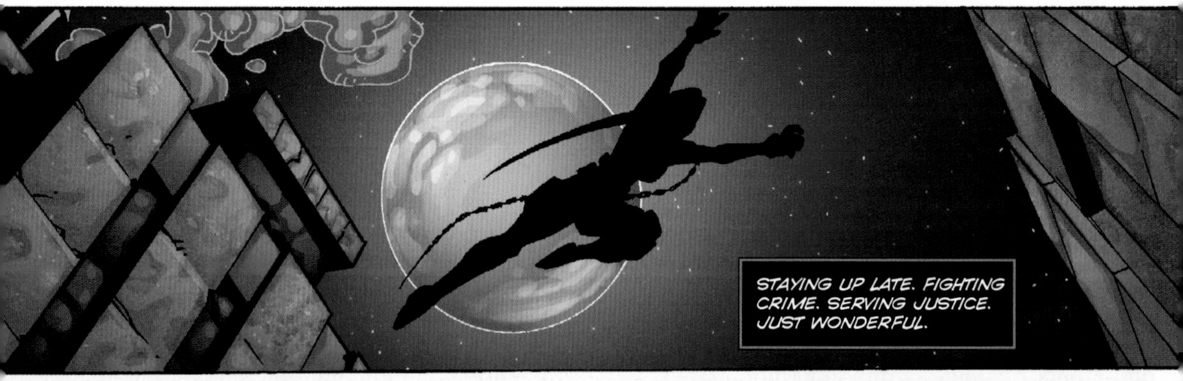
STAYING UP LATE. FIGHTING CRIME. SERVING JUSTICE. JUST WONDERFUL.

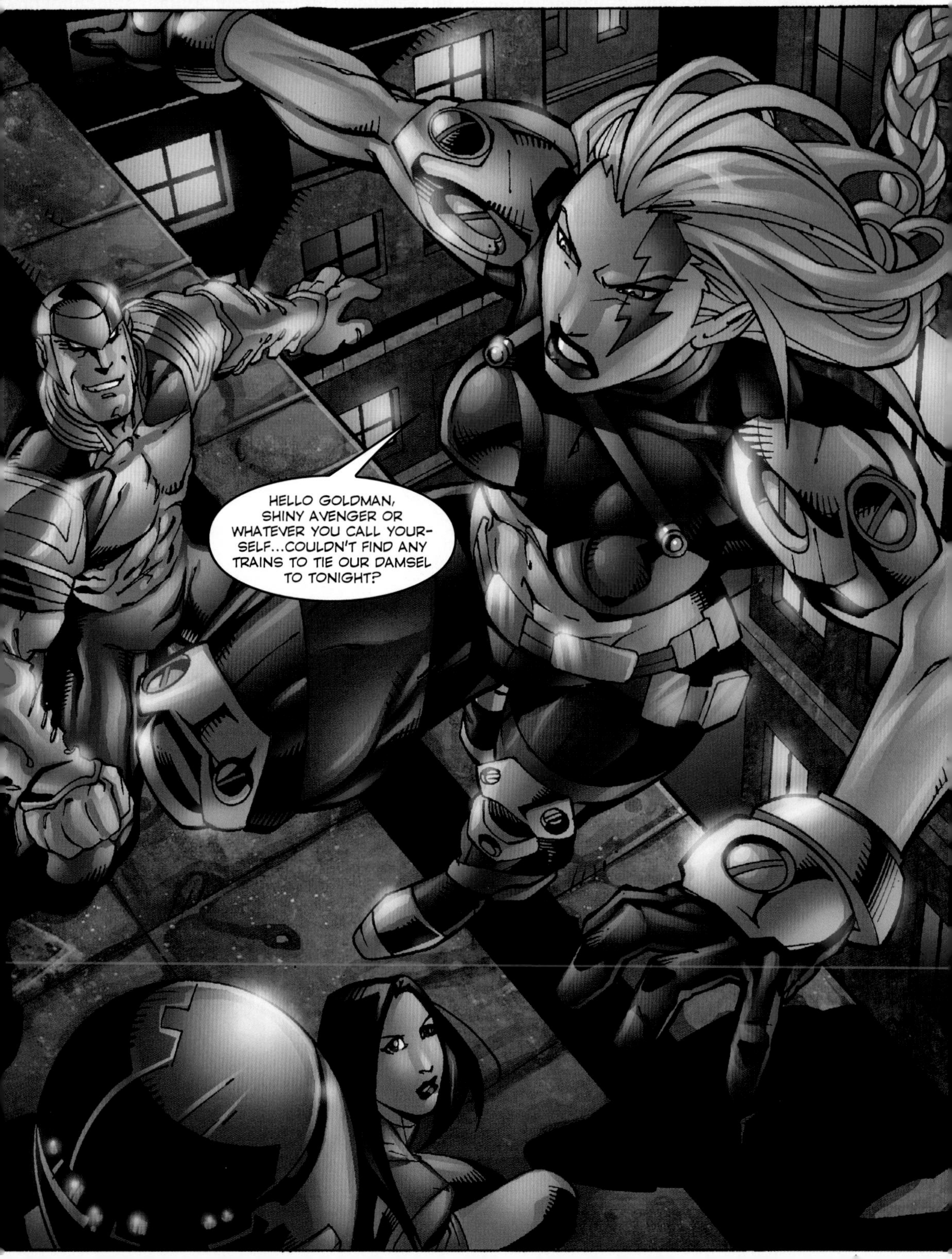
HELLO GOLDMAN, SHINY AVENGER OR WHATEVER YOU CALL YOUR-SELF...COULDN'T FIND ANY TRAINS TO TIE OUR DAMSEL TO TONIGHT?

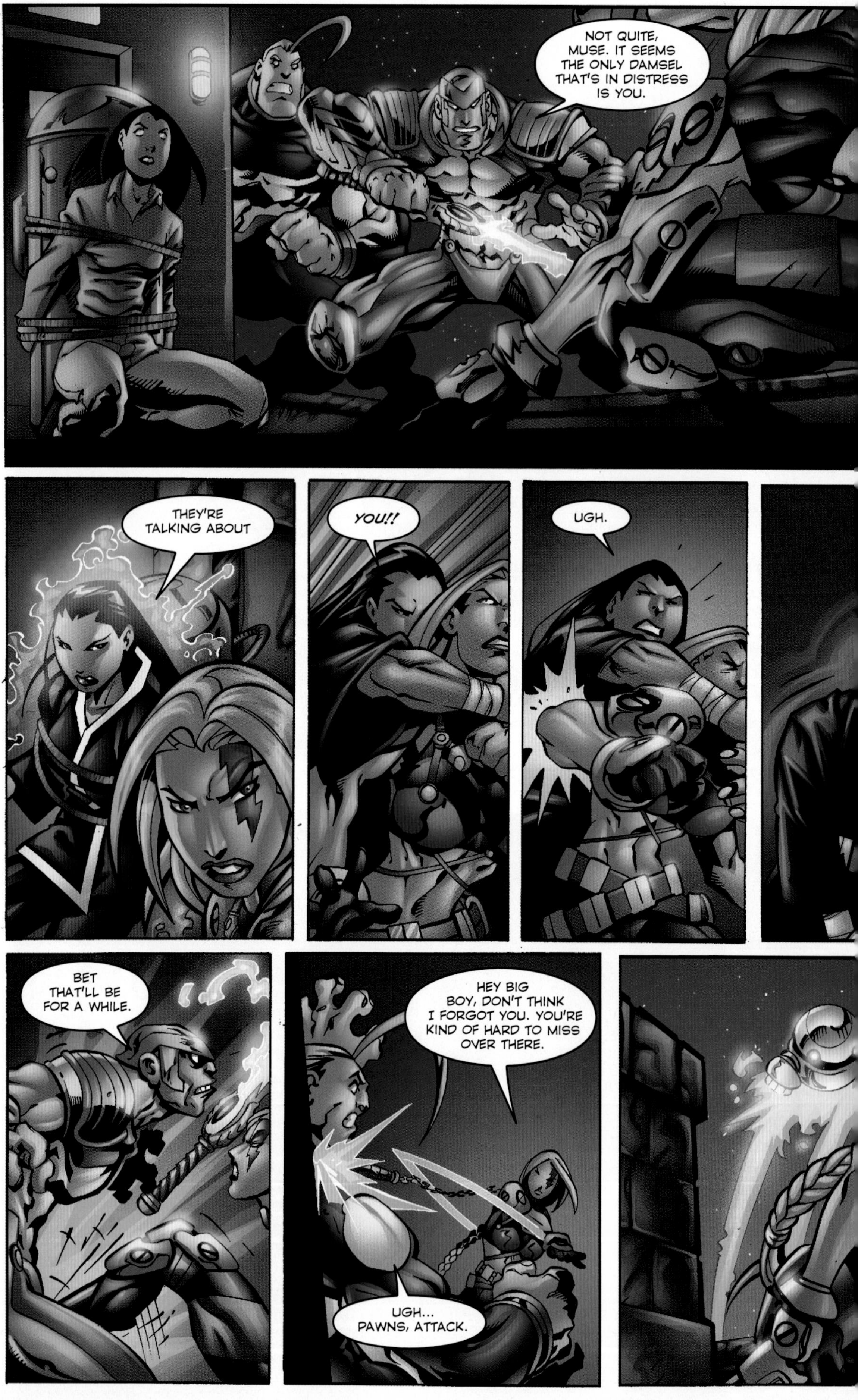
NOT QUITE, MUSE. IT SEEMS THE ONLY DAMSEL THAT'S IN DISTRESS IS YOU.
THEY'RE TALKING ABOUT
YOU!!
UGH.
BET THAT'LL BE FOR A WHILE.
HEY BIG BOY, DON'T THINK I FORGOT YOU. YOU'RE KIND OF HARD TO MISS OVER THERE.
UGH... PAWNS, ATTACK.

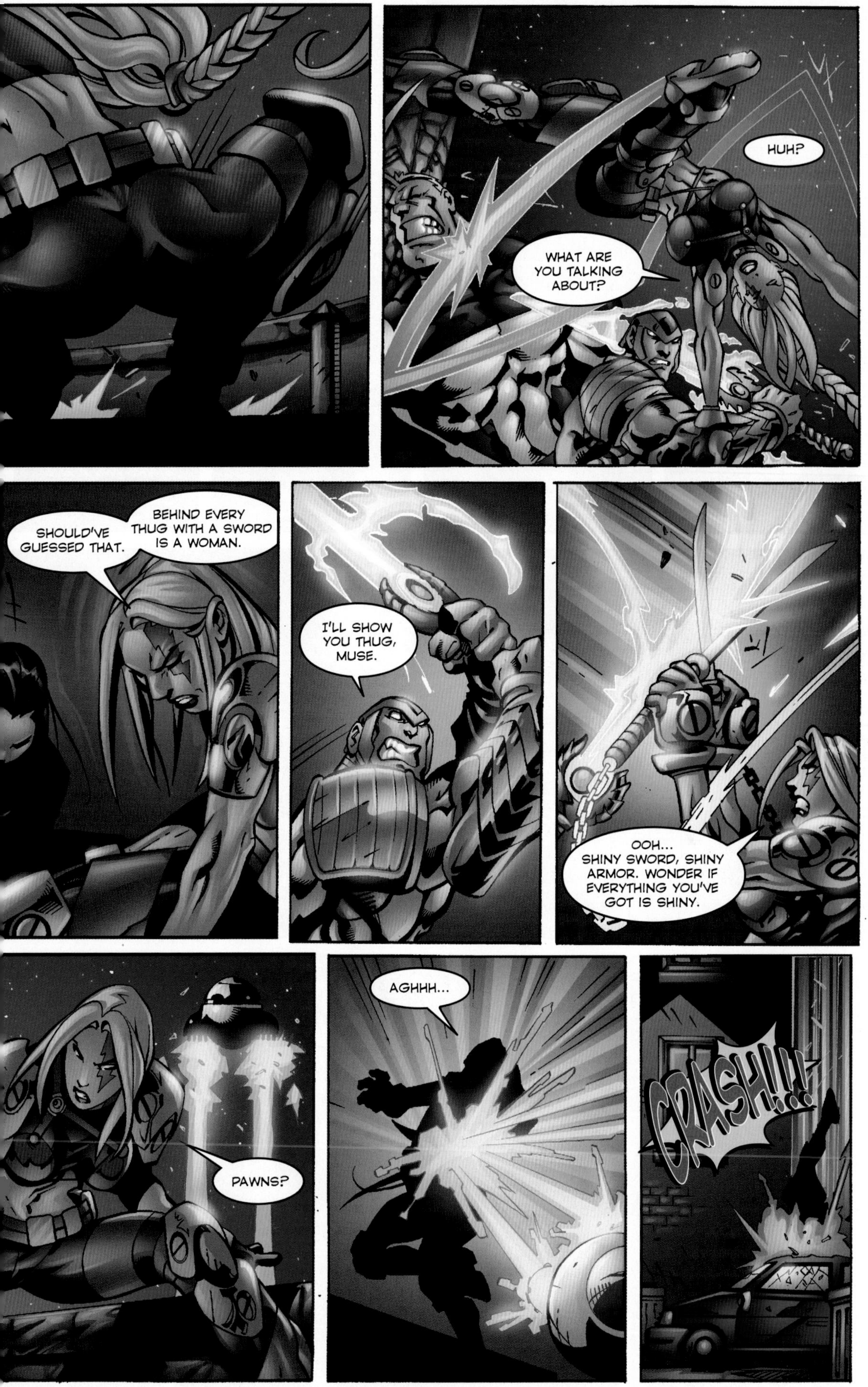
HUH?
WHAT ARE YOU TALKING ABOUT?
SHOULD'VE GUESSED THAT.
BEHIND EVERY THUG WITH A SWORD IS A WOMAN.
I'LL SHOW YOU THUG, MUSE.
OOH... SHINY SWORD, SHINY ARMOR. WONDER IF EVERYTHING YOU'VE GOT IS SHINY.
PAWNS?
AGHHH...
CRASH!!!

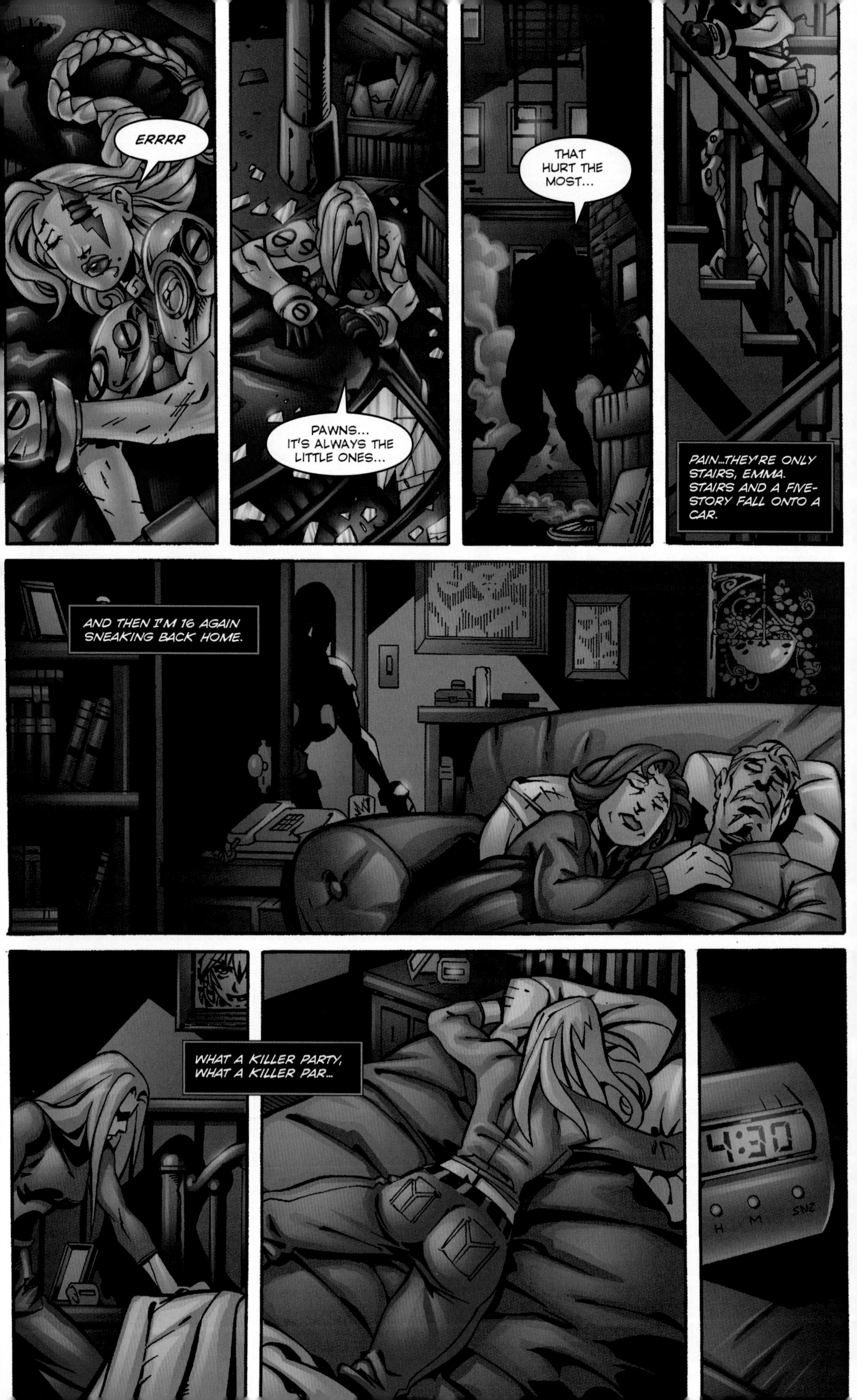
ERRRR
PAWNS... IT'S ALWAYS THE LITTLE ONES...
THAT HURT THE MOST...
PAIN...THEY'RE ONLY STAIRS, EMMA. STAIRS AND A FIVE-STORY FALL ONTO A CAR.
AND THEN I'M 16 AGAIN SNEAKING BACK HOME.
WHAT A KILLER PARTY, WHAT A KILLER PAR...
4:30
H M SNZ

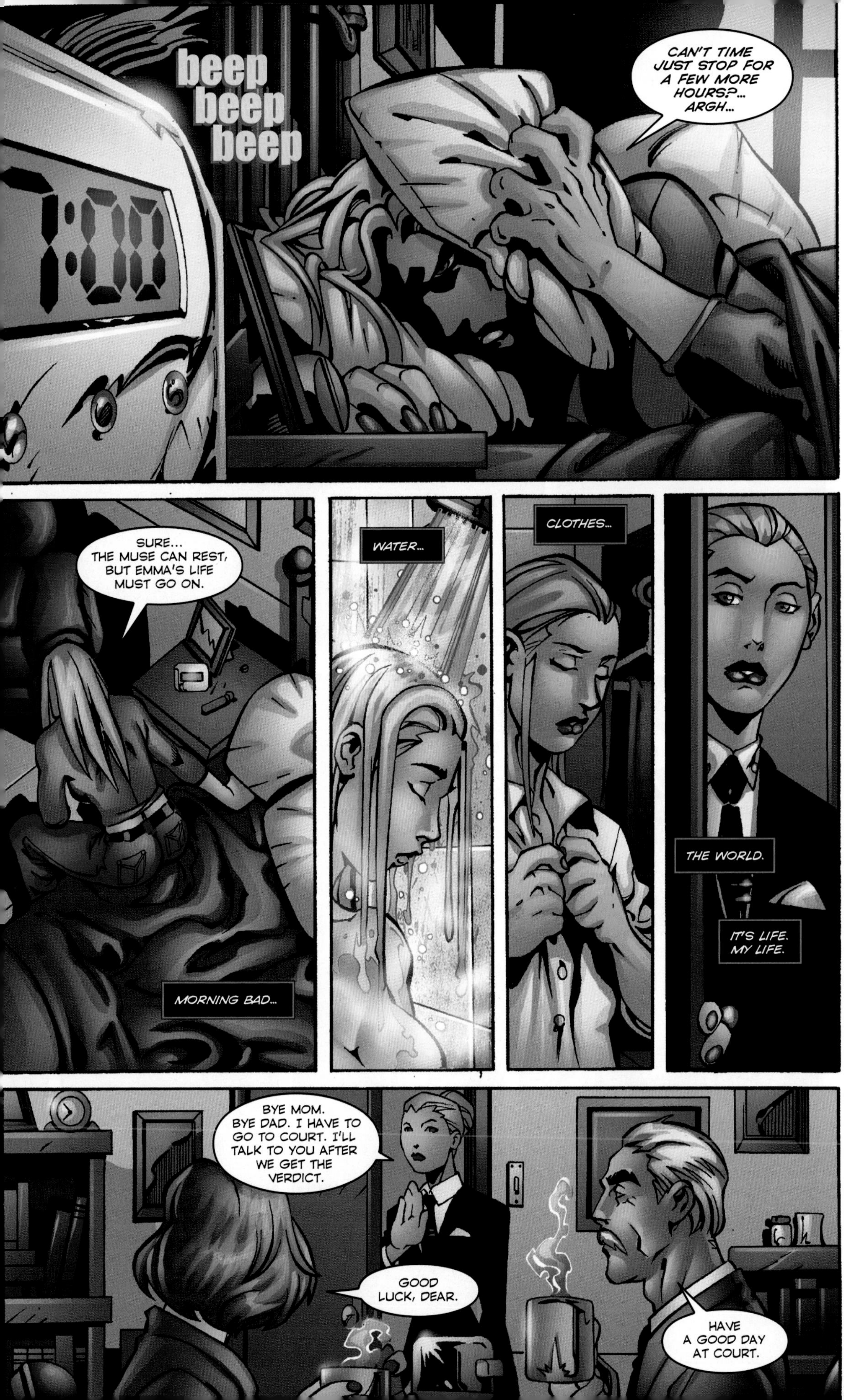
beep beep beep
CAN'T TIME JUST STOP FOR A FEW MORE HOURS?... ARGH...
SURE... THE MUSE CAN REST, BUT EMMA'S LIFE MUST GO ON.
MORNING BAD...
WATER...
CLOTHES...
THE WORLD.
IT'S LIFE. MY LIFE.
BYE MOM. BYE DAD. I HAVE TO GO TO COURT. I'LL TALK TO YOU AFTER WE GET THE VERDICT.
GOOD LUCK, DEAR.
HAVE A GOOD DAY AT COURT.

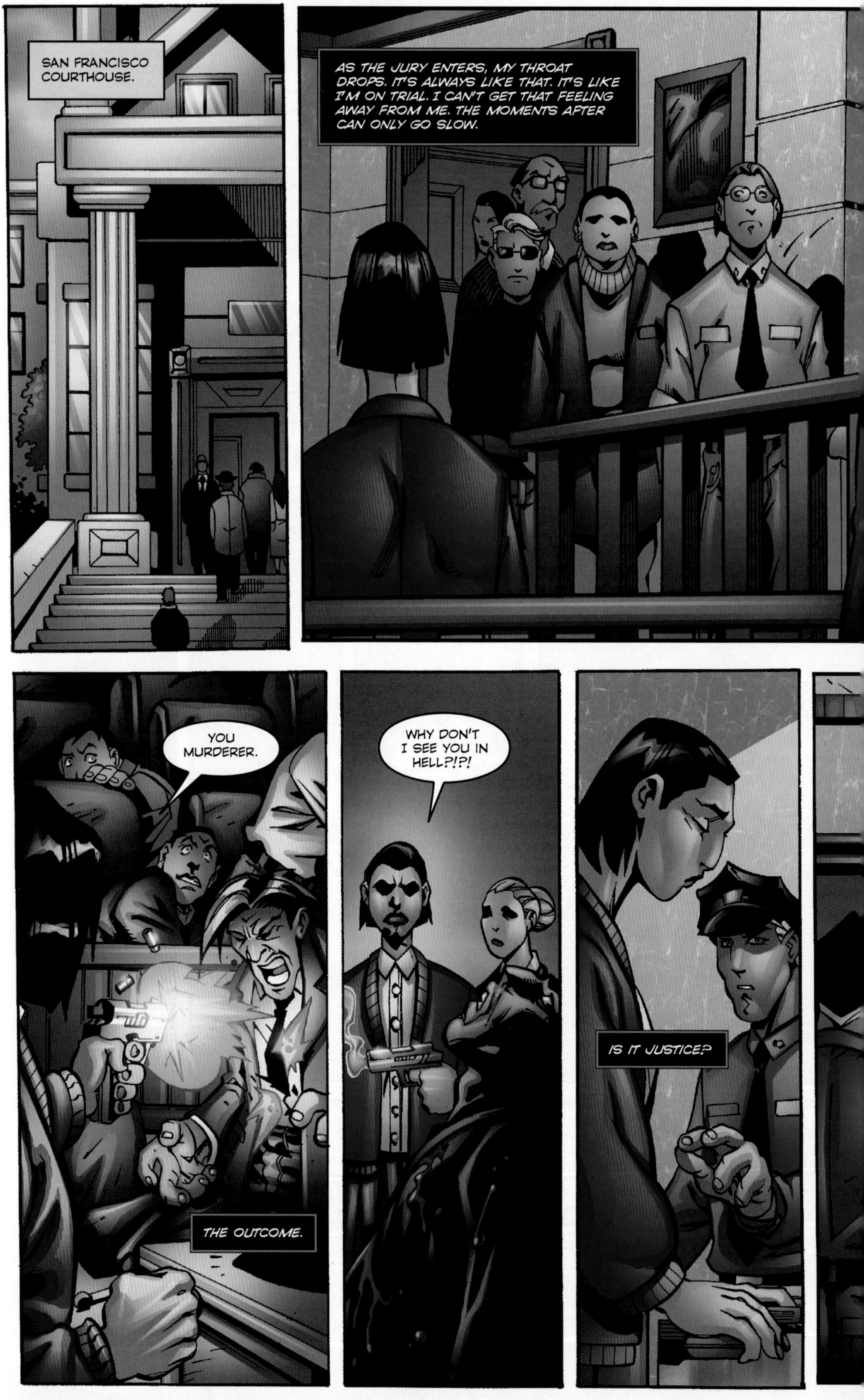
SAN FRANCISCO COURTHOUSE.
AS THE JURY ENTERS, MY THROAT DROPS. IT'S ALWAYS LIKE THAT. IT'S LIKE I'M ON TRIAL. I CAN'T GET THAT FEELING AWAY FROM ME. THE MOMENTS AFTER CAN ONLY GO SLOW.
YOU MURDERER.
THE OUTCOME.
WHY DON'T I SEE YOU IN HELL?!?!
IS IT JUSTICE?

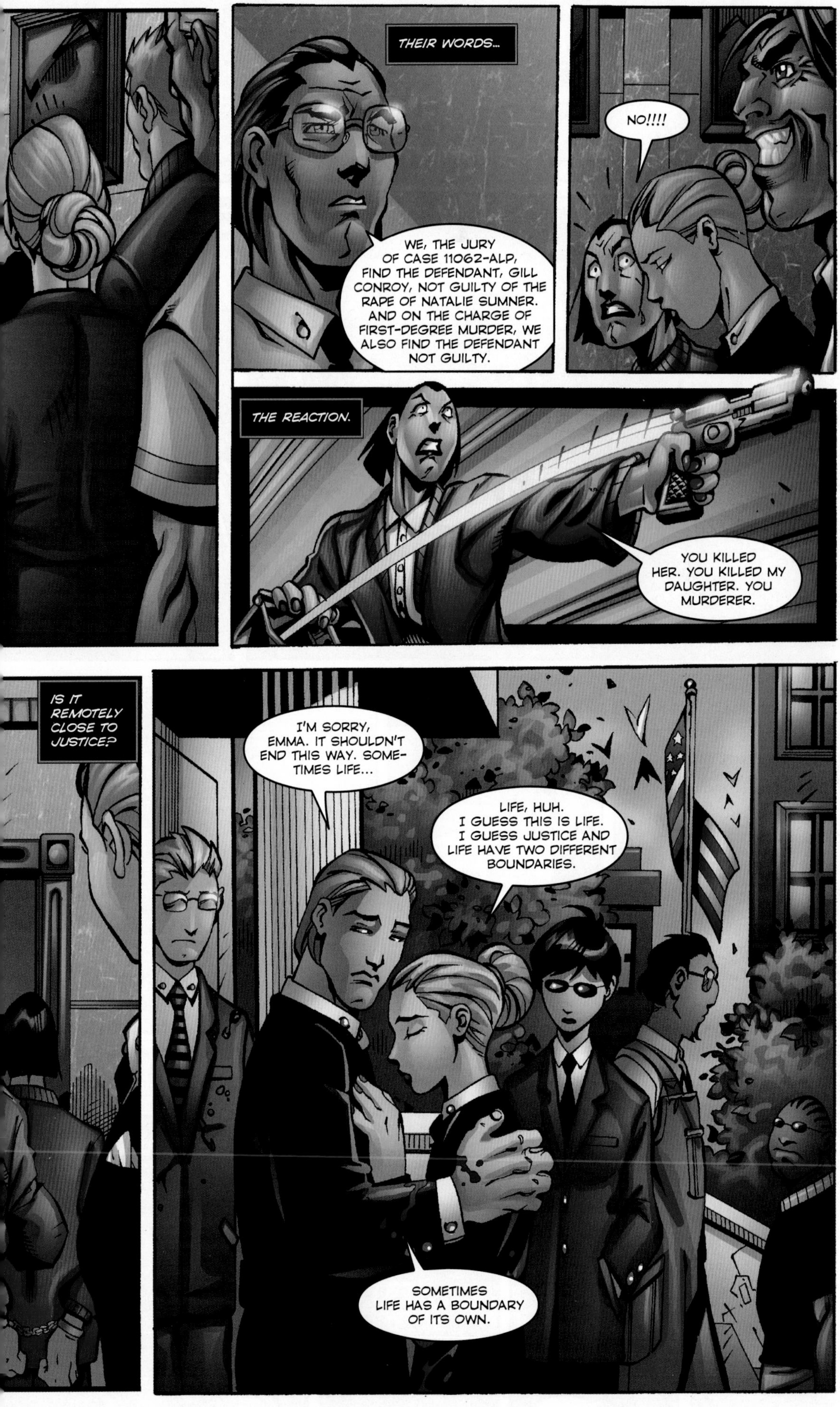
THEIR WORDS...
WE, THE JURY OF CASE 11062-ALP, FIND THE DEFENDANT, GILL CONROY, NOT GUILTY OF THE RAPE OF NATALIE SUMNER. AND ON THE CHARGE OF FIRST-DEGREE MURDER, WE ALSO FIND THE DEFENDANT NOT GUILTY.
NO!!!!
THE REACTION.
YOU KILLED HER. YOU KILLED MY DAUGHTER. YOU MURDERER.
IS IT REMOTELY CLOSE TO JUSTICE?
I'M SORRY, EMMA. IT SHOULDN'T END THIS WAY. SOME-TIMES LIFE...
LIFE, HUH. I GUESS THIS IS LIFE. I GUESS JUSTICE AND LIFE HAVE TWO DIFFERENT BOUNDARIES.
SOMETIMES LIFE HAS A BOUNDARY OF ITS OWN.

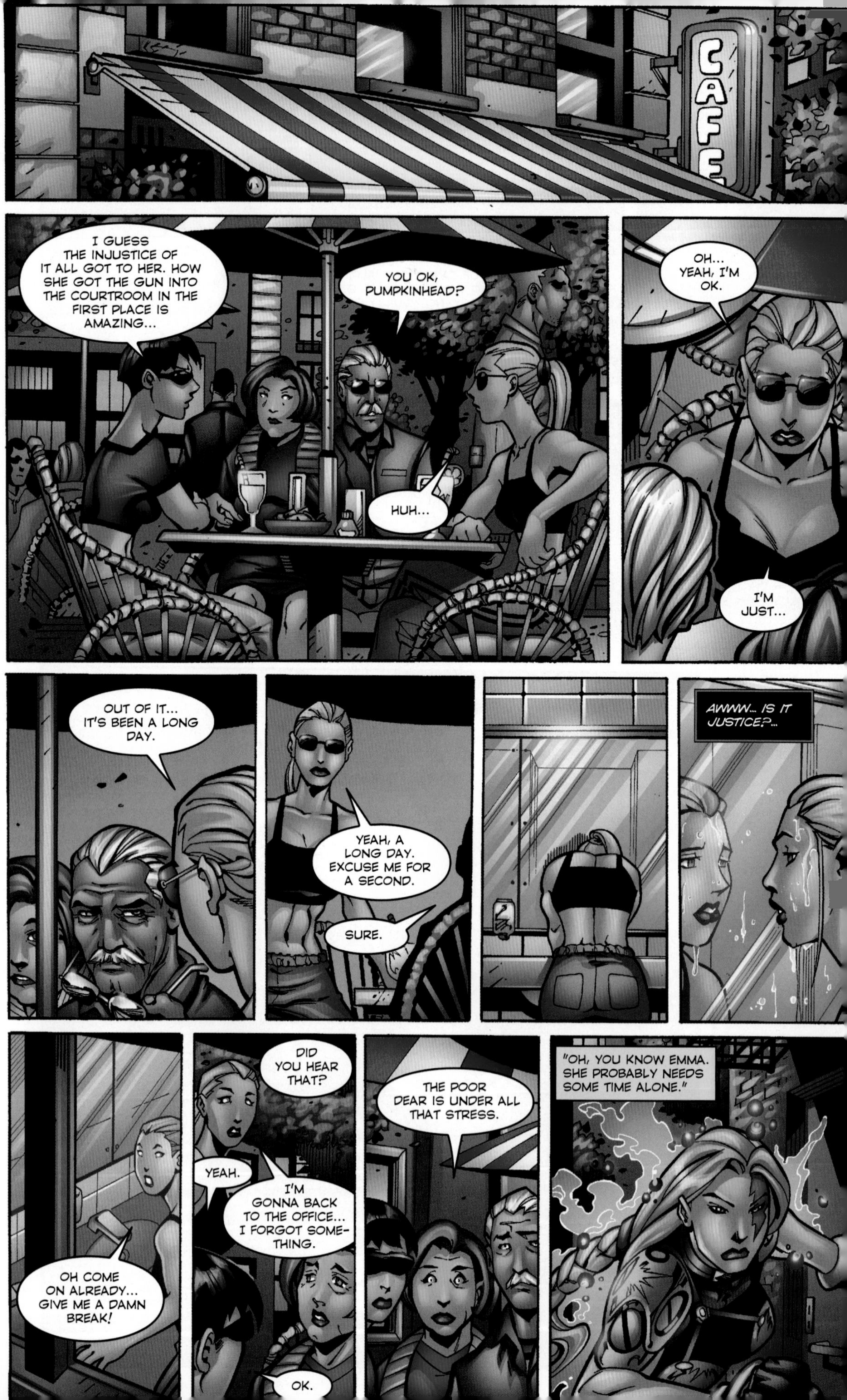
CAFE
I GUESS THE INJUSTICE OF IT ALL GOT TO HER. HOW SHE GOT THE GUN INTO THE COURTROOM IN THE FIRST PLACE IS AMAZING...
YOU OK, PUMPKINHEAD?
HUH...
OH... YEAH, I'M OK.
I'M JUST...
OUT OF IT... IT'S BEEN A LONG DAY.
YEAH, A LONG DAY. EXCUSE ME FOR A SECOND.
SURE.
AWWW... IS IT JUSTICE?...
OH COME ON ALREADY... GIVE ME A DAMN BREAK!
DID YOU HEAR THAT?
YEAH.
I'M GONNA BACK TO THE OFFICE... I FORGOT SOME-THING.
OK.
THE POOR DEAR IS UNDER ALL THAT STRESS.
"OH, YOU KNOW EMMA. SHE PROBABLY NEEDS SOME TIME ALONE."

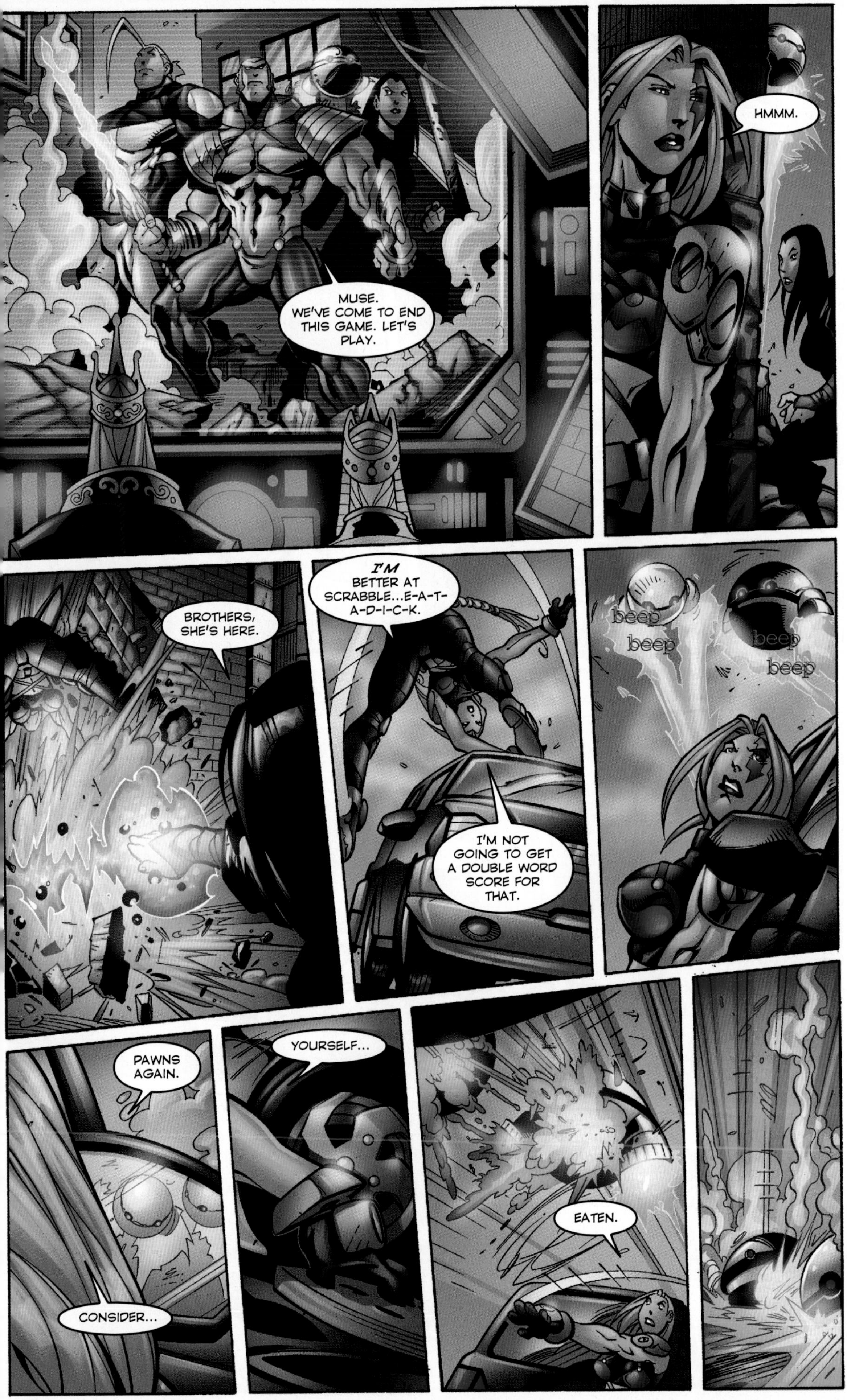
MUSE. WE'VE COME TO END THIS GAME. LET'S PLAY.
HMMM.
BROTHERS, SHE'S HERE.
I'M BETTER AT SCRABBLE...E-A-T-A-D-I-C-K.
I'M NOT GOING TO GET A DOUBLE WORD SCORE FOR THAT.
beep
beep
beep
beep
PAWNS AGAIN.
CONSIDER...
YOURSELF...
EATEN.

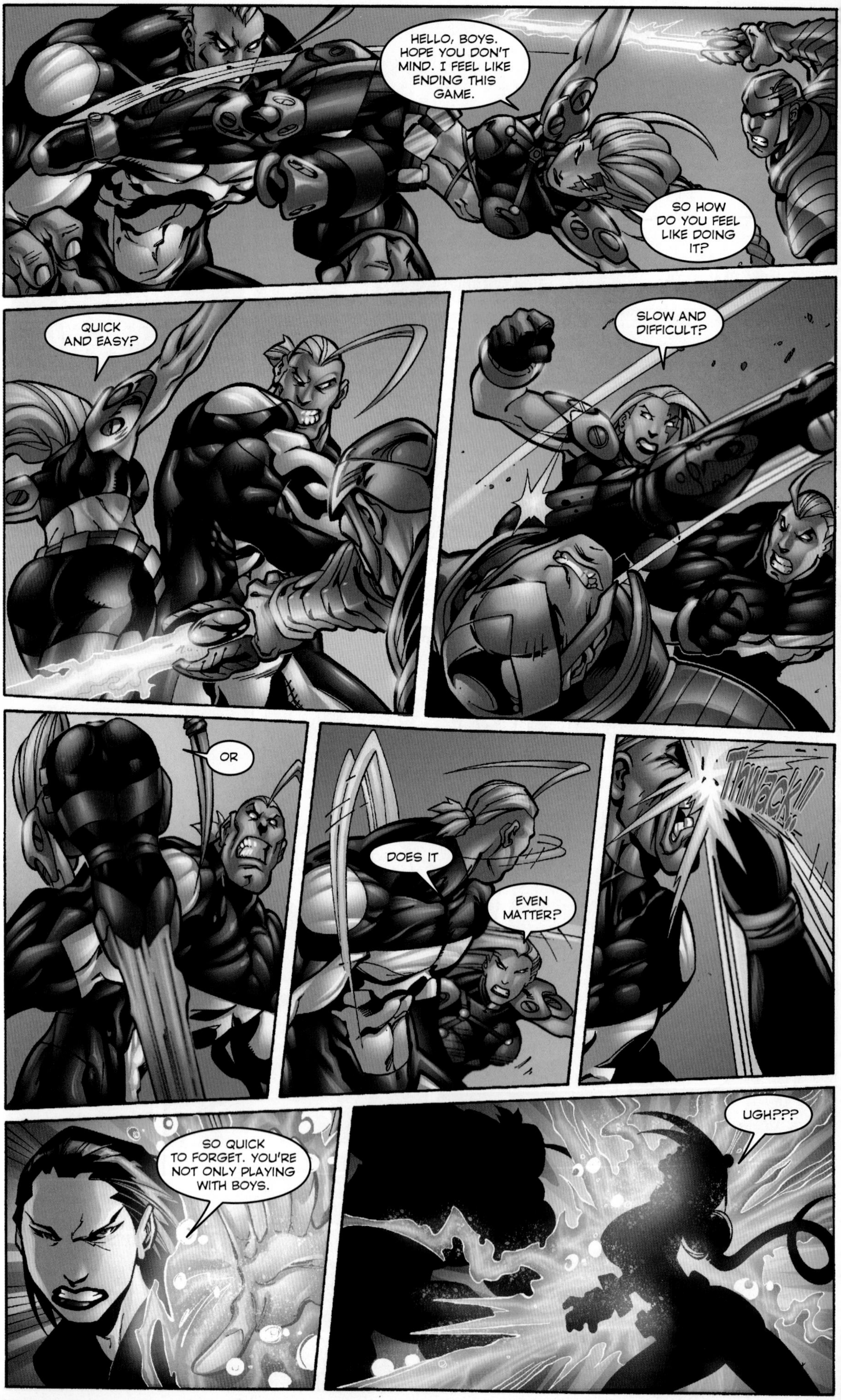
HELLO, BOYS. HOPE YOU DON'T MIND. I FEEL LIKE ENDING THIS GAME.
SO HOW DO YOU FEEL LIKE DOING IT?
QUICK AND EASY?
SLOW AND DIFFICULT?
OR
DOES IT
EVEN MATTER?
THWACK!!
SO QUICK TO FORGET. YOU'RE NOT ONLY PLAYING WITH BOYS.
UGH???

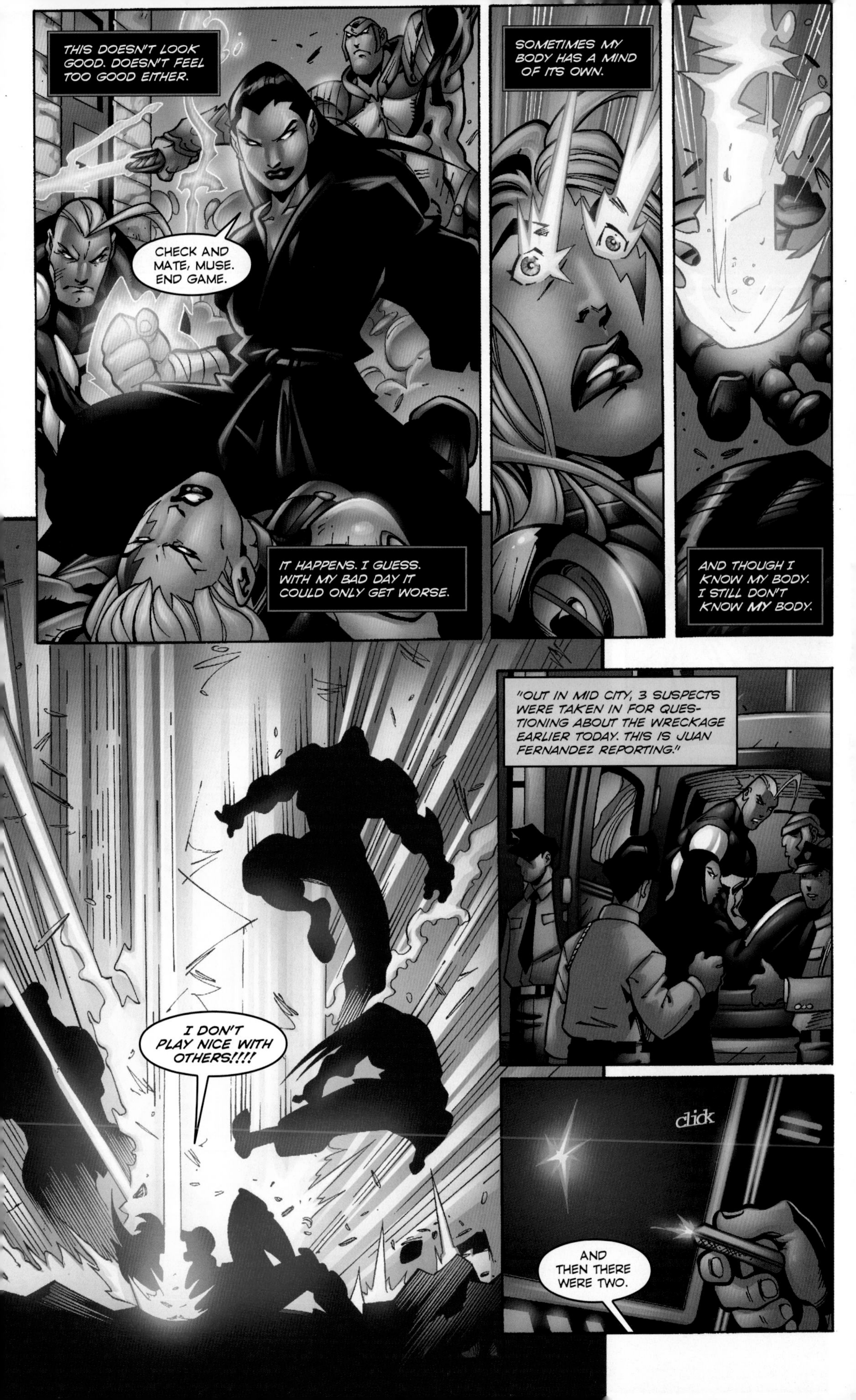
THIS DOESN'T LOOK GOOD. DOESN'T FEEL TOO GOOD EITHER.
CHECK AND MATE, MUSE. END GAME.
IT HAPPENS. I GUESS. WITH MY BAD DAY IT COULD ONLY GET WORSE.
SOMETIMES MY BODY HAS A MIND OF ITS OWN.
AND THOUGH I KNOW MY BODY. I STILL DON'T KNOW MY BODY.
I DON'T PLAY NICE WITH OTHERS!!!!
"OUT IN MID CITY, 3 SUSPECTS WERE TAKEN IN FOR QUESTIONING ABOUT THE WRECKAGE EARLIER TODAY. THIS IS JUAN FERNANDEZ REPORTING."
click
AND THEN THERE WERE TWO.

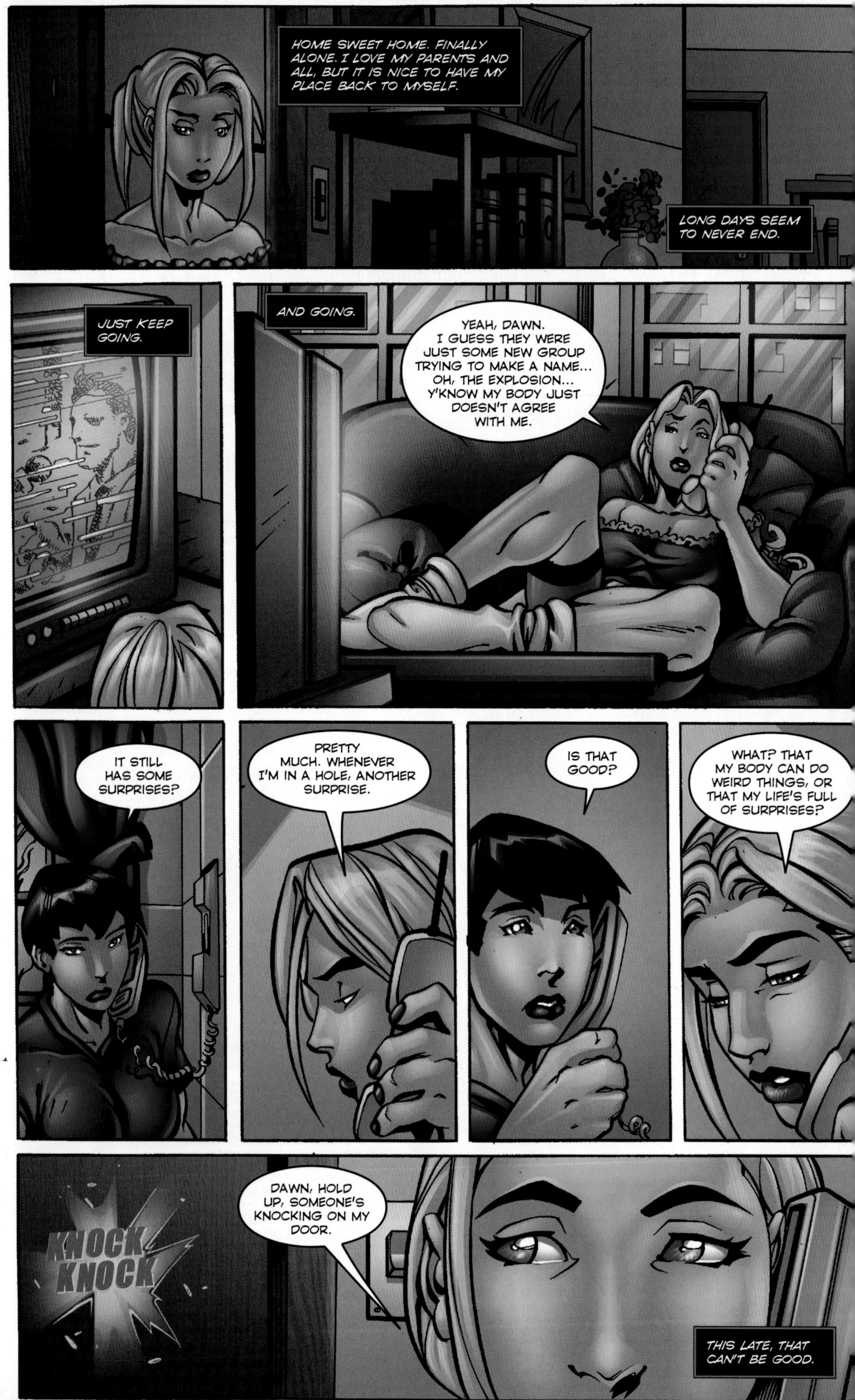
HOME SWEET HOME. FINALLY ALONE. I LOVE MY PARENTS AND ALL, BUT IT IS NICE TO HAVE MY PLACE BACK TO MYSELF.
LONG DAYS SEEM TO NEVER END.
JUST KEEP GOING.
AND GOING.
YEAH, DAWN. I GUESS THEY WERE JUST SOME NEW GROUP TRYING TO MAKE A NAME... OH, THE EXPLOSION... Y'KNOW MY BODY JUST DOESN'T AGREE WITH ME.
IT STILL HAS SOME SURPRISES?
PRETTY MUCH. WHENEVER I'M IN A HOLE, ANOTHER SURPRISE.
IS THAT GOOD?
WHAT? THAT MY BODY CAN DO WEIRD THINGS, OR THAT MY LIFE'S FULL OF SURPRISES?
KNOCK KNOCK
DAWN, HOLD UP, SOMEONE'S KNOCKING ON MY DOOR.
THIS LATE, THAT CAN'T BE GOOD.

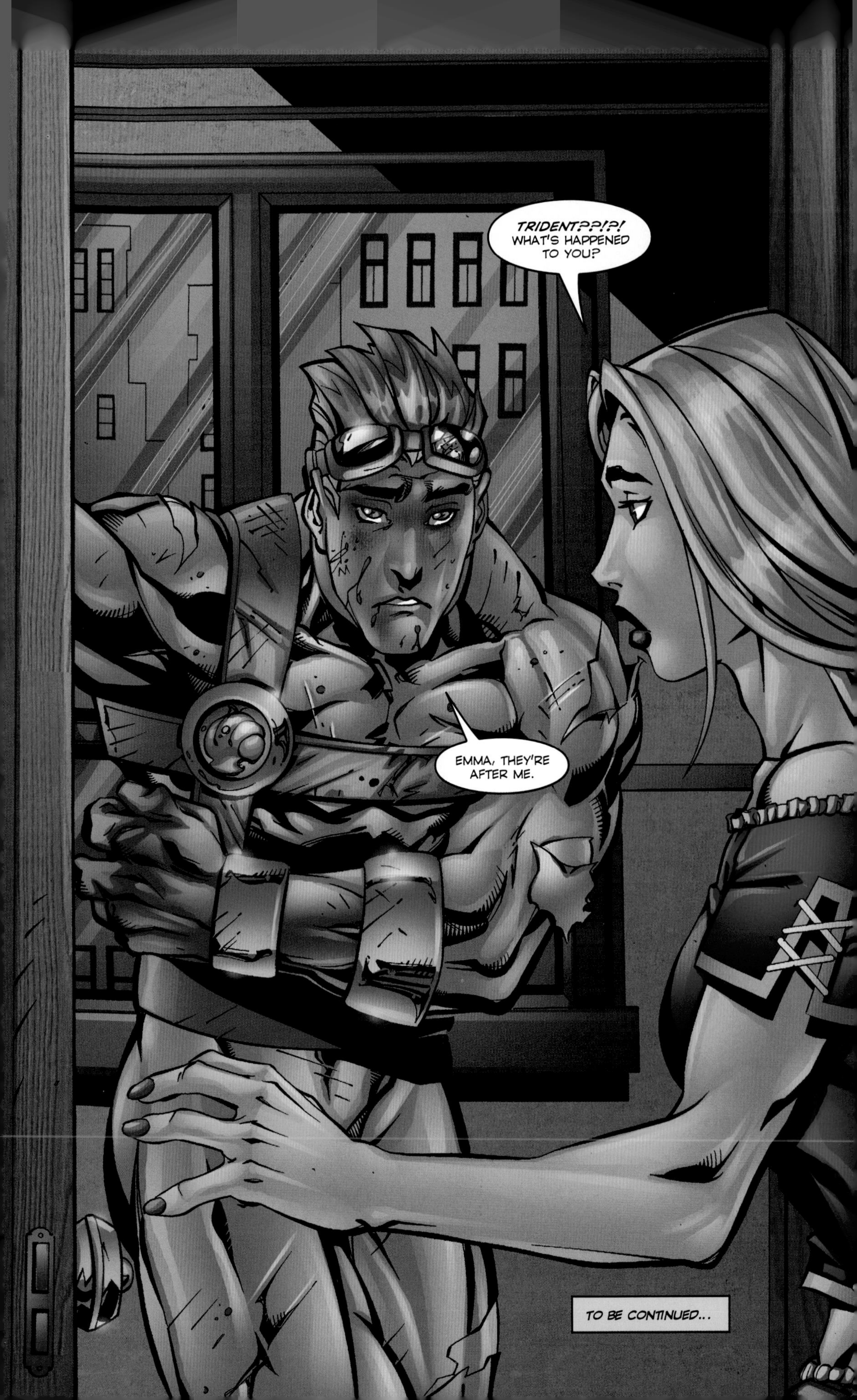
TRIDENT??!?! WHAT'S HAPPENED TO YOU?
EMMA, THEY'RE AFTER ME.
TO BE CONTINUED...

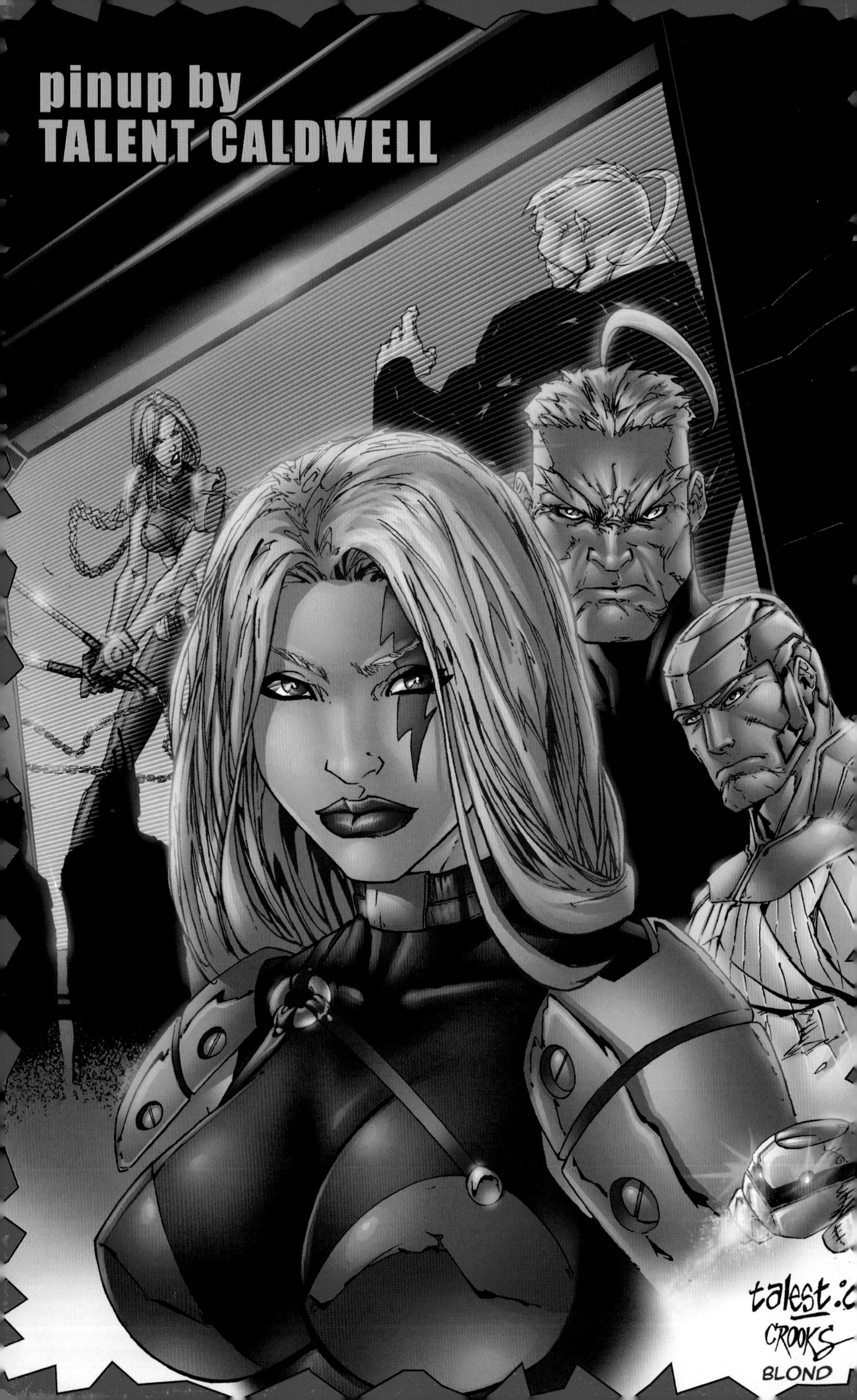
pinup by
TALENT CALDWELL
CROOKS
BLOND